T0354408

LIFE
Through These Eyes, Vol II

Michael S. Lambiotte

authorHOUSE°

AuthorHouse™
1663 Liberty Drive
Bloomington, IN 47403
www.authorhouse.com
Phone: 1 (800) 839-8640

Published by AuthorHouse 04/26/2017

ISBN: 978-1-5246-8911-7 (sc)
ISBN: 978-1-5246-8909-4 (hc)
ISBN: 978-1-5246-8910-0 (e)

TO
Merry

Our precious Labrador Retriever
She taught me love, loyalty and forgiveness

Merry "Wiggles"

Contents

Chapter 3

A Child of the 50's Memories

Chapter 4

Really Special People & Places

Chapter 5

Being a Man...It's Not Easy

Chapter 6

My Home Sweet Home

Chapter 7

In My Garden

Chapter 8

Sitting in A Tree...K I S S I N G

Chapter 9

Holidays – Time to Dream

Chapter 10

My Community Soap Box

Chapter 11

Family and Friends

Chapter 12

Oh, Those Beautiful Brown Eyes

Chapter 13

When You Stop Learning – You Stop!

Chapter 14

The Shape of Mean

Introduction

Welcome to Volume II of *Life Through These Eyes*. When my book was completed in 2015, I was at peace. Four and a half years of work was before me. I was pleased, exhausted, and excited – all at the same time. Walking into the post office with manuscript in hand was a surreal experience. Handing over years of work to a stranger who would hand it off to strangers, bound for even more strangers, created feelings which made me very uneasy.

My original manuscript was 800 pages, as it turned out, much too long for a book of this type. So, I was told, "You need to divide it into two volumes." This task was given to my wife Sandra because I was too emotionally connected and, if I do say so myself, she did a masterful job.

If you read Volume I, you understand why I refer to myself as "The Man Least Likely to Become an Author." Writing came to me in the oddest of ways: I was not professionally trained. Did not grow up in a family or community of writers. Nor was I driven at an early age or influenced by other writers. However, oddly enough, I found a passion for writing – at age 58. I discovered I had a message I wanted to share with others. I wanted to share my memories from childhood to retirement. I wanted to share many of my wonderful, and sometimes painful, life-lessons. I wanted to write about my community and events and people which made me angry and disillusioned. I found an outlet for many hurtful experiences and I found a way to channel my political feelings.

Something noteworthy: This book contains fourteen chapters. Fourteen different topics. Topics which include holiday memories, respecting individual ways and beliefs, special people who came into and out of my life, my beloved pets and how they trained me, love and romance, gardening, education, politics and much more. What you receive is 60 years of me – uncensored, straight forward, and close to the edge.

As I said in Volume I, "I can honestly say that every story has a personal connection." There is always a story within a story. I am often asked, "Are you characters real?" I immediately respond with, "Oh yes, they are all real - very real to me. I loved a few. Despised many. And spent years trying to forget some."

Under each story title is a quote. Pay attention to the quote. It is the key to understanding the story behind the story. This is not a book that will capture your imagination for hours at a time. It is not full of complex characters. There is no overall social statement. However, it is a book full of emotion, frustrations, successes, failures, and memories. Many of the stories will make you laugh. Several stories will make you cry. But above all, I hope all of the stories will make you THINK!

60 years of *"Life Through These Eyes."* Eyes that see the world a little differently.

CHAPTER 1

RESPECT

Riding with Miss Manners

"Things may happen to you, but the only things that matter are the things that happen in you." – Eric Butterworth

Raise your hand if you have never done anything dangerous or just plain dumb while driving an automobile? For those with their hands up, let me remind you about: That recent red light you went through. No, pink doesn't mean go with caution.

What about the person you pulled in front of and you proceeded to drive at snail speed. They almost had your tail pipe as a hood ornament. Or the time you cut off the driver in front of you because the Sale' sign was just too damn compelling. And I distinctively remember a "Stop" sign doesn't mean proceed slowly with vigilance. Furthermore, remember backing into that car in the parking lot? You thought, "That car wasn't behind me when I arrived two hours ago."

Just as I thought, all hands are down. Now, raise your hand if you have ever witnessed another driver doing something dangerous or just plain dumb? Here are a few of my favorites: The early morning "I'm late I'm late" driver finishing her make up 1o miles over the speed limit. Or the man putting the final touches on that last-minute shave during his NASCAR-like commute.

How about the youthful driver cruising at 60 mph and texting a very important message? Oops! That tree interrupted the texting. "Sorry Mom and Dad. I'll never be home for dinner." And one of my all-time favorites:

1

The driver who was approaching "Suicide Central," the intersection of Rt. 50 and Emily Drive in Clarksburg, West Virginia. She was proceeding through a pink light, cigarette in one hand, coffee in the other and head tilted to the left holding a cell phone against their shoulder. Obviously well coordinated and very stupid. Their juggling might get them a circus job, but it might also get them (or someone) unexpected coverage in the obituaries.

My point: Through these eyes, every driver (sooner or later) either initiates or becomes the victim of highway stupidity. Too often this stupidity results in further stupidity... (aka) "Road Rage." I would like to devote the rest of this story to my unique solutions for highway temper tantrums.

First, I believe people make obscene gestures, yell obscenities, or otherwise react in socially unacceptable ways toward other drivers because they "know they can." It's almost like making that unpleasant phone call rather then talking with the individual in person. You become disconnected and safe. And can easily run away by hanging up. As a driver, you can 'salute' or yell at an offending motorist and drive (run) away. Avoid the face-to-face.

Here are my unique (sort of) solutions for highway tantrums: For the perpetrator (the cause of the incident) – Ignore the obscenities, stare straight ahead, and close your ears. Or simply apologize with the windows up and the doors locked. An exaggerated, "I'm sorry. I'm stupid" usually works.

Don't try to get creative or throw them off balance like I once did. After apparently irritating the driver behind me, he pulled alongside and presented me with a very unkind salute. I looked at him, smiled, and threw him a kiss. Not smart! In hind sight, my actions could have enraged him further or could have gotten me a date...neither of which would have been desirable.

For the victim– If another driver does something beside, in front of, or behind you that is stupid, dangerous, or dumb, take a deep breath before you do or say something that is stupid, dangerous, or dumb. Think: That person could be a serial killer wanted by the FBI. Or, would you react in a belligerent or obscene way if you suddenly recognized the offender as your best friend? Well, come to think of it you might. But it would probably be with a smile and friendly salute!

Before you do or say something obscene to another driver remember, "Quit lying to your self! We all drive dumb at times." And my best solution for highway tantrums is, "Oh, high Mom. I didn't know that was you. We need to talk later."

I've never committed a thoughtless act while behind the wheel of a car.
Except lie frequently.

Send Them Back – They're Illegal!

"The greatest good you can do for another is not to just share your riches, but to reveal to him his own." – Benjamin Disraeli

Send e'm back, they wear funny clothes!
Send e'm back, they can't speak our language!
Send e'm back, they have a different religion!
Send e'm back, they have foreign diseases!
No doubt, Powhatan, the Algonquian Indian Chief, and many of his followers thought and said these very words. For the record, they were directed at the English – in 1607. I think I still hear these words today. Listen, do you? Oh yea, this story is about immigration. No personal opinions though. Because, my opinions are just that – personal. However, I hope it will make you think. Think about your relatives and why they came to a strange and different land...America.

My family came from Belgium and Germany. Legally, I think. It doesn't really make any difference now. That was over a hundred years ago. But, what if it was last week? At one time, immigration was mainly an historical topic for me, to be taught and analyzed in the classroom. While living in Virginia, it became personal. We lived in a city that was a political, religious, and ethnic melting pot.

Those years opened my eyes to ethnic diversity. I met adults and children who fled unimaginable suffering, inhumanity, poverty, and political persecution. Those years also opened my eyes to Americans who made an art form of using the system. Those who can work and should work, but choose not to work.

I had a friend who worked for the INS (Immigration and Naturalization Service). They raided an open-air vegetable market in Washington, D.C. looking for illegal immigrants. As they were loading the illegals, he noticed a large crowd gathering. He said, "Go on in. I think they're hiring now." Someone in the crowd said, "F_ _ k no!! I ain't working for no piss-ass wages!" "Mike, I was so angry I felt like arresting the crowd. Maybe we were deporting the wrong group."

After retiring from education, I sold automobiles while Sandra, my wife, finished her tour of duty in education. One of my customers was a young man from Mexico. One day he said, "Mike, I love Mexico, but down there you work hard and get nothing. Here, you work hard and get something. I work hard for my family, here and in Mexico. One day, I want them to have what I have in my new country."

At that point, I didn't care if he was illegal or not. Over the years, I knew several immigrants who became citizens. I found out obtaining visas, sponsors, application fees, Green Cards, permanent resident status, and finally citizenship takes years and cost thousands. Entering illegally...can cost you your life. Imagine selling everything you own to pay smugglers to get you across the border. The lucky ones make it. Some die trying.

Why do they risk everything? "Here, you work hard and get something!" Using my best Nixon imitation "Let me make one thing perfectly clear," illegal immigration is just that – illegal. But we better find a way to deal with it, and fast. Forget deporting. It doesn't work.

Yes, "illegals" strain our economy, schools, and health care system. But, so does "can work and won't work." Think - you're living where you do now, in extreme poverty, and under a brutal corrupt government. Yet in Virginia, there was promise and hope. But, you must sneak across a dangerous border. What would you do? Me... "These boots are made for walking." Or running real fast!

Through these eyes, we must find a way to help the illegal immigrants become legal. We have no other realistic choice. Skills, desire, and work ethics are there. We must streamline the legal process for admittance and citizenship. Democratic and Republican lawmakers, put down your swords! Just once, do what is right, without checking your political playbook. Maybe it's our time – "to not only share our riches, but help them reveal their own."

If I had not lived in a diverse environment, I would
have lived my life one dimensional.

The Magic Mirror

"The greatest discovery of my generation is that man can alter his life simply by altering his attitude of mind." – William James

"Mirror mirror on the wall, who's the fairest of them all? Tis you my queen. You are fair so true." Many times, the wicked queen looked into her magical mirror for answers. Always pleased. Until one day her mirror said, "But Snow White is fairer than you." The queen was expecting truth, honesty, and a 'fairest' reflection. hat she received on that one eventful morning created anger, conflict, and jealousy. But the mirror spoke only the truth.

Magic mirrors only exist in fairy tales. But I wonder? I wonder what it would be like to have a magic mirror to help me (us) deal with life's conflicts? One that would tell the truth. Be honest and fair. However, accepting what we see deep in the mirror might not always please. For how we deal with conflict separates the successful from the unproductive and the happy from the discontented. Yet, it can lead to the incompatible seeing as one. Or it can rebuild bridges destroyed by anger and misunderstandings.

When we first glance into the mirror we see conflicts everywhere: At work, family, with friends, and neighbors. We're seeing a reflection of life. And we go to the mirror and say, "OK - mirror mirror on the wall, be honest. Tell me the truth! Tell me when I am right and when I am wrong." But, are we prepared for the fairest of them all. Remember, mirrors lie not.

A mirror sees most conflicts as a failure to communicate or our unwillingness to accept the possibility we might be wrong. Conflicts at work are unavoidable: Your boss never considers your ideas. Jealousy over promotions will happen. Colleagues will steal ideas or take credit for the work of others.

Also, show me a family without conflict and I will show you a very unhappy single person: Siblings yell and parents argue. Dance recitals will conflict with soccer games and anniversaries. Furthermore, if you know someone or live in a certain neighborhood long enough, disagreements are as certain as the sun rising and setting. The difference is…will you believe what you see in the mirror?

But if you are willing to look deep enough, you will see reflections that please and offend. You will be pleased when you see your image writing a note that says, "I'm sorry. I know my words stung." However, you will be offended when the mirror asks, "Why didn't you invite them to lunch so you could talk." Taking that giant step (talking) is not always easy.

You will be delighted when you see your image not engaging in hurtful gossip about a dear friend, club member, or a co-worker. On the other hand, you will be upset by your reflection being rude to a guest in your home, especially when you didn't realize you were offensive.

And you were thrilled when your mirror complimented you by saying. "The gift of your time is a gift never forgotten." Yet, you were embarrassed (or were you) when you saw your likeness canceling an invitation already accepted. Something better came up.

In the fairy tale *Snow White and the Seven Dwarfs*, a magic mirror created conflict by speaking the truth. I think the authors of *Snow White*, the Brothers Grimm, may have stumbled onto something – a mirror that tells the truth and reflects who we really are. However, we need to use this mirror to resolve conflicts and never allowing it to create conflicts.

I hope the next time you look in your mirror, wherever it may be, you will be able to see more than a simple reflection. I truly believe magic mirrors do exist. And if we look deep enough, I hope we will be able to see the person other people see.

And for the fortunate ones, who have a true friend, don't be afraid to exchange reflections. That's the magic of the mirror!

Magic mirrors really do exist for some people.
It's the reflection of a friend.

The Title Fight

"I will speak ill of no man and speak all the good I know of everybody." Ben Franklin

In the red corner, at 6'5" and 285 lbs. is…Gossip! In the blue corner, at 6'3" and 260 lbs. is …Knowledge! Both fighters are powerful and strong and have enormous influence with those around them. Gossip can destroy his opponent with a single punch. Not only his career, but possibly his life. He charges to the center of the ring…fast and furious.

Knowledge is more of a finesse fighter. He works slowly, calculating and analyzing his opponent. Then, and only then, will he make his move. Knowledge is as powerful, but not as flamboyant or quick to strike with devastating blows. In the end, how each uses his power will decide victory.

For an insider look at these two heavy weights, let's go to their training camps and observe their techniques. First, is Gossip. At 6'5" and 285 lbs. and very intimidating. His training is secretive, always surrounded by rumors and idle chatter. The chatter about his opponent is always personal, designed to distract from the task at hand.

Gossip's rumors are about self- promotion.. His press conferences are always sensational and meant to hurt his opponent. To many, he may even appear as "acid-dripping" sweet. Beware! Let's look at who's in his corner. There's Bob (Gossip), who tells anyone who will listen about a dying child when that child is doing quite well thanks to science and God. Beside him is Carol (Gossip), who talks about a friend's battle with alcoholism, as she accepts that third glass of wine. To her left is Ted (Gossip), who loves spreading vicious rumors about his political opponents, the day before the election.

Never forget Alice (Gossip). She loves to speculate, at her social club, why the police are frequent visitors to the house a block from her home. Remember, being the center of attention is important to Alice.

However, despite Gossip's power and destruction, Knowledge knows he will defeat Gossip. It may not be in the first round, but certainly before the final round. Let's look at Knowledge's training camp. Knowledge's camp is open to the public. He is aware of his popularity and encourages others to watch and learn. Knowledge understands the importance of studying an opponent's every move. He analyzes Gossip's past fights and pays careful attention to how he hurts his opponents.

Knowledge is also powerful, but he's constantly aware of how his power influences others. He wants to win as badly as Gossip, but hurting and humiliating an opponent is not part of his strategy. Knowledge always tries to share and spread his successes because for Knowledge, there is no me, it's all about we.

Look who's in Knowledge's corner. I see Martin Luther King, standing on the steps of the Lincoln Memorial saying, "I have a Dream." Beside him is Mother Theresa, in the squalor of Calcutta, praying with a young husband, as he cradles his dying wife in his arms. I see Rachel Carson, holding a copy of her book *Silent Spring* in one hand and the upraised hand of Knowledge with her other hand. The public outcry to her book in 1962 was instrumental in launching the environmental movement.

Beside her, with arms raised to a higher power is the Rev. Billy Graham, at 86, preparing his last sermon after 67 years on the pulpit. Directly behind Knowledge is a man wearing a brown suit with his right hand in his jacket pocket. As Knowledge looks around, the man in the suit says, "In a time of turbulence and change, it is more important today than ever that knowledge is power." Mr. President, you died way too young.

In this heavy weight title fight called "Life," Gossip can land a devastating blow at any time. While Knowledge can defeat any foe. Within each of us...Gossip and Knowledge are waiting for their chance.

When your bell sounds, and you walk toward the center of the ring, which corner will you choose?

The difference between spreading gossip and
fact is the motive of the tongue.

What's Your Pedigree?

Every man has a history worth knowing, if he could tell it,
or if we could draw it from him." – Ralph Waldo Emerson

The individuals portrayed in this story are purely fictional. Any resemblance to anyone living or dead is purely coincidental. However, feel free to interject your own opinions.

If you have had the privilege of a dog as a companion, chances are they were AKC registered (American Kennel Club) or good ole AMB (American Mixed Breed). For registration purposes, the AKC groups dogs into eight categories: Sporting, Non-Sporting, Hound, Working, Terrier, Toy, Herding and Miscellaneous.

However, did you ever notice dogs don't care about categories, pedigree or papers And most of the owners don't either. Yet occasionally you'll run into a "snobby" owner who says with an arrogant tone and a tipped-up nose, "Myyyyy dog is the same breed that won 'Best in Show' at the Westminster Kennel Club Dog Show. Is that really a dog you're walking? It looks like a collage of leftover parts." Incidentally, the 2010 Best in Show was a Scottish terrier named Ch Roundtown Mercedes of Maryscot (aka Sadie). No AMB's allowed in this event.

Last February I watched Sadie (Yes, I watched the event) strut her winning stuff with her proud owner parading beside her and thought, "What if we had to register our own pedigree or divided into categories? 'What would the categories be based on? Would it be based on money or possessions? Education? A family name? Political power? Job status? What? Would we be judged based on our perceived pedigree rather than our character?"

Once in, would we be treated fairly by the old guard or as second-class citizens because they feel our pedigree isn't that impressive, even though theirs was bought or borrowed. And what would happen when someone feels they have a strong pedigree yet no papers to back it up? Then what do we do?"

Taking all this into account, I have decided to title this new categorical system the "American Social Ranking System" (ASRS). And unlike the Westminster Kennel Club which judges how close a dog matches the standard of the ideal specimen, the ASRS is based on wealth…money, pure and simple. Face it, many to most of us judge people initially by the size of their house or the emblem on their car.

See if you or anyone you know fits any of these categories: Inherited Money – One of the easiest pedigrees to acquire. The real test is, "Will you put it to good use or will you squander it?" Self-Made Money: Hard work. One of the most admired pedigrees. Through "Blood, Sweat & Tears" you've achieved "Best in Show." Enjoy it. You deserve all the benefits. Married Money: Admirable, if it's for the right reasons and you remain humble. Nobody can stand a person who suddenly says, "Excuse me! I'm Mrs. or Mr. so-and-so. It's time to bow." Judge me for who I am, not who I married.

Another category is Won Money: One of the least desirable pedigrees. Where do you think the saying "Easy come - Easy go" originated? And this kind of money usually attracts fleas…friends and relatives. Stolen Money: The least desirable. For in its wake is a trail of tears, anger, heartbreak and a lifetime of regret. Ask Bernie Madoff. See anybody you know?

The AKC, the Westminster Kennel Club and the ASRS have a lot in common. All three are judgmental based on pedigree. Yet the biggest difference is, the dogs don't care! And humans are always judging or being judged. We can learn much from our canine friends.

Next time you go to a dog park, watch how the dogs interact. After the initial sniff and check, it's play time. Pedigrees and papers mean nothing. They don't care whose AKC or AMB. True, they may develop a little pecking order, but it has nothing to do with pedigree. It's the same with the new dog on the farm.

Come to think of it, wouldn't we all be better off if after an initial "sniff and check" we treated everyone as equals…and played fairly.

This was personal. Since our return to Clarksburg, we've met far too many people who have married money. And, that is their only claim to fame. Others have inherited money. And, have never added a brick to the family building.

CHAPTER 2

Some Get It – Some Don't

A Tale of Two Cities

Addressing community friction through an advice column

"Dear Mike"

DEAR HOPEFUL: As promised, here is your entire letter from last week. Your concerns were too important to address in the space allowed.

DEAR MIKE: I'm new to the area and honestly don't understand the friction between my adjoining cities. They both seem like nice places to work and live, although one appears more progressive than the other. When I was transferred, I didn't have a lot of time for house shopping so I relied on colleagues in the area.

They suggested a real estate broker in the city where my company is located. When I asked about homes in the other, the agent's response was, "Trust me, you'll like this one much better. It's a community on the move." Being pressed for time, I bought in the city she suggested. It wasn't long before a few of my neighbors began talking about the adjacent town like it was a depressed third world nation.

Adding to my confusion, one of my best friends lives there and constantly asks, "Why did you buy in that city? They're a bunch of 'haughty tot tots" I didn't understand what a "haughty tot tot" was, but I assumed it wasn't a compliment.

I really like living where I am, but I've come to realize the adjacent city isn't all "doom and gloom" as portrayed by a 'few' of my neighbors. The people living around me aren't a bunch of haughty tot tots. Unless you consider successful people, who care about their family and community and willing to get up and do as haughty (I looked it up).

I see a lot of good in both cities and the constant friction and rivalries are discouraging. Some say, "They'll never come together." And I say, "Why not!" Being new allows me to see through smudge-less glasses. What can I do? – HOPEFUL

DEAR HOPEFUL: I felt I needed to know more about your cities. Therefore, I sent a team to visit both, ask questions, and above all... listen. As I suggested last week, most rivalries stem from jealousy: Either economic, athletic, political, or some combination of the three. In your situation, it's all three. But being new, you couldn't be expected to understand their history.

Let's look at some interesting facts: The income level of one is about double the other and their square miles are similar. One has a much higher high school graduation rate and much higher percentage of college degreed people. One pays over double the median real estate taxes of the other. However, ironically, their 2008-09 budget is about the same.

You can form your own conclusions. The perception is that one is the "Have's" and the other the "Have Nots." However, my team found that this is not a universal perception. For some, the athletic rivalry is the heart and soul of the controversy. But, kept in check, that can be a positive.

On the other hand, they discovered there was a similar perception between two high schools in the older of the two cities in the 50's and 60's. When its economy crashed and one school closed, the rivalry switched to and intensified with the high school in the city you now live. Of course, the income and educational differences have added to the friction/rivalry. At least that's the perception.

But remember, perceptions differ depending on whose glasses you're looking through. On the political end, they're both competing for a bigger piece of the economic pie. The key is being able to adapt to the economics of change. It appears one city is better at adapting.

Yet, my team uncovered some wonderful qualities within each city. Qualities, if properly showcased, will benefit all. Understand: Solving big differences usually requires bigger solutions! As I see it, your mission (if you choose to accept) is to help them find a common ground...and there is always common ground.

And stress these words to anyone who will listen "There's no limit to what can be accomplished if it doesn't matter who gets the credit." – unknown.

> Knowing both cities very well, they will never
> solve their differences – egos!

Beginners Guide to Successful "Festivalizing"

"I loaf and invite my soul" – Walt Whitman

Festivalizing: "Attending area events that bring pleasure while minimizing stress, sibling arguments, and uttering bad words." At least that's the definition I found.

Yes, it's festival season where I live, finally! It all begins May 4 and continues through the first week of October. Every Week! A festival. A fair. A celebration. A jubilee. No traffic congestion. No shuttle busses. Easy Parking. Short Walks. I love it!

However, after being gone for 32 years from my home town, I was sadly unprepared for my first two festival seasons. Do you realize the planning that goes into (or should) a successful festival visit? Oh, I was once like you. Check the date, time, location and drive. A rookie mistake. I want to share my failures, poor judgment, embarrassing moments, and just dumbness from the past, in hopes it might be of some value.

Therefore, I have prepared the *"Beginners Guide to Successful Festivalizing,"*

Rule 1: Check your calendar. Nothing ruins a good festival like an anniversary, your child's birthday, graduation, or your mother-in-laws visit.

Rule 2: Contact the organizers. Ask about dos and don'ts. Merry (our Lab) loves festivals. Two years ago, we went to one and saw a few dogs walking their companions.

Merry wanted to go last year, so we bought her a new bandana and packed her water jug. By the way, be responsible and take plastic bags for your dog's waste. When we arrived, she was so excited. But, the signs said, "No Dogs Allowed." We would never leave her in the car, so we decided to take her home and return. After arriving home, you guessed it. One look in those disappointed eyes and we all stayed home.

Rule 3: The go bag. Certain essentials are important but leave them in the car. An old duffle bag works great for the small stuff. Include folding chairs and those cheap little rain coats that you can never get back in the pouches. Don't forget sweatshirts, old hats, and extra socks. Don't laugh. I have stories that belong in a survival manual. Ah yes, suntan lotion. Red body parts might not spoil the day, but it will spoil the next day.

Rule 4: Weather check. Dress appropriately. Sneakers are a must. Spiked heels and fishnet stockings might have their place, but not at festivals. I arrived to one festival wearing a tank top and shorts. In two hours, the temperature dropped 20 degrees and it rained. No go bag!

Rule 5: Emergency rations. Put some protein bars and small water bottles in a back pack. I know. Protein bars taste awful but they can prevent starvation. Festival food is usually great but can wreck havoc with your digestive system, leading to other disasters.

Rule 6: Map. Get one (if available) and highlight restrooms and first aid centers.

Restrooms…know where they are. Funnel cakes are wonderful, but not six plates. Fact: Restrooms are farther apart the older you get. First Aide Centers: Great for bee stings and applying ice to the back of your neck to treat hand prints when you forgot the meaning of, "enough is enough!"

Rule 7: Enough is enough. Know when it's time to go home. When your companion's (or spouse's) face turns blotchy and her skin is cold and clammy, call it a day. By the way, I don't recommend getting them a milk shake in that condition. Learn from my mistakes.

Rule 8: Head count. Which is worse? Leaving with four and returning with three or returning with five. Tempting as it might be, come home with the correct number.

Rule 9: Opportunities abound. I've heard some say, "There's nothing to do around here." Open your eyes and embrace the opportunities! Festivals are only the beginning.

When your child comes to you and says, "Can we go to the fair?" Think! Is a round of golf that important?

Epilogue. Whether it's a festival, a concert, a fair, or a craft show, it doesn't matter. In the words of my Uncle Jess, "Never let work interfere with a good opportunity to loaf."

One final point: Always check ahead of time regarding
taking you pets and make sure you have plenty of water.
And remember, a festival is not a training ground!

"Build It and They Will Come"

"Determine that the thing can and shall be done and then we shall find the way." – Abraham Lincoln

Lompoc, California. Norfolk, Virginia. Bangor, Maine. Martinsburg, West Virginia. They all did it. Clarksburg, West Virginia, my town, can do it. This is not about Clarksburg, past or present. It's about what Clarksburg can become. Although far apart, these cities have a common thread. They once had a thriving downtown and for various reasons, fell upon hard times.

The one thread Clarksburg doesn't share…the others have recovered. Rest easy, I'm not going to talk about the Clarksburg of my childhood. I do want to talk about what I see and what I've been told. I have been told the Oak Hall building (on Main Street) and much of the block may be demolished and replaced by offices. The old City Hall is budgeted for demolition. The former Jack's Furniture building is being demolished. The Waldo Hotel, the once proud grand dame built at the turn of the century, cries for help and is so worth saving. There are more vacant than occupied stores on Main Street and Fourth Street.

I haven't been back in Clarksburg long enough to know the business "movers and shakers." The politicians, I know their names only because I knew their fathers. but I don't know them. I don't know who is connected or disconnected because I don't know. However, I can speak freely about what I do know.

I have a vision for Clarksburg, my "Field of Dreams." In the movie, Ray (Kevin Costner) kept hearing a voice that said, "Build it and they will come." As I walked the streets of Clarksburg, I thought about those other cities. Each had a vision and found a way, just as Ray did in that Iowa cornfield, despite the doubters.

Walk with me while I share my "vision." Remember though…if you build it (what people want) they will come (back to downtown). Let's begin at the Waldo Hotel. She still has good "bones." Could we possibly do what Norfolk did with some of their vacant warehouses? Turn them into luxury condos, with many amenities. Baby boomer bungalows.

Let's turn the corner and walk Fourth Street. Woo, how about this.

Block off the street and keep Traders Alley open. Replace the asphalt with brick or cobblestones. Plant some trees, have nice benches, and maybe a fountain. Very old-world, like Taormina, Sicily. Sidewalk cafes, a tea room, coffee shops, upscale gift shops, and music.

This is making me hungry, so let's keep walking. Look at this old building on the corner. I think this was once Friedlander's dress shop. Wouldn't it make a grand art gallery? It could host student art shows, support local artists, and teach classes. A small gift shop would be perfect. Look across the street. There is Oak Hall. An office building would be good and would bring a lot of business to Fourth Street. Do you think a little space could be used to build a small amphitheater? What a great place for concerts, plays, and even movies in the summer. I love live events.

Concerts make me hungry and thirsty. Remember Fourth Street? Maybe a venue could be built where Jack's Furniture store was? You don't remember it, let's walk down Main Street. There it is...or was. Oh yes, I have a Main Street vision, but I'm saving that for later.

Now, let's walk Third Street. There's the old City Hall. I was told the lot might become "green space." How about a gazebo, benches, trees and flowers? What a nice place for lunch. Maybe a little music on the weekends. Look, there's a nice restaurant across the street.

Well, that's about it. This is my Clarksburg "Field of Dreams." Just like the movie, "Build it and they will come" ...if they have a reason! Unlike Ray (in the movie), it takes more than one builder. To our movers and shakers. Its time to put aside egos, end power struggles and work together and find a way. Sandra and I volunteer!

Like the motto of a soccer team I once knew, "Play with one brain, one heart, and one vision."

If you grew up in a small town, you could probably change a
few names and mine would become yours. Sad, isn't it.
As one friend said, "What we need is a few well timed 'natural' deaths."

"Come together right now…over me"

"You don't live in a world all your own. Your brothers are here, too." - Albert Switzer

In 1969, the Beatles released their final album *Abbey Road*. The album opener was a song by John Lennon titled "Come Together. "For me, that song took on a whole new meaning the evening of May 30, 2008.

Two weeks earlier, an old high school teammate (Jim Christie) called me and asked if I would be interested in playing in a benefit basketball game. After hearing the details, I agreed. After all, old athletes are young athletes with many years of experience.

Jim told me several former basketball players from Roosevelt – Wilson and Washington Irving high schools were getting together to raise money for Doug Hogue, principal at WI Middle. Jim said Doug's wife had recently passed away from cancer and Doug is now battling the disease. The benefit was called "Do It for Doug," with proceeds going to the American Cancer Society.

Although I never knew Doug, his wife, or most of the players participating, it was certainly a worthy cause, a cause that eventually touches most of our families. Little did I realize the impact the evening would have for me…and the community. When I entered the gym at RCB (Robert C. Byrd High School), only a handful of players were there. The volunteers were setting up and a few fans were in the stands. I grabbed a basketball and tried to remember what it was like to make a basket and dribble without looking at the ball.

The mind of an 18-year-old was telling the body of a 58-year-old what to do but the body wasn't listening. Very Frustrating! Other people get old. I just gain experience, at least through these eyes. As we came closer to game time, the stands started to fill and I recognized a few old teammates.

The beginning of the evening was about "Sharing" memories and 'posin' for oldie pictures, arm-in-arm, possibly holding each other up. As it turned out, the players of the 60's would play each other, followed by 70's, 80's and 90's. 'Pickins' were a bit thin. for the WI Toppers of the 60's (my team). It seems most were unable to play or too far away. The starting 5 for

WI were Jim Christie (bad knee and all), Mike Erwin, Bud Henderson, Pete Bowie, and me. That's it. That's all we had.

For R-W, it was Bob Ferrell, Butch Sutton, Dave Garvin, Mark DeFazio, and 'Duck' Webster. Having left in 1972, names like Chris Meighen, Billy Childers, and Jeff Schneider meant nothing to me. Until I found out they were All-Staters. To non-sports readers, that means they were (are) really good! I asked Jim who those two girls were, "Oh, that's Suzanne Pettrey and Trisha Talkington. They were on the 1983 WI State Championship team." Suddenly, I felt very inferior.

All-in-all, there were about 50 players from each school. Right before tip-off, the gym was almost filled and I began to understand. that something very special was taking place. Chris Meighen (the event organizer) was right when he said, "I just thought this would be a great way to honor two people (Doug and Janice) who have meant so much to so many."

And honor them we did: Players ranging in age from 70 to 31 came together as teammates...for a common cause. Former and current coaches and officials came together...for a common cause. Doug's current students sat beside the fathers and mothers of past students (with their children) ...for a common cause.

Friends and colleagues came together on this special May evening... for a common cause. And there were supporters (like me) who never knew Doug and Janice, yet came together...for a common cause.

Toward the end of the game, Tom Dyer (a teammate from the 80's) summed it all up when he said to me, "Mike, just look around. Look at all these people. What does this say about our community?" And I thought: When we come together we may not always win...But we will never fail!

If we could come together over a basketball game, why can't our leaders come together over other issues?

Maybe we should play more basketball.

Fall clean-up – trash or treasure?

"I see a lot of people who love their jobs. I see some garbage collectors smiling as they go about their jobs. – Willie Stargell

To the city of Clarksburg, West Virginia, my hometown, thank you for providing the fall and spring clean-up. Many may not take advantage of this service but take it from a world-class never throw it away person, it will make your life a lot cleaner – in many ways!

In case you were unaware, not every city has this service. For instance, before moving back to Clarksburg, I lived in a city with over 500,000 people. This city did not have a seasonal clean-up, but it did have a special pick-up service. It happened twice a month and required a call to schedule a pick-up. It sounds better than it was.

The trash had to be four feet away from the curb, not on the sidewalk, put out the night before, and bagged, boxed or bundled. The list of "no I won't take it' was longer than what they would take. Unfortunately, many would resort to illegal burning or dumping. Well guess what, we have a city service that is efficient, thorough, and the restrictions are reasonable, Imagine that!

I first learned about our service shortly after I moved back to Clarksburg. My neighbor told me that the city would take just about everything, if it wasn't toxic or would explode. So, I began a new phase of my life called de-cluttering, with the encouragement (prodding) of my wife Sandra, who pursued me with the exuberance of a Marine drill sergeant. Keep in mind, I had saved everything from the age of six. Sandra's rule was (is), "If you haven't worn it, picked it up, started it, or looked at it the last two years, it goes" This was very painful, very painful indeed.

My neighbor also told me that most of my "stuff" would be gone before the actual pick-up day. I was a bit confused but he said, "Just wait, you'll see." It didn't take long for me to understand what he said.

Now we begin the "trash or treasure" part of the story. A week before my neighborhood pick-up date, there was a constant stream of bargain seekers combing my alley. These were not the average seekers. These were seasoned professionals with an eye for that special deal or need. My father-in-law always said, "Somebody always wants your stuff more than you do".

What was once my trash became someone else's treasure." By the official pick- up date, my Mt. Hood of treasures was reduced to a speed bump of trash.

As I drove around the city, I was amazed to see what people were throwing out, or in some cases didn't throw out and should. I admit that Fred Sanford of "Sanford and Son" would have been envious of my garage before the clean-up - but wait! After last years clean up, I saw many homes and yards that must have belonged to Fred's son, sister, brother, or uncle. Many front porches and yards were still littered with trash or treasures .

Cluttering your garage or even the inside of your home is one thing, but when it spills onto the porch and into the yard and becomes an eyesore for your neighbors, you have crossed the line, I my opinion. Sandra, my wife/drill sergeant, has this favorite saying, "A cluttered home is the sign of a cluttered mind". The fall and spring clean-up is an opportunity to de-clutter our homes, neighborhoods, and minds.

Our homes reflect who we are. Who are you? In the words of John Ruskin, "Much of the character of every man may be read in his house". If you have a Fred Sanford living beside you, talk with them. Maybe they are physically unable to do the work or they might not know where to start. Clutter is like that. Offer your help. That is what neighbors do. If they tell you to mind your own business, go to plan C - C is for City. Call the city. That is why we have codes and inspectors. They can't be everywhere so we need to help them.

Clean-up. Fix-up. Put-up. It's all about pride! In many cities around the country, our children grow up around graffiti, garbage, and clutter. What do you want for your child?

Remember, pride and effort does not cost the first penny!

If more towns had similar programs, perhaps we
would see less dumped along side the road.

Many priceless objects have been created from garbage,
namely Ann P. Smith's "Awesome Owl."

For Every Lock, There Is a Key!

"To do as you would be done by, in the plain, sure, and undisputed rule of morality and justice." - Lord Chesterfield

For years, it had been in his garage, as it had been in his grandfather's garage before him gathering dust and drawing little attention, although it was being moved from shelf to shelf. Then one day, out of curiosity he picked up the old cigar box. So many years had gone by, he had forgotten why he saved it. He couldn't even remember what was inside.

After laying it on his work bench, he wiped away the dust so he could see what was written on the outside. Under the years of grime was a brown box with a gold, blue and red band around the edge. In the center was printed "Muriel Cigars" with the word Senators underneath. On the inside of the lid was the image of a woman wearing a red scarf and red beads, with red lipstick and large hoop earrings.

Inside were dozens and dozens if not hundreds of keys. Keys of all shapes and sizes.

Where they came from and why they were in that cigar box, who knows? There were long and short barrel keys (skeleton keys) some with solid and some with hollow shafts. Some were brass and some silver. He recognized a few as safety deposit box keys because of the name Diebold. There were a few small silver keys that were probably luggage keys, but he couldn't really tell.

Several of the keys had Yale, Excelsior, Crouch and Fitzgerald and Corbin printed on them. Flat keys. Square keys. Funny shaped keys. There were several old automobile keys: Buick, Chevrolet and Oldsmobile, among some which were unrecognizable. As he finished dumping the contents of the box, one lone padlock fell onto the bench. It was 3 ½ inches tall and 2 inches wide. There were no markings or key attached. He wondered, "What was so special about this one lock?"

As he looked at this odd collection of keys he thought, "Somewhere, someplace, and at sometime there was a lock for each of these." Determined to open the padlock, he tried every key that could remotely fit the cylinder. Many of them slid in but would not turn. Close, but not close enough.

And finally, as he was about to give up, the shackle of the lock popped up. Opening a lock that had been secured for decades.

A very profound lesson was learned that day: For every lock, there is a key! A key called persistence. The right key can unlock so much but you must recognize it and try it!

As the years went by he thought back to when he was a child and his father was out of work for nine months because of a union strike. Everyone suffered, workers and management. When union and management finally found their "key," it was the same one they picked up during month number one. It took eight months of suffering before the impasse was unlocked.

He never forgot the child he met years ago, the child who had difficulty learning but his parents never gave up. They were committed to unlocking the mystery. And finally, they found the right key. A teacher who saw what no one else saw.

To the people who have very complex and unsatisfying personal or professional lives; your cigar box is out there. Just find it and try each key. For eventually, one key will unlock a new world of happiness and satisfaction.

And as he looks around his community he sees some governments, agencies, businesses and organizations that are "locked tight." Compromise. Cooperation. Mutual good. Integrity. None of their keys are stamped with these names. Just like union and management when he was a child. He remembered how everyone suffered. And the key was right in front of them all along.

He still has that Muriel cigar box full of keys. And a brass lock with a key inserted in the cylinder.

A constant reminder that, "For every lock, there is a key!"

Never stop looking!

"Heigh – Ho Heigh – Ho It's Off to Town I Go"

"Vision helps us see the possibilities of tomorrow within the realities of today, and motivates us to do what needs to be done." - Steven Covey

Sandra! Sandra! Mike, quit yelling. I'm right here. Sandra, I'm going to town. But it's Saturday morning. Nothing's open yet. Oh, yes there is. It's opening today and I need to get to the new parking facility before all the good stuff is gone. Oh yea, I remember reading about it. Don't spend all day. Remember 'The List.'

I'm 'outa' here. Yes, I have my license, money, phone, hat, and I put on sunscreen. Geez, I'm not a child. 30 seconds later...Back so soon! I forgot my keys! Don't look at me that way. I'll be back by noon...as Sandra handed me my watch.

Finally, I was out of the garage and driving toward town. And I started thinking, "I wish Dad was here. He would've loved this." And suddenly, I was pulling into the lower level of the parking facility. How is it we can drive for miles and not remember the trip? Oh well, that's another story by itself.

As I looked up I saw a sign, "Welcome to the Clarksburg's Outdoor Market."

Today was opening day. The possibility had been discussed for a long time but today it became reality. As I walked up the side steps, I thought to my self, "Well Dad what do you think? Yea, it looks very old world. Nothing fancy." The trucks and cars of the local growers lined Traders Alley. A reminder of bygone days. Under the cover of the upper level were dozens of tables. Faces of the familiar and unfamiliar behind each stand. And I smiled at the simplicity and creativity of the signs.

As I (we) walked around, nature's bounty was a plenty. The aromas confused my senses. So many tomatoes, cucumbers, melons, corn, peppers, berries, homemade breads, and cookies. A beekeeper even had a demonstration hive (it's safe and behind glass) and jars of golden honey for sale. Some local churches were selling homemade jams and pies. Oh, those pies. One garden club was selling flowers.

There were several tables full of organic produce for those who dislike pesticides and other man-made bad stuff. I stopped (very briefly) at a few specialty and exotic stands selling food that looked more like bark, twigs, grass clippings, and very small bird eggs.

And then I saw a very familiar face. The sign said, "Angelo and Gus' Summit Park Produce - Grown Where Dad Grew." Their gardens (today) are on the same terraced land their father grew vegetables in the 1920's. No doubt, their hands are guided by his. As we talked (imagine that), one of the organizers responsible for the market came by and joined the conversation. "Great idea," I said. "Giving people a reason to come downtown early on a Saturday (every Saturday) to buy fresh produce and other treats."

How convenient. I can visit the shops on Main, 3rd and 4th Streets and take home fresh produce. Life is good! As I've said before, "Build it and they will come." Food vendors were preparing lunch and a small bluegrass band was setting up.

As I was walking around, I heard someone say, "It's really nice to buy locally grown produce. No contaminated spinach or tomatoes. And everyone knows mountain air, soil, and water makes everything taste better." And just to be super safe, the Health Department makes random inspections. Later, Angelo said one of the requirements to receive a vendor's license is everything must be grown or produced in West Virginia. No foreign stuff allowed! Nothing from Ohio or Pennsylvania.

Before I left, I sat down on a bench to enjoy a cup of coffee. And I could hear Dad saying, "Mike, just look around. Look what leadership with vision can accomplish. Just one more reason to come to town. Oops! Look at your watch. Its 1:00 and you're late. You better stop by the flower shop. Say goodbye to Angelo for me and don't forget the leeks."

Having a farmer's market allows local money to stay local and for the most part, we consume much healthier products. And, sometimes, it's just nice to visit with old friends and meet new friends.

He Held the Power

"The strength of criticism lies in the weakness of the thing criticized." – Henry Wadsworth Longfellow

He held the power to ruin your life or make you a success. He was both feared and respected. When he entered a room, the atmosphere changed. What began as a quiet and casual evening quickly turned tense. He was treated differently. Special. He was given the best seat available.

The owner personally greeted him. Attention to detail was critical: The linen tablecloth perfectly placed. The silverware polished and appropriately set. They knew he always looked for fresh flowers and a never-burned candle in the center of the table. The most experienced wait-staff was assigned to him.. When he left, there was a unified sigh of relief, only to be followed by nervous anticipation.

For Sunday morning was the moment of truth. He was no eccentric movie star, professional athlete, talent scout, or agent. Politics wasn't his profession. However, he was well known throughout the city. Respected because he had studied with some of the greats in their profession and was a master in his own right. He was feared because his opinions, either complimentary or critical, could mean triumph or failure for those he visited.

The moment of truth came every Sunday morning. He was simply called 'The Critic.' Yes, he was a restaurant critic, but not any critic. His column was potentially read by over a million people. As his reputation increased, he found it necessary to alter his appearance and wear a variety of clothes when he visited different establishments.

Different accents became the norm. He would go alone. Sometimes with a companion. And occasionally as a family. This way owners never knew his face. His rules, from the beginning were: Be objective. Fair. Honest. He reviewed the restaurants outside appearance, décor, service, atmosphere, cuisine, and of course prices.

His goals: Keep the established and successful on their toes and give the newcomers a chance to become established and successful. In his own unique way, he was simply encouraging businesses to provide a pleasant environment, quality service and excellent food at a fair price.

Wow, what a novel idea! I thought, "He's just what we need. Right here! Right now!" We need someone who is respected to do what this famous critic was doing: Keeping the established on their toes and telling us about the new ones in an objective, fair and honest way.

Far too many times success (decades or years) can breed complacency and/or a false sense of accomplishment causing people to overlook the little details. Just like the well-established (for decades) restaurant whose food has remained consistently good but their service has declined. It's inexcusable to wait an hour and a half for service for a party of 10 which had reservations. People also need to know about the up-scale restaurant which has significantly reduced their portion size and has difficulty providing quality service for groups larger than four.

It would also be reassuring to read about the quaint little place which raised generations and is still providing quality service and excellent food at a fair price. How about that new restaurant which just recently opened? What's it like? What kind of food do they serve? Is it child-friendly? Do they add the wow to their dining experience? Do they have a dress code? It might be nice to know what's behind the door before we enter.

And this is exactly what "The Critic" provided. Yes, 'He held the power," but only because he was respected and his opinion mattered. Come to think of it, in addition to a restaurant critic, we also need a General Business Critic. I can see it now, every Sunday morning. The moment of truth. Reviews of our local banks, law firms, hardware stores, fraternal organizations, grocery stores, or (insert your own business).

Reviews based on: Objectivity. Fairness. Honesty. With goals aimed at keeping the established on their toes and giving the new ones a chance for success. Revolutionary idea - maybe! Needed - yes, at least in my opinion.

To stay on your toes, you need good balance.

Magical Mystery Tour

"There are only two creatures of value on the face of the earth. Those with a commitment and those who require the commitment of others." – John Adams

A walk-about town with an old friend.

I can't believe it! It's almost been a year since we last visited Clarksburg, West Virginia, my hometown. So much has happened. I must show you Main Street. Yes, the Waldo Hotel, built at the turn of the century, is now luxury condos and 4th Street is booming. Blocking it off was a great idea. It has an old world feeling. The fountain is beautiful. The tea room, sidewalk cafés and upscale gift shops are bustling with customers.

Remember last May when I said I had a vision for Main Street? Well, it's no longer a vision. Main Street is once again magical. No, it's not like it once was. Nothing is like it once was. But, I think you'll be surprised. Pleasantly! Let's park in front of the Chamber of Commerce's new home so we can tour Main Street. I don't have any change either, but don't worry. The parking meters are gone. Let's walk down this side first. Look across the street. Wow is right! Yes, that new federal office building is where Oak Hall Cafeteria used to stand. Finally, all the players made a commitment to get it done. Yes, I think Senator Byrd (D.WV) had a hand in it. If only he was 60.

Look across 4th street. Remember Friedlander's lady clothing store? I thought it was going to be an art gallery, but a law firm moved in. Something about downtown that attracts lawyers. However, the building beside it is our new art gallery. They're teaching classes and next month they're hosting the first Harrison County Student Art Show. I thought you'd like that, being an artsy person.

Before we cross 4th street, just stop and take in the beautiful streetscape. Looks a lot different doesn't it. The city worked with the garden clubs and planted trees on both sides of the street.Yeah. Yeah. Some people objected because of the birds but I guess our city leaders thought beauty was more important than an occasional dry cleaning bill.

Let's cross the street and sit on one of the benches in front of the art gallery. Look on both sides of the street. Benches everywhere. Everyone donated by local service clubs. No, I don't know who provided the planters, but I do know the garden clubs plant and maintain them. The clubs also do the hanging baskets on the light posts. I think they're petunias. It's a pretty good relationship. The clubs plant and the city waters.

Well, we've sat here long enough. We've got a lot to see. Yes, this used to be a vacant building but it's now the Harrison County Historical Society Museum. It was in the Stealey-Goff-Vance House on West Main. The house has been restored and furnished like it must have looked in 1807. We'll stop there when we leave.

In the meantime, check out our newest addition, The Main Street Internet Café. In the evenings, they host your kind of stuff (artsy stuff): poetry readings, book discussions, guest authors, and book signings.

The last vacant building between 3rd and 4th street is now called "The Chocolate Rose." Gourmet chocolates and intimate flowers...food for the soul. It's especially convenient when we (boys) say or do stupid things. Now, turn around and look at the Court House Plaza and tell me what you see? Yep, it's flat and beautiful. They pulled up all the marble and reset it. A good choice to recycle than replace, considering some of the Egyptian marble walkways have been around for centuries, I guess it wasn't a bad idea.

Yes, down town is coming alive...once again. Sure, it's different. And in some ways, better. It's an eclectic mixture of restaurants, salons, high-end shops, government buildings, banking, offices, and cultural activities. I think one word sums up why it all happened. Commitment! A commitment to working together. Putting aside political differences and personal agendas, working together to secure federal and state grants.

You're right. The results can be amazing when the goal is bigger than the players! How about a cup of coffee?

When I shared this vision with some city leaders, they just stared.

And I thought, "Who is really in control"

May I Have the Envelope Please?

"When you experience true beauty, you find yourself being lifted by the wings of harmony." – Alexandra Stoddard

Applause! Applause! Applause! Thank you very much. I'm Woody Mulch and I will be your host for tonight's One Great Bloom awards. Before we identify this year's recipients and our Grand Prize Winners, I want to recognize the person responsible for this magnificent program. Please welcome Ima Bloom.

Ima, please tell us the story (the history) behind tonight's awards. Why here! Why now! How you put it together? Yes Woody, it was my idea, but it took the commitment of a lot of people and the support of the business community to make it a success.

Let's start from the beginning. I always knew this was a wonderful place to live. And one day, sitting in my garden, I began to realize how beauty has elevated my life. I started thinking, "What a wonderful place to live. I wonder what it would take to make this a beautiful place to live."

At first, some snickered and even laughed at my ideas. But, I asked them how they felt the first time they saw Blackwater Falls State Park, in northcentral West Virginia. Or when the door bell rang and there was a bouquet of flowers with their name on the card. And how alive they felt after a nature walk through the wild and wonderful areas close by.

I remember the peace within after leaving the Hospice Garden at the Veteran's Memorial Park in Clarksburg, West Virginia. Beauty takes many forms. At that moment, Woody, an idea was born. An idea to recognize people in our community who are trying not only to elevate their lives, but the lives of others. I called it the "Yard of the Month." I wanted to keep it simple but it soon took on a life of its own.

Knowing I needed a lot of help, I turned to the local garden clubs. I contacted the Harrison County Garden Council, the governing body for the local clubs, and asked if I could speak at their next meeting. Here's what I presented: The existing clubs would adopt neighborhoods not currently represented by a club, keeping the numbers equal. The criteria for the "Yard of the Month" award would be established by the Garden Council. Remembering…it's all about improvement, taste, pride, creativity, and beauty. It's not about who can spend the most money. It's not about competition. It's more about who can do the most with the least.

Club members would not be eligible. Too many scandals in the news already. But Ima, what's to keep the same people from winning all the time. Elementary my dear Woody. You can only win once in two years. Remember, it's about spreading and encouraging beauty. Bear in mind, beauty takes many forms.

What makes this award so unique is it's presented every month, 12 times per- year, by each club. With seven clubs, that's 84 winners. On a set week, the boards from each club would tour their areas and pick their "Yard of the Month" and present their award.

Yes, they receive more than a sign for their yard. Thanks to the generosity of local businesses, each club collected wonderful donations. Woody, just look at what one club awarded this year: WVU (West Virginia University) football tickets, golf packages, a $200 gift certificate from a home and garden store, a spa visit for two, $200 gas card, one month house cleaning service, one month free baby sitting, weekend stay at a local hotel, and home catering for a week.

Ima, your vision has truly elevated the lives of many. Would everyone please direct their attention to our large screen while we look at this year's monthly winners, through the eyes of Ima Bloom.

Please note, our four grand prize winners will each receive an all expenses paid three-day weekend for two at the Stonewall Resort, compliments of the Harrison County Wings of Harmony Foundation. And now, "May I hve the envelope please." Our spring, summer, fall and winter Grand Prize Winners of the "One Great Bloom award are…

Once again, this story was personal. My frustration with visionless people is evident. This is my home and I see it dying right before my eyes. And, it doesn't have to be.

Never Say You Are from West Virginia, Especially Clarksburg

This was my very first story as a professional writer.

Yes, that is exactly what I mean. Before you read any further, let me say that I was born, grew up, worked, and left Clarksburg, West Virginia. Now, I have returned after being in a very progressive Southern state for thirty-two years. I saw the boom-times in the 50's and 60's and would never have left Clarksburg if the city would have been better to me job-wise.

However, I like many, went south for greener pastures. Yes, my adopted state was good to me in many ways. Yet, being from West Virginia had its drawbacks. I, like many who followed my path, was subjected to all the hillbilly jokes. I would always grit my teeth and swallow hard when southern gentlemen and ladies asked me where I was from.

After a while, I would even muffle the West in West Virginia to prevent further ridicule. As I found out, many people would say, "Oh, where in western Virginia are you from. On a few occasions, I would just answer by saying that it was a small town you never heard of. This usually kept the wall of protection in place.

Even with all the tasteless jokes (no need to relive them now), history and Hollywood have not made it easy being from West Virginia. Movies like *Coal Miner's Daughter* made outsiders think that every town in West Virginia was like the one in the film. I kept telling everyone that the movie was set in a town in Kentucky, but it made no difference. Kentucky, West Virginia, Appalachia, they are all the same to many of the refined people in my adopted state south of the Mason-Dixon.

I also became very frustrated saying that the movie *Deliverance* was not filmed in the hills around Clarksburg. Come to think of it, some pretty interesting events took place on Lowndes Hill, located in the center of Clarksburg in the 60's. At least no one got killed (that I knew of), although a lot of car windows did get fogged up by generations of teenagers.

Oh yes, on more than one occasion, I had to show my driver's license to prove that my middle name is not Hatfield or McCoy. Even my side job (raising sheep) was the source of ridicule. After a few years, I finally convinced my southern city- friends that I raised mine for the wool. Over the years, I developed a hard shell that no one ever broke. A few possible cracks, but it was never broken.

Don't take me wrong, I was never ashamed of being from West Virginia but I must admit being a Mountaineer (our nickname) had its trying moments. These moments tried my spirit, my beliefs, and my courage. As the state motto says "Montani Semper Liberi" - Mountaineers are always free! Freedom, I guess this also includes the freedom to be narrow-minded, misguided, misinformed and just plain rude.

Shortly after my return to Clarksburg, words such as pride, majestic beauty, family, hard work, freedom, fierce patriotism, and many more came flooding back. These words describe the West Virginia I knew and once again know. You see, I left West Virginia and Clarksburg because I felt I had to. I came home because I wanted to.

Clarksburg and West Virginia is one of the best kept secrets around, in my opinion. Perhaps you must get away for a while before you realize how much you really take for granted, like we did. The person who said, "You can't go home", never went home. So, as this title says, "Never Say You Are from West Virginia, Especially Clarksburg." Instead of just saying it, I encourage you to **"Yell"** as loud as you can, "I am from West Virginia, especially Clarksburg".

So, from now on, when you travel outside the state and meet someone from West Virginia, just point to that missing front tooth (our secret salute), we all have a missing one (or so they say). And remember to keep the best kept secret a secret.

Many times, we are our own worst enemies.

One Piece at A Time!

"Flaming enthusiasm, backed up by horse sense and persistence, is the quality that most frequently makes for success. — Dale Carnegie

This is for all you car guys and gals. Do you remember the Johnny Cash song "One piece at a time?" If not, it's about a man who appropriated automobile parts from a General Motors plant over a 20-year period, hoping to build his dream car. The final product was unique, to say the least.

When I first returned to West Virginia, I was taken back by the number of cars that reminded me of Cash's song or possibly my Grandmother's patch-work quilt. Please understand, where I lived in Virginia for 32 years took automobile materialism to a new level. If it wasn't new, shiny, and expensive, it just wasn't driven! Many of the high school parking lots looked like exotic car shows, with real-world shock only a graduation away.

I forgot how creative Mountaineers are when it comes to keeping old faithful on the road. I admit, I raised many an eyebrow upon seeing some cars in the parking lots and on the highways. One reminded me of a zebra…was it white with black stripes or black with white stripes? I couldn't tell. One fender was red, one was gray primer, and the trunk was green.

There was the Falcon I saw in Gore, West Virginia that was so jacked up (body lifted), the driver must have needed an oxygen mask. It was a station wagon for heaven's sake! I'll never forget the old Pontiac that pulled beside me at Eastpointe shopping Center in Clarksburg. It looked like Rocky Balboa after his last fight - bruised and bloodied, but still on its feet. His eye (headlight) was taped open with duct tape. Do you know that there are books written about duct tape? However, the editors must visit West Virginia for the revised addition. My friend, who owns a local barber shop, calls it "West Virginia Chrome."

Upon close observation, I now understand the term West Virginia Chrome. It can cover up a rusty bumper, hold down a broken trunk lid, hold a tail light in place, keep a convertible top from leaking, replace a broken window, and even hold tight an outside mirror that had a fight with a post and lost.

However, the one car (loosely called) that still tops my list was one I passed driving to Shinnston, West Virginia. It was a pickup body on tank (or bull dozer) treads. Yes, a pick up tank! I'm sure they didn't sneak it out in a lunch box as Cash's song indicated, but, they will surely "have the only one there is a round," in Johnny's words. Ingenious – Creative – and only in West Virginia...a pickup tank! The ultimate ATV.

Yes, I now have a greater appreciation for the West Virginia automobile. Some may not be pretty, but they get their creators to and from work. For many years, my Father-in-law (Lester Ogden) had a very successful trucking business in Enterprise, West Virginia. His trucks may not have been shinny, clean, or new, but they were always on the road – making a living! One of the many reasons I have grown to respect the automotive resourcefulness of many West Virginia rides. Some may be put together "one piece at a time" but they are on the road – useful to the family and helping make a living! As Lester also said, "A clean truck doesn't make any more money that a dirty one."

There may be some flaws in his philosophy but, oh so much truth! These patch- work quilt cars may be the result of necessity but are also serving their owners the same as the owner of the shiny new one, without the hefty monthly payment.

I no longer raise an eyebrow at the duct taped head light, the red fender and green trunk, the spare tire tied to the roof, or the tail light with red cellophane paper. Now, I just think about what Lester said. These "one piece at a time" cars are just one more example of the Whatever It Takes West Virginia grittiness! Now, "Every day, I watch them beauties roll by".

Oh, yes, Mom, Goo Gone" will remove duck tape residue from your trunk!

Thanks Mr. Cash!

Our cars might not always be the cleanest, prettiest or
the fastest – but they get us to and from work.

The "Good News Paper"

"I am part of all I have read" – John Kiernan

I taught Political Science for 17 years.

Friday, November 18, 1997. As my students entered the classroom, they knew it was "Current Event Friday." Every Friday, we would discuss significant international, national, Virginia, and local political events. Week after week, we talked about murder, earthquakes, robberies, assassinations, and domestic violence. One morning, a young lady with a frustrated tone in her voice asked, "Mr. Lambiotte, isn't there any good news out there?" Ah Ha! I felt another assignment building.

"Yes Michelle, there are a lot of wonderful things happening. But, they're not always right in front of us. Sometimes we must look for them," I said. "But Mr. Lambiotte, why aren't they on the front page?"

A new project was born that day. The students were to take a piece of poster board (teachers love poster board) and recreate the front page of our local paper: Headlines, weather, date, pictures, stories, and all the 'stuff' editors put on a front page.

It was called "The Good News Paper," with a twist. Only articles that were uplifting, people helping people, feel good, warm and fuzzy stories were allowed. No stories about suicide bombings, traffic fatalities, arson, or illegal political deals. No pictures of monster hurricanes, quakes or mine disasters, no matter where they occur.

Yes, (tragedy) is news and events we need to know about, but my students were saying, "Enough is Enough!" I'm tired of being depressed or angry after I read the front page. Give me something that makes me feel good about life," they said. And feel good they did. Because on their front page...it was a "Good News Paper."

I still think about these students and the ones that came after them every time I read the paper. A friend once said, "Mike, the news is about violence, disease, disgust, and mayhem. The papers just report it. They don't create it. Besides, we need to be informed." I looked at him and said, "It's also about beauty, art, music, kindness, charity and helping."

We also need to be informed about the good! I accused him of being negative, cynical, and always jumping to conclusions. He told me to take off my rose colored glasses. I looked at him and said, "Careful, it is easy to become what we see, smell, taste, and read – without realizing it. A man is what he thinks about all day long." - Emerson

Eventually, we won each other over. I agreed, we needed to know about the blood, guts, and gore. And he agreed, positive human interest stories help create a balance in a somewhat unbalanced world. I admit I know little about journalism. especially about the decision-making process in what to print, if to print, and where to place the article.

All I want is to enjoy writing. Maybe help you laugh occasionally and maybe, just maybe, give you something to think about. For the record, my journalistic role models were Candice Bergen of *Murphy Brown* and Mary Richards and Lou Grant from *The Mary Tyler Moore Show*. Although fictional characters, I admired their qualities. They never embraced sensationalism. They reported the facts and never forgot the sensitive human element. They made us cry, laugh, gave us hope, and above all, made us think!

As an editor, it's probably easy to flood the front page with blood, guts and gore. There's plenty to choose from and it happens everywhere and way too often. But it's nice to read about the "Seven Wonders of West Virginia," and JROTC programs on the rise on the front page!

Good News. On the front page. What a fresh idea. In 1997, I challenged my students to create a "Good News Paper." Now, it's time for a different challenge: To the real Murphy Brown's of the world; Every day, give me something positive and give me hope – Hope the front page. Every day, give me a reason to smile. And never forget…make me think!

> I received much criticism for this story. To those who
> heaped the criticism, truth be known, we know why.

The Village That Ate Itself

What experience and history teaches is this – that people and governments never have learned anything from history, or acted upon principles." – George Wilhelm Hegel

Variations of my opening quote have surfaced throughout history. And sadly enough, the quote remains true. However, as you read this story, I ask you to consider, "What would it take to prove Hegel wrong?"

Once upon a time in another century, there was a small village in Transylvania, a region in central Romania. Counting every man, women, child and farm animal, there was no more than 1,000 residents. Although small, they were very united. Most families had lived there for several generations as a very tight-knit village.

Independent yet interdependent people. They shared the good times and pulled together during hard times, but that did not last forever. Although their roots were in agriculture, the center of the economy was now mining. With the discovery of coal, a railroad soon followed which provided needed supplies and left with what the locals called "black gold."

With the success of the mine and railroad, the village prospered. In the beginning, there was a blacksmith shop, livery, general store and of course a tavern. Continued prosperity brought with it a more civilized lifestyle: Within a few years they built a church and a school.

With the addition of a newspaper, the villagers no longer relied on outsiders for information. Because of the smallness of the village, leadership was intertwined and very complicated. The mayor was the great-grand son of one of the founding fathers. Even the village elders who advised the mayor had similar roots. The sheriff was the son of an elder and his deputy was his brother-in-law who he didn't really want to hire, but wifely pressures prevailed. The tax collector, appointed by the mayor was a distant cousin.

The school teacher's father had been the town crier walking the streets with a hand bell making public announcements, "Oyez, Oyez…" However, the newspaper forced him into an early retirement. The teacher ended up marrying the newspaper editor and he hired her father as a copy boy.

The only true outsider was the traveling minister who decided to make this village his home. In the end, it was only he who saw what was happening. But no one was listening to his messages. When mine production slowed, everyone brushed it off as temporary, ignoring the signs. Everyone heard but no one listened to the minister's Sunday messages, "Vision, change, diversity, sacrifice, and compromise. Village good transcends personal gain." His message fell upon deaf ears. Within a few years, the coal was depleted and the railroad tracks fell silent - the beginning of the end.

First to close was the bakery. Then the butcher shop and the shoemaker. Soon, empty storefronts outnumbered the occupied. Over one third of the population left for more progressive areas. Areas with diversity and vision. Without a plan, this once tight-knit village became divisive. The mayor and village elders argued violently over what were once minor issues. Instead of one working unit, the elders championed their own agendas. The tavern became a place for scheming and back-stabbing instead of singing and celebrating.

The sheriff tried to arrest the tax collector for stealing village money but was stopped by the mayor. The collector was his cousin. Gradually, corruption and greed consumed the village leaders and apathy quickly spread throughout the citizenry like the plague a century before. This once beautiful prosperous village in the foothills of the Hateg Mountains began to slowly consume itself. Still, no one listened. The school closed because there were no more children. The once bustling market place where everyone gathered each Saturday was nearly empty.

Neighboring communities referred to them as "The village that ate itself." Yet through the eyes of the minister and eventually the teacher and a small handful of villagers, there was still hope. They were determined to learn from their past and thus, change their future. In one memorable sermon, the minister looked at his congregation and said, "The mighty pyramids of Egypt began with the laying of a single stone."

I really struggled to make this sound fictitious, because it was fact.

This Ain't Mayberry Anymore!

"The greatest thing in life is not where you are, but the direction in which you are moving." – Oliver Wendell Holmes

Many of us grew up watching *The Andy Griffith Show*. Sheriff Andy Taylor, every little boy's role model. When asked why he never carried a gun he said, "I want the people of Mayberry to respect me, not fear a gun." We all loved Aunt Bee, "Andy, did you like the white beans we had for supper?" "Well I ate four bowls," he said. "If that ain't a tribute to white beans I don't know what is."

And there was a little of Opie (Andy's son) in all of us. "Pa, just what can you do with a grown woman?" Also, anyone who has eaten a P B & J can sympathize with Opie, "Pa, it ain't easy getting a peanut butter and jelly sandwich down dry. Yesterday, I almost choked."

We laughed at the bumbling antics of Deputy Barney Fife, yet at the same time knew there was a sincere, kind and loyal side to Barney. Deputy B's signature line, "Nip it! Just nip it in the bud!" Remember? "Oh, you're just full of fun today aren't you Andy? Why don't we go to the old people's home and wax the steps!"

The Andy Griffith Show – Mayberry: Small town America. Shared values. Everyone knew and looked out for one another. Mayberry, not too far removed from where I and many of my friends grew up – Clarksburg, West Virginia. There were our neighborhoods: Stealey, Hartland, Broad Oaks, North View, East View, Bridgeport or Shinnston...it made little difference. We had our own little Mayberry right here in Harrison County, West Virginia. A place where 11-year-old girls could safely walk to town for choir practice and stop by Bland's Drugstore for a cherry coke and a package of crackers.

Children would sit on a neighbor's step or under a street light until way after dark, laughing, catching fireflies and telling ghost stories. That is, until mom yelled, "Opie, time to come in!" We continually fished and swam in the river. Yea, we knew swimming was illegal, that was part of the thrill. Boys rode their bikes to baseball practice, spent their allowance on baseball cards and at the neighborhood lemonade stand. Big spenders impressing little girls.

We camped in the wilds at night, listening to the untamed animals roar - from our back yards. We slept with our windows open, seldom locked the doors and if Dad forgot to close the garage, no one gave it a thought.

How fortunate we were to grow up in a kinder and gentler time. However, as I look around today, "This ain't Mayberry anymore!" Drugs, gun crimes, domestic violence, pedophilia, apathy and going ostrich (burying our heads in the sand) have all contributed to the death of our Mayberry. Today, parents fear letting their children out of sight. The elderly and young have become prime targets.

We stand and demand greater police presence, faster court action and longer jail sentences, but we resist providing needed resources. We need to open our eyes. Andy didn't need to carry a gun. Barney only had one bullet, which he kept in his shirt pocket. But, "This ain't Mayberry anymore!" When our police need more resources, and they desperately do, we must find a way. But, we also must help ourselves. Get to know your neighbor. Look out for one another, be aware in parking lots and expand (or create) 'Neighborhood Watch' programs.

Be conscious of the unusual: An influx of out-of-state cars in a quite neighborhood. A child who doesn't play outside anymore. Your neighbor, who starts wearing excessive make-up, won't make eye contact and suddenly is too busy to talk.

In the coming years, if I wrote a story about my (our) hometown, I would like to title it "Return to Mayberry – How a small town woke up." The dedication would say, "To those who saw a better way…and together, made it happen!" The final sentence would be, "Oh mom, do I have to come in now? Yes Opie!"

By the way, Mayberry was based on Griffith's real-life hometown, Mt. Airy North Carolina.

The past may not be better than the present.
But, in many cases, it was far safer.

Through Madame Merimee's Crystal Ball

"The Wright brothers flew right through the smoke screen of impossibility." – Charles Franklin Kettering (1876-1958) American inventor, engineer and businessman

Like most of us, I've always been interested in what the future holds. Like many of us, I don't want to wait until the future becomes the present. So, I decided to consult someone who can see into the future. Unfortunately, I don't know any Chinese fortune tellers who can read the dark tea leaves from the bottom of a china symbol cup. Nor do I know someone skilled in reading tarot cards. And I'm not traveling to Hungary or northern Italy where the practice originated. Plus, I can't find my Ouija board we used in the late 60's. Probably a good thing. That board still spooks me.

Nonetheless, I did stumble upon Madame Merimee, a famous Romanian gypsy during one of my many voyages to the outer limits of my imagination. She was dressed just like the gypsy fortune teller in the movie *Lacho Drom* – colorful floor length pleated skirt, a puffed sleeved blouse sparkling with sequins, head scarf and very ornate jewelry, lots of jewelry! When we sat down, I couldn't help but notice the crystal ball in the center of her small round table.

As we sat across from one another, she looked into my eyes and said, "Michael (gypsies always use formal names) tell me what you want to learn?" "Madame Merimee," I said, "Tell me what the future holds. Not for me personally. But, for the community I love. What will be the future of our town? Will we grow? When will the economy begin to improve? What will become of our struggling neighborhoods? Madame Merimee, tell me where we're heading."

She held up her hand, as to quiet me, and said, "Michael, let me look deep into my crystal ball for answers." After a few minutes, she smiled and said, "Michael, I see very positive things happening. I see new faces among your village elders. I think you call them council persons."

She stopped for a few seconds, then looked at me and said, "And your elders have learned to play with one brain. Petty differences have vanished! I see many of your neighbors, far and near, with a resurgence of pride in their homes and yards. Paint brushes and garden spades have replaced broken beer bottles and sagging fences.

"And to fight the growing drug problem, your village elders and law enforcement agencies have expanded the sorely needed drug task force. "Yes Michael, I see many positive events taking place. Wait, there's more! I see many small villages (towns, excuse me) which made the common-sense decision to combine resources."

"I see a sign saying, Eliminate Bickering – Enjoy Benefits, Regional Government Works! How nice. I see one of your side streets has been closed: Sidewalk cafes with roving minstrels. I think you call them musicians. Reminds me of my small Romanian village."

"Your downtown is rising from the ashes. I hear two of your elders (councilmen, sorry) talking with a new business owner. I hear positive business climate being mentioned. Ah yes, even the soaring gas prices will be a blessing." I looked at her with bewilderment. "Michael, use this (gas prices) as an opportunity to explore the beauty of your state of West Virginia - Wild and Wonderful,' it truly is! Plus, you stimulate your own economy."

"I see family's white water rafting and biking. An elderly couple sitting on a park bench holding hands – still in love. "I see people relaxing in a cozy bed and breakfast inn. There's a couple on the patio of a mountain lodge in the Potomac highlands."

"I see some people dressed like me. Ah, it's the color, sounds and smells of your ethnic festivals. More will attend this year. I see your schools working closely with businesses and universities to better prepare their students for their future – our future is their future."

Then, Madame Merimee stopped and looked straight into my eyes, "Michael, you have nothing to worry about. Your future is in good hands." "Madame Merimee, do you speak the truth?" I asked. She smiled and said, "We shall see. We shall see."

Instead of gypsy I thought about using a Ouija
board as the basis for this story.
But, I liked the beauty and mystery of a gypsy.
I'm still spooked by the board.

Through These Eyes, I Can See Clearly...Now!

Being from West Virginia isn't easy.

"I like to see a man proud of the place in which he lives. I like to see a man live so his place will be proud of him." - Abraham Lincoln

In an earlier story, I talked about emotional walls, hillbilly jokes, Clarksburg and how difficult it was (at times) being from West Virginia. As a native of Clarksburg who lived in the South for the past 32 years, you can imagine (or maybe you can't) what it is like to be the brunt of jokes and movie references.

At times, I would even go along with the jokes or even enhance them. Yes, making fun of West Virginia has made the career of some comics, at our expense. Although I rarely showed my anger toward these jokes to anyone but my wife (who is also a Clarksburg native), I really got tired of being asked, "Is the state flower actually the satellite dish?" Remember when they were the size of a television station dish?

I was constantly asked state political questions. I lost track of the times I said, "No, the governor's mansion did not burn all the way to the axle." I would simple say axle(s). It was a doublewide with new vinyl windows. These quick-witted answers would usually quiet my southern colleagues. However, there were always some who would delight in showing their ignorance time and time again with the shoeless and one leg longer than the other jokes.

The quickest way to prevent ignorant ridicule is to head it off at the pass. I always made it a point to show off my new black Converse high tops and to show them one heel was not built up for hill walking. I have now graduated to designer sneakers and I must admit that I am 'gellen.' with both shoes the same height. For some reason, those Converse shoes are not as comfortable as they were 40 years ago, the quality must be in decline.

As my years in the South multiplied, I slowly regained my appreciation for the internal and external beauty of West Virginia, Harrison County, and Clarksburg. Oh yes, now I remember, this is called "**Mountaineer Spirit**".

If you remember from an earlier story, I had talked about how Hollywood hasn't been kind to my state with Movies like *Coal Miners Daughter* (I know, it was about Kentucky), and *Deliverance*."

Today, when I think of "Coal Miner's Daughter," my heart swells with pride and my eyes tear. For I think of the hard, dangerous, necessary work these men and women perform. Their sense of family and work ethics could teach my former colleagues much about life and much more about living. In this movie, I also think of one little girl's dream of success and the struggles she overcame…AKA "Mountaineer Spirit".

When I watch *Deliverance* I think of many scenes, but one I will always remember is where the young boy, sitting on his porch and playing the banjo and duels with the guitar player, hence the song "Dueling Banjos." I remember the look in the young boy's eyes when he out-played the outsider. A look that said, "Come on back when you want some more… AKA "Mountaineer Spirit".

So, my fellow West Virginians and Clarksburgians (sic), when we are joked about the mountain state and our city and Hollywood is unkind to us and comedians launch their careers at our expense, show your "Mountaineer Spirit" and pride and say, "Hell yes I am from West Virginia. I do dangerous work, necessary work, provide for my family, look out for my neighbor, raise my children (just don't let them grow up), love life and living in West Virginia. Now, come on back when you want some more!

After returning home, I can see so much more clearly now!

Pride in one's heritage is pride in oneself.

Welcome to WMSL

"I fear there will be no future for those who do not change." –
Louis L'Amour

With a blinding flash, lightning struck the ground! Then, thunder shook the old weathered Victorian home! Suddenly, the door handle began to turn. Then, the dissonant chords of an organ could be heard. As the door opened, an eerie 'creek' sent chills down my spine. A voice from the shadows said, "My name is Raymond. I'll be your host for the *New Inner Sanctum Mysteries.*"

"Yes, I'm the same Raymond from long ago. As a child in the 1940's and early 50's, you may remember me from the original *Inner Sanctum Mysteries*. I entertained you. I frightened you. But, I kept you awake (very awake) on those long dark trips home with your parents."

"Ah yes, the suspense and spine-tingling stories. Do you remember how the voices of Boris Karloff, Peter Lorre, and Claude Rains kept you on the edge of your seat? There all gone now. And you're all grown up. But my friends, it's time for a whole new generation of listeners to understand and feel what you felt…a long time ago."

"Thanks to some visionaries who embrace change (not resist it), it's time for a new radio program from the past. Welcome to WMSL. North Central West Virginia's newest and most innovative radio station. The only music you will hear will be from this old pipe organ. No sports or political banter. No weather report, unless it is dark and stormy night."

"For those who remember me, I won't disappoint you. There will be plenty of suspenseful stories. But these stories will be different. You will write the stories and the mysteries. I want to give local writers an opportunity. Especially our high school students. Imagine… writing and performing on *The New Inner Sanctum.*"

"But my friends, we'll offer much more than before. We'll also air episodes examining local myths and legends. Occasionally, we will feature short stories written by children. Add a little history and stories about colorful local characters and you have a truly new and dynamic radio program. A program that not only entertains…but also educates and makes you think."

"Let's look at some of our upcoming programs: Have you ever heard of the "Mystery Hole" along Rt. 60 on the way to Hawk's Nest, West Virginia? It's close to Ansted, West Virginia. Water flows up hill. Take a drive to Point Pleasant, West Virginia. Most of the locals know about the mysterious creature called Mothman. The first reported sighting was in 1966. The sightings ended on December 15, 1967...the day the Silver Bridge collapsed."

"If you live near Salem, West Virginia, visit the old train station. No doubt, you'll hear stories about the tragic train wreck in the Flinderation railroad tunnel. Reportedly, the sounds from that tragedy still come from that tunnel! We'll look at the Black Hand Gang that reportedly had some influence in Clarksburg, West Virginia. Many deny their presence, but I remember as a child seeing a badly faded black hand painted underneath a highway overpass. My father said it was just graffiti. Later, my grandfather simply said, "It was part of the past. It was nothing.""

"And stories still circulate about tunnels connecting various buildings and hotels in Clarksburg. The *New Inner Sanctum Mysteries* will attempt to locate one or more of these tunnels and find someone who remembers why they were built and who built them. Who knows what lurks below? With a little imagination, we will interview the abolitionist John Brown. He led the assault on the federal arsenal in Harpers Ferry, West Virginia in 1859. One of my special guests will be retired Brigadier General Chuck Yeager, the first man to fly faster than sound. He was born in Myra, West Virginia."

"WMSL knows you're ready for a change. The question is: Are you ready for something that's not only exciting and stimulating... but makes make you think? Especially, on dark rainy nights."

"For now, WMSL is only a vision. It exists in my mind. But who knows what tomorrow will bring."

"This is Raymond saying, "Pleasant Dreeeammsss.""

WMSL – taking us from where we are, to where we want to be, and then, to where we never thought we could be.

CHAPTER 3

A Child of the 50's Memories

If we're lucky, there will come a time when memories are all we have.

A Knight to Remember

"Elegance does not consist in putting on a new dress." – Coco Chanel

It was May, 1993…high school prom season. The "hype" surrounding prom signaled the end of the school year. Although there were still a few weeks left, most seniors had already pressed cruise control, "School's Over!"

For the girls: It was all about the perfect dress, shoes, jewelry, and getting that all-important hair and nail appointment. For the guys: It was about renting a tux which would compliment her dress and making dinner reservations at a fine restaurant. Rent a limousine or a fancy car from one of the luxury dealers.

This was not the Emmy's or Academy Awards. This was high school, yet the spending was equally obscene. The theme for the evening was "A Knight to Remember." Their mascot was a knight. The prom, red carpet and all, was to be held at the naval base officer's club. As the students said, "It was time to let the big dogs out!" After all, it was prom season.

But not everyone was equally excited. For one student, it was a reminder of how John and his family struggled. His father worked for a landscape company and his mother was a stay-at-home mom with four children.

John worked part-time at a local fast food restaurant and gave his entire pay check to his mother. For him, there would be no "Knight to Remember." He was embarrassed because he couldn't afford to take Linda, his girlfriend since their freshmen year, to their senior prom in the manner expected. A tux, dinner, fancy car or a limo was out of the question. He didn't even own a sport jacket.

Linda understood and said, "It's all right. I didn't want to go anyway." But he saw the disappointment in her eyes. The truth is she couldn't afford a dress, let alone all the accessories. Her father deserted them years ago. It was just her, her younger sister, and her mom.

When his teacher heard, they weren't going to the prom he asked John to come by his room after school one day. This is all John's teacher said, "The extravagance isn't what's important. What's important is who you're with and that you make them feel special. Here's your prom ticket. We'll take care of the rest." John looked at him and said, "I have no suit. Linda doesn't have a dress and our car's a piece of junk."

"Don't worry," he said, "Miss T (the Home Economics teacher) is talking with Linda." Getting defensive, John said, "We're no charity couple." "We're not offering charity. You two are going to work this off," the teacher said. John thought for a minute, smiled and said, "Deal."

The next day, operation 'A Knight to Remember" was set in motion. Miss T got the fabric for her dress donated by an exclusive fabric shop. Together Linda and Miss T sewed the dress after school. All the accessories were on loan from a local jewelry store.

The shoes were purchased from a thrift store and redone free of charge by a local cobbler. No one dare turn down Miss T.

The male teachers combed their closets and put together an outfit for John worthy of the cover of *GQ (Gentlemen's Quarterly)* magazine. A local car dealership provided transportation. When John's manager at the fast food restaurant heard what was going on, he wanted to help. "I'll take care of dinner at the restaurant," he said.

Do not snicker. Look at what they did: A wing of the restaurant was blocked off and made very private. The employees brought plants and decorations from home. A linen table cloth, a candle and one red rose were on the center table which was set for two with real china, cloth napkins, and silverware, all from the employees.

On prom night John and Linda were served an extraordinary meal, especially prepared from their menu. On that one special evening in May, two young teenagers shared 'A Knight to Remember.'

Memories that would last a lifetime. And lessons they would carry with them forever.

A few years later someone told me they got
married and now have two children.
Values passed down.

"Devine Secrets of a (Real) Ya -Ya Sisterhood"

"It is one of the blessings of old friends that you can afford to be stupid with them." - Ralph Waldo Emerson

In 1996 Rebecca Wells wrote *Devine Secrets of the Ya-Ya Sisterhood*, a fictional story about a group of young women in 1930's Louisiana who became best friends as children and remained close into their 70's. Over the years, they kept a scrapbook of their lives chronicling tragedies, celebrations, pranks and loves (won and lost).

That book is fiction, however, my story is factual: "The Devine Secrets of a (Real) Ya-Ya Sisterhood." Their friendship began at Morgan Elementary School, in Clarksburg, West Virginial in the 1950's. As children, they played together in the Stealey and Hartland neighborhoods. This friendship continued during their years at Central Junior High. While at Washington Irving High School, they ate lunch together every day for four years.

During college, they remained good friends but careers, marriages and children led them in different directions and different states. And then one day several years ago, one of them came up with the idea of getting the entire group together for a few days of Remember when! and Did you know?

That first reunion was so enjoyable and special they decided to get together every two years at various locations for some serious girl updates. This is where I enter the picture. Recently, I was invited to spend an evening with these six life-long friends, girls I have known since elementary school.

While waiting for them on the upper deck of the tour boat on Stonewall Lake near Roanoke, West Virginia. I found myself uncharacteristically nervous. Not sure why, but I was. However, once they boarded the boat it was like a high school cruise - without all the drama!

Let me introduce you to a real-life "Ya-Ya Sisterhood." Cindy King (Shaver) is a speech pathologist who lives in Weston, West Virginia. She was the host of this year's reunion. Ellen Colvin (Condron) lives in Bridgeport, West Virginia and is an Associate Professor of Nursing at Fairmont State University. Susan Martin (Watson) lives in Lexington, Kentucky and has taught English for 28 years and is currently a Literacy Coach. Peggy Grimes (Semesco) lives in Ocala, Florida and was the office manager for her husband's dental practice. Amy Robinson (Algee) lives in Nashville, Tennessee and is an accountant and controller. And the final member of the sisterhood is Nancy Hersman (Harvey) who lives in Clarksburg, West Virginia and teaches second grade at Norwood Elementary.

Six incredibly bright, successful, and fun-loving girls (as I remember them) who are successful career women. And yet, despite many life-obstacles placed in their paths, they can maintain and even build upon a friendship that started when they were children.

While listening to their stories, I saw one little girl who I delighted teasing by pulling her hair as we walked home from elementary school. Another, whom I fell in love with in probably third or fourth grade. She was my secret girlfriend, so secret, she never knew.

By the time our reminiscing reached our high school years, those little girls sitting on that boat deck had all grown up. I now saw a high school Yearbook Editor, a Candystriper (a teen hospital volunteer), a Head Cheerleader and a Senior Homecoming Attendant, two *Memoirs* (our Yearbook*)* Princesses who were also Majorettes. My oh my…how I loved a girl in uniform!

After returning from "Fantasy Island," I listened, asked questions and took notes. Many of their stories were punctuated with, "You're not going to print that, are you?" Or, "You better not print that! I know where you live." I just laughed. That is until Cindy looked at me with an icy-cold stare and using perfect diction (speech pathologist) said, "Remember, we are on a boat in the middle of a lake." She convinced me that discretion was the better part of valor.

To be continued! I was having too much fun to end this story now.

Next page, "Secrets from the Ya-Ya Scrapbook:" Revealing stories about psychics, exotic dancing, 6 in-a- tub, temptation, the allure of dental school, marriage, and a little insight into real friends…having one and being one.

I love them all, in different ways. But I love them all.

Secrets from the Ya-Ya Scrapbook

"I'm learning to live close to the lives of my friends without ever seeing them. No miles of any measurement can separate your soul from mine." – John Muir

Part 2: Previously, you met Cindy, Susan, Nancy, Amy, Ellen, and Peggy. Six girls who became friends at Morgan Elementary School and have remained close to this very day… "A (Real) Ya-Ya Sisterhood." They went from playing with crayons to perfume and are now playing with (their) grandchildren. Friends who discovered what it means to be a friend and have a friend.

And now, "Secrets from the Ya-Ya Scrapbook." As we sat on the upper deck of the boat and talked about life, I began to realize how special 50-some years of friendship can be. I just wanted to hear their stories: What's in your scrapbook? When did the reunions start? Who started them? What do you talk about? What's an adult slumber party like? Tell me some secrets!

Peggy spoke up and said, "Sorry Mike, we're actually pretty boring. We just talk about life as it was and is. No soap opera drama." They all just shrugged their shoulders and nodded in agreement. But I did notice a couple of playful grins. The next few hours didn't reveal any deep dark secrets or tabloid headlines. However, they did reveal a lot about the teenage girls I once knew…now all grown up! Such as: A reunion was Amy's idea and she hosted the first one. Now, every two years they pick a location and get together for three or four days of girl talk.

They have found the secret for successful marriages. Combined, they have been married 216 years with only one divorce and have 12 children. Nancy proudly said, "And I have seven grandchildren." "Grandchildren! My God, she still looks like a majorette," I thought. Cindy said the secret ingredient was in the Morgan (elementary) School water.

Ellen said the secret was to marry a dentist. Three of them (Ellen, Cindy, and Peggy) married dentists.

It seems all three girls and their future dentist-husbands knew each other in college. Ellen tried to explain it but I got confused, to no one's surprise. I think those dental students put more than fluoride in their water. Susan (I think it was Susan) told me about the time they all shared a hot tub. No doubt their discussion was limited to politics and the state of the economy.

Oh yes, Amy said she would joke with her co-workers about being a Go-Go dancer in her spare time. We all laughed. That is until I saw Amy's mischievous grin as we exited the ship. Cindy talked about the psychic who came to read their fortunes. The psychic foresaw one of them being tempted by a younger man; a second would have two husbands, and a third would find a companion who likes to dance. Believe me, their stories were far from boring, especially the ones I promised not to publish.

More interesting than the stories was the insight they provided about real friendship - having one and being one. Much was left unsaid. Yet there was so much I could sense. Things I knew without asking. For fifty years, they have been there for each other. They have been there when needed, not just when it was convenient. There's nothing transparent or fake about this sisterhood...they're real! They were there for each other during their turbulent teenage years. Then shared the joys of adulthood: Marriage, children and grandchildren. They have been there for each other during tragic times. None more tragic then the death of a child. Please visit the Andrew J. Semesco Foundation website: www.ajsfoundation.org

I can say this with all certainty, "They don't pass judgment on one another and they don't waive their or their husband's credentials." They don't have to! When they're together, it's all about celebrating a beautiful friendship that has withstood the test of time... "A Real Ya-Ya Sisterhood."

To Cindy, Susan, Nancy, Amy, Peggy and Ellen: Thank you for giving me a glimpse of what few people ever have.

p.s. You're still stunning!

How many "real" friends can you count on one finger?

I Just Can't Wait to Get Old(er)!

"For beauty, truth, and goodness are not obsolete; they spring eternal in the breast of man. " - Ralph Waldo Emerson

They say age waits for no man. But man (and woman) always waits for age. As a child, we can't wait to begin elementary school. At least I couldn't. So many games to play. So many girls to tease.

And of course, the learning thing. Can't forget the 3-R's. Then we can't wait for junior high school, middle school for you "newbie's." And then there's high school: Driving, dating, sports and the drama connected with being a teenager. We can't wait until we're finally 18. A fully feathered adult with the, "I can do what I want to do attitude." Free at last...that is until we really need mom or dad. In so many ways, being an adult is highly overrated. Way too much responsibility and decision making and not enough play time.

Then we reach 21. We do our Rocky dance and then suddenly realize it's all downhill. But is it? Through these eyes, eyes that can't even remember 21, "I can't wait to get old(er)." Old enough to say what I want, when I want, where I want and as often as I want without worrying what others think. No more tongue biting and being forced to make the all-important politically correct statements. I'm weary of hearing, "You can't say that! You don't want to offend anyone." Or, "Perhaps you need to phrase it another way, using less intense words. We wouldn't want to shock someone into actually thinking."

And that is the heart of my most recent dilemma. A question I keep asking myself over and over, "How old do you have to be before you can say what you want and not care what people think?" I want to be that old(er) person who speaks the truth regardless of where they are and to who (or is it whom) they're speaking! "Oh, don't pay any attention to that old fart, he doesn't know what he's saying. But he's telling the truth. He just doesn't care what you think." I want to be that guy!

That's where I need your help. How old must be to become that guy? I want to be old enough to look at my minister and say, "Did you give a sermon today? If so, you need to speak up. I thought you were a mime." Or,

"Father, my false teeth were rattling so loud I couldn't hear your sermon. How about turning up the heat next Sunday?"

I want to be the guy at his club meeting who says to the consistently late or seldom-comer, "I see we have a visitor. Oh, Tom it's you? When are you going to pay your $200 in back dues? Wow, nice new Mercedes." Or, "Alice, why the hell are you signing up for this committee? You always sign up but never show up."

I want to be the guy who tells the father and son sitting in the restaurant wearing their ball caps, "Nice example. No wonder mom wants to stay home." Or, "Wow, the lights in here are bright, do you have an extra cap I can wear." Or, to the maître de, "Your portions are like women's swim suits; the smaller they get the more expensive they become."

I want to be the guy who goes to his town hall meeting and says to the mayor, "Brad just because your dad was a jerk doesn't mean you have to be. Quit arguing and do what's right!" Or to the lady who is against higher taxes yet wants a stoplight at the end of her alley, "For goodness sake Hazel, just shut up. You were an idiot in high school and now you're just an old(er) idiot."

He may shock some people. Some may laugh. Some may even ignore him, "He's just a senile old fart." However, they will remember him.

But how old do I must be before I can become that guy, the guy who's not afraid to say the truth?

Someday, I hope I have the nerve to be the guy I want to be.

June 17, 1949 ... Six Decades Later

"There is a fountain of youth: it is your mind, your talents, the creativity you bring to your life and the lives of people you love. When you learn to tap this source, you will have truly defeated age." – Sofia Loren

June 17, 1949 is my birthday. And last week, six decades later, I celebrated my 60th birthday. When I reflect, several age-related milestones seem to stand out. I couldn't wait until I reached 16. Look out world! I'm now "Heading down the highway, lookin for adventure." I had my driver's license.

And then I waited for 18. In 1967, you could legally purchase beer at 18. Then 21. In 1970, you could legally purchase other spirits and could vote. Hey, what did you expect, I was young and self-centered.

Reaching those milestones seemed to take forever. Then, the age-related highs and low points came by the decade. Hitting 40 wasn't too bad. Sandra threw a big surprise party to help me ease into that decade. Reaching 50 was another story. All the years of doing dumb boy stuff (physical stuff) began catching up with me. I now had a bad back, sore feet, climbing a ladder was no longer fun, and working on your knees was work.

But once again, for my 50th, Sandra came to the rescue with a surprise vacation to Bald Head Island, North Carolina. At first I took the bald head personal, but big surf, warm sand, and plenty of sun was the panacea I needed for entering my 5th decade.

Now I'm entering my 6th decade and the best way for me to express how I feel about being 60 is to share some of my favorite quotes about maturing. *"Men grow old. Pearls grow yellow; there is no cure for it."* - Chinese proverb. I don't embrace growing old(er). In fact, I fight it at every twist and turn by trying to take care of my body and mind as best I can. But in the end, growing old is better than not growing old.

"When I was younger I could remember anything, whether it happened or not." – Mark Twain. As I go through this and future decades (hopefully) maybe I won't be able to remember yesterday. And in many ways, that might be a good thing. But I still have today. And I'm going to enjoy it!

"Wake up and see for yourself, with your own eyes, all you dreamed of, all

of your days!" - Homer. I'm going to try my best to accomplish something positive each day...a positive thought, a positive action. And at the end of each day, I will smile at what I achieved.

"Inside every older person is a younger person wondering what the hell happened?" – Cora Harvey Armstrong. When I look back at my life it reminds me of driving a Lamborghini (the Italian super car). It seems like I went from 0 -60 (years old) in 3.7 seconds. I remember the trip but it was way too fast. Rest assured, in my remaining years I will drive slower, stop often, and enjoy the flowers.

"The virtue of a person is measured not by his outstanding efforts, but by his everyday behavior." – Blaise Pascal. At the end of each day, it's the little things that become most important: Flowers for no special occasion. Watching a ball game with your son. Canceling that meeting so you can attend your daughter's soccer game. Greeting your dog with the same affection she shows you.

"I still find each day too short for all the thoughts I want to think, all the walks I want to take, all the books I want to read, and all the friends I want to see." – *John Burroughs.* At 60, I know I won't have enough time to do all I want. But age has slowed me just enough to allow me to enjoy what I have.

And finally, from Eli Cass, *"Old age is when a guy keeps turning off the lights for economical rather than romantic reasons."*

For me, I choose the latter... "Click!"

I pray I will never get old – in spirit.

Just Look at Them Now

"The young man I was is quite different from the man I am. And when I become old, another I is beginning." - George Sand

Sitting there, I was very nervous. He assured me everything would be fine. And I assured him my high pain threshold stopped at my neck. He laughed and said, "Mike, you've been telling me the same thing every time you're here. How long has it been – 15 years?" And I said, "The past is the past." He smiled and guaranteed me his new dental hygienist was the best and most gentle assistant he ever had.

My confidence was immediately shattered when she entered the room. Dora is that you? Mr. Lambiotte is that you? The Dora (I saw) standing before me was the poster child for every (undeserved) blonde, air-head, cheerleader joke ever uttered.. I know. I taught her as a senior. She was bright, pleasant, and spent most of her senior year in 'never never land.'

The thought of her approaching my mouth with sharp pointy objects and whining devices was paralyzing. She laughed and said, "I know what you're thinking but look over your shoulder." I saw a Bachelor and Master degree, plus a Dental Radiation Safety Certification from Old Dominion University. "Don't worry; I graduated at the top of my class from ODU." She was right. There wasn't anything to worry about. Because the professional standing over me was quite different from the bouncy bobble head I once knew.

That was my first encounter with 'then and now.' That is, until I returned home after 32 years. When I left West Virginia, most of my friends were in their late teens or early twenties. Some I hadn't seen for 32 years and a few, only occasionally. The "young I knew are quite different from the person (s) I see before me." Today, they're respectable, mature, and successful. At least most of them! A far cry from the wide-eyed, I have all the answers, turn me loose on the world teen-twenty something I remember. Join me for a "Look at them now," through the eyes of yesterday.

As a child, he loved astronomy. We spent countless hours looking at the stars and counting the bulbs on the Veterans Hospital star at Christmas. Did you know there are 50 bulbs in that star! When I was 11 and he was

14, he doctored my hand after burning it camping on the West Fork River. Today, he's the leading ophthalmologist in our area and secretly wants to be a professional fisherman.

And there was another friend who spent most of his high school years avoiding the police. Nothing serious, but the potential for becoming a career criminal was always close by. Look at him now! He retired as a successful and decorated police officer. He once said, "I was almost a bad guy. I know how they think and where they hang out. The rest was easy."

My next-door neighbor was always playing with her chemistry set. Really mixing bad smelling stuff. Again, a sign. She became a doctor. I guess that wasn't challenging enough so she became a lawyer. Way too many brains in one head. I guess that explains why I could never beat her at Monopoly.

And there are my two politician friends. We played basketball and football together. I just can't help it. Every time I see them I think of the locker room pranks and high jinks. – major league boy stuff. It's like *Cold Case.* I keep flashing back to that 17-year-old team mate. And 'look at them now' – they make our laws.

One of my very best friends, who loved his Marlboro's and beer, fought his own addictions and demons from Vietnam. With God's intervention, he's now a minister with a beautiful family. No one would have ever guessed...back then.

I'm curious, when they look at me, what do they see? And I wonder, what will we become tomorrow?

Treat that child in the playground with kindness.
In a few years, she may be your cardiologist.

Reunions... 40 Years
Never Be Afraid to be 17 - Again

"The most beautiful discovery true friends make is that they can grow separately without growing apart." – Elizabeth Foley

This story is about reunions - memories, friendships, and growing up. I just returned from my 40th high school reunion. Nothing says life's so unfair louder than going to a reunion. Remember when you were 15, waiting to get that driver's license?

The clock never moved. The days crept by. You kept saying, "Life's not fair!"

Then, you couldn't wait for graduation. As graduation approached, you thought little about elementary friendships. It never dawned on you, the years would scatter you and your classmates around the world. Then, as Captain Kirk said, "Scotty, take her to warp speed." Your life changes and you begin doing adult things.

Soon, all too soon, reunion notices arrive. Along with their arrival come memories and questions." I wonder where Linda and John are now?" I miss the old gang and so many of my teammates. What's great about reunions is they allow you to turn back the clock to a happy carefree time, at least for me they do. I guess I am one of the fortunate ones.

I realize not everyone has pleasant memories of high school. Maybe, just maybe, that's why some don't attend. I remember our 10th reunion. Very interesting to say the least. This was the one where we gave all those silly awards. Remember the "Person who changed the most." – Go Christina!

Fast-forward. It's 30 years later. Sandra and I were on our way to my 40th reunion. As I got out of the car, I felt 17 again. Until my back reminded me differently and I looked in the mirror. Then I remembered what Paul said, "Oh, what the hell, we all a little dinged up." Thank God for name tags with pictures. "Hey, how are you? You look great. You haven't changed a bit." As your eyes drop down to find the name tag. This brings me back to the adult version of 'Life's not Fair.'

Call it genetics, working out, eating right – call it whatever you like.

But, it's just not fair that at 58, some look as good at they did when they were 17, and not nipped and tucked or otherwise enhanced. Then there were, guys with dropped chests, bald heads reflecting light, and knobby knees. Others were trim, tanned, and had hair. Life's just not fair!

A funny thing happened that Friday and Saturday night in July – we became 17 again. We did hours of remember when. We hugged and danced all night. Soaked our feet the next day and became good friends with Advil. But it was worth it. We have five years to recover, until our 45th All evening, pictures were flashing on large screens, pictures of a carefree time. So many beautiful pictures of elementary friends, high school friendships, and romances.

Little did we realize (back then) we would grow separately without growing apart.

One never grows too old to relive the memories or moments. This October, my Mother will attend her 63rd high school reunion at Hundred High School in West Virginia. Yes, there will be a new dress and shoes. And a lot of old memories. She will probably get the award for the oldest cheerleader and band member again this year. Don't tell her I said this, but I think she is the only one left. I will look forward to hearing her stories as much as she looks forward to telling them.

That's what reunions are about. It's not about physical changes – who cares!

"Were all a little dinged up." It's not about living up to expectations or sharing resumes. Reunions are about then, not now. They're about friendships, dances, and cruising your favorite drive-in or burger place. They're about football and basketball games, band camp, bonfires, and sled rides. It's a time to think about that special person and what you thought would last forever.

So, when your time comes...don't be afraid to be 17 again.

Remember, someone is looking forward to seeing you.

I truly believe reunions should be without
spouses, partners, or significant others.

Rock – Paper – Scissors

"When I look at a patch of dandelions, I see a bunch of weeds that are going to take over my yard. A child sees flowers for mom and blowing white fluff you can wish on." – Author Unknown

I wonder if we are given children to teach, or to learn from? Children seem to make choices in the most simplistic of ways. It's unfortunate that as adults, we generally seem to forget how easy it was to make decisions as children.

We (adults) seem to have this burning desire to complicate everything, sometimes turning potentially enjoyable activities into major power struggles. Think back? Have any of these ever escalated into a domestic 'War of the Worlds?' What movie do you want to go and see? Where would you like to go for dinner? Why are you taking this road?

Let's go away for a long weekend. Where would you like to go? Sure, you can play golf, but what about the painting?

Take a few moments and pencil in your own personal favorite. Now, let's board our time machine and go back to being 9 or 10 years old. And relive how simple it was to make decisions. Several of the neighborhood kids have gathered on the local baseball field at the VA Park (Veterans Administration). How do we pick teams? Simple: the two biggest, oldest or best players do the bat toss. You don't remember the bat toss? One captain holds the barrel (fat part) and tosses it to the other captain. He grabs it somewhere between the barrel and the knob.

Then they alternate placing their hands on the bat by either using a scissor method or grabbing it like they were making a fist around the bat. The first to cover the knob wins and gets first choice. Simple and final! No arguments. No what if's.

The only problem for adults is not everyone has a baseball bat handy. Not everyone has one hanging on their office wall, in the back seat of their car, or behind the kitchen door. For those who don't, you might choose a decision-making prop that is always with you...your hands.

Ever play 'Rock – Paper – Scissors?' For those who haven't (sheltered lives) it's very simple. The 'rock' sign is a fist. 'Paper' a flat hand. 'Scissors' is made with the thumb, fourth, and fifth finger folded toward the palm and the index and middle finger wide apart…like a pair of scissors. The critical role in preventing arguments is, "How many times do we do it: once, best of three or best of five."

After that's established, here's how it goes: One hand is open, palm up. The other hand is in a fist. On the count of one, fist hits the palm. On two, fist hits the palm. And on three the players hit their palms but with the option of making a fist, scissor, or paper sign. The rules are: Rock crushes scissors. Paper covers rock. Scissors cuts paper. If there's a tie, it's a 'do over.' Simple and final. No arguments. No what if's. We made many a movie choices using this method.

Shooting basketball foul shots is another practical way to make choices or decisions. First to make one, two, or three shots gets to choose. First three to make a shot are on the same team. You get the idea. Simple and final. No arguments. Either you make it or you don't. The obvious drawback to this decision-making process is the need for props. You need quick access to a basketball and rim. But can you imagine the number of decisions or choices that were made over the years at the Stealey playground in Clarksburg, West Virginia, a regular hangout for many of us growing up.

And my final childhood decision-making memory is, 'Spaces or Seams.' Grab a football on the sides and spin it real fast as you toss it up in the air. The other person calls out either spaces or seam' and then catches the ball on the sides. The catcher either wins or loses depending on what is pointing up.

Children have it figured out. Simple and final. No arguments. No maybes. No what if's

Too bad they turn into us.

> Maybe we should turn over the Middle East crisis to
> six Palestinian and Israeli children – ones who haven't
> been indoctrinated by the book of hate.

Wooo! I think I'm afraid of heights.

"There are only two lasting bequests we can hope to give our children. One is roots; the other, wings." – Hooding Carter

One of life's simple pleasures (at least for us) is sitting on our patio in the spring. This year we watched a robin meticulously build her nest in the exact same spot as last year. Sheltered by the porch roof and supported by the elbow of the downspout, she was high and safe.

Out front, another robin was building her nest in the rhododendron only inches from the front steps railing. She was low and vulnerable. And on our front door a dove was trying to build a nest in Sandra's forsythia wreath. One fearless dove.

It was a very busy spring at the Lambiotte home. Because the dove was "pruning" the forsythia to her liking, Sandra was determined to discourage her, "I can't let her tear up my wreath. She needs to go away! Go build your nest in a tree." she said. So down came the wreath.

A week later, Sandra placed it back on the front door. And with in minutes (so it seemed), the dove was back...building with a vengeance. And there, on the forsythia wreath we encountered the icy cold stare of a very persistent and bold dove with two small white eggs in her nest. She had won!

Over the next several days, part of our yard entertainment was noting the different parenting skills between door dove, gutter robin and paranoid robin in the rhododendron. Door dove would stay put and go along for the ride each time the door was opened. Gutter robin completely ignored us and sat tight in her nest. Even Merry's (our black Lab) curious stares and attempts at standing on her hind legs never rattled her. Paranoid robin fled every time the front door opened. Of course, Merry's big nose inches from her nest might have added to her paranoia. She would fly high into the dogwood or Japanese maple and chirp insistently, trying to distract us and protect her nest. When we left, she would immediately return to keep her eggs warm.

Each, in her own individual way, was protecting her young. When the eggs hatched, the real circus began. Each robin had four babies with furious appetites. Both mom and dad fed them tasty morsels. It seemed each nest had one baby who tried to hog the best worms. However, the parents made sure each had plenty to eat. And at night, they made sure their kids were safe and warm.

The dove was equally attentive with her two young. But instead of worms and bugs she fed them 'crop milk,' something doves produce to feed their young. Sometimes she would stare at us through the glass with a look that said, "Can I have some privacy?"

A couple weeks later, it was time for the teenagers to leave their nests. The back-yard robins went first. Sandra saw two babies flapping their stubby wings from atop our brick wall, one was missing in action, and the fourth was teetering on the edge of his nest.

He was flapping and wobbling as if to say, "Wooo! I think I'm afraid of heights." "Mom, can I stay home a little longer?" From the brick wall mom was chirping and bobbing her head as if to say, "Son, it's time to leave. Time to fly." Then he launched himself toward a scary new world.

We didn't witness the robin exodus in the front yard. But I knew the teenagers were close because several adult robins were "buzzing" me as I tried to enjoy my morning coffee. The dove...well, she and her two babies left on Memorial Day morning. How appropriate.

It was then I realized how much we have in common...humans and birds. We both do our best to protect and nurture our children. Yet there is no perfect formula for success. What works for the robin may not work for the dove. Yet in both worlds, the time will come when every parent will say, "Remember your roots, yet don't be afraid to fly."

In today's world, once you push them out of the nest, lock the doors!

CHAPTER 4

Really Special People & Places

Four Generations of Dental History

"There is a persuasion in the soul of man that he is here for a cause, that he was put down in this place by the Creator to do the work for which inspires him." – Ralph Waldo Emerson

This story is dedicated to the Davis family. A family of dentists who have served our community for 116 years and counting. When I returned to Harrison County five years ago, I needed to locate a good dentist, among other doctors. After being gone for thirty years, most of the doctors I knew before I left were either dead or retired. I met Dr. John Davis at a service club meeting and asked if he was accepting new patients.

When I went to his office for my first visit I saw five pictures on his foyer wall: Dr's Dorsey Davis, Robert H. Davis, John B. Davis, Robert B. Davis and (another) John B. Davis. The walls are also adorned with many old photos. One I recognized from a picture in the newspaper. It was Dorsey standing beside a patient in his dental chair with an assistant to the rear.

Dr. John explained that Dorsey was his great grandfather and he was the fourth generation of Davis-dentists. Later he introduced me to his father, Dr. Robert B. Davis who still practices with his son. After talking with them, I knew I wanted to share their story.

What they told me was not only a fascinating history lesson about the dental profession, but also an intriguing human interest story. Because of the amount of information, I felt it was necessary to present this in two parts. This story will be a dental history lesson through the eyes of Dr's. Robert and John Davis.

Let's begin with **Dr's. Dorsey and Claude Davis:** The brothers established their practice in 1894 and in 1907 moved into the St. Charles Hotel on the corner of 4th and Main Street in Clarksburg, West Virginia. Kerosene lamps provided light. Tooth extractions were $1.00 or patients could pay 25 cents a week. Dorsey was known to barter for services. Gold crowns were $35.00. And fillings were made of tin, mercury (yes mercury), silver or gold.

They practiced without anesthetics or antibiotics which had not yet been developed. However, opiates (morphine) and cocaine could be administered for pain. Yes, cocaine was legal then. The only way to treat an infection was to drain the tooth. Infections could turn into brain abscesses and abscesses could lead to death. All from a bad tooth.

Dorsey and Claude did use drills but they were waterless foot-powered drills. Pass the whiskey! In 1929 Dorsey passed his drill to his son Robert H., although they continued to work together for a few years. With **Robert H. Davis** and the beginning of the 1930's, dentistry saw significant advancements. Electric drills replaced the foot powered ones. Just the very thought of a foot drill gives me the 'heebeegeebes.' The really good news was by the mid 1930's dentists had antibiotics and sulfur drugs and by WWII, penicillin was available.

In 1959 Robert passed his drill to his son **Robert B. Davis**, Dr. John's father. With this pass came even more advancements: High speed drills with water, bridges, and composite and amalgam fillings, which look like silver. Dr. Davis also saw the introduction of Vicodin and other synthetics for pain relief. I'm saving what he told me about denture history for my next story. I will tell you this: He clarified one long-standing myth.

In 1988, it was time for Robert to pass his drill to his son, **Dr. John Davis**. Dr. John began practicing in 1988 and joined his father in 1997 in the Goff Building in Clarksburg, West Virginia's Main Street. In 2001, they moved their practice to its present location in Medwood Plaza off Route 98, between Nutter Fort and Clarksburg, West Virginia.

Dr. John's tools and procedures are a far cry from those of his great grandfather's. He has the benefit of digital x-rays, super high speed drills, composite resin materials, dental implants and so much more. I wonder what the next generation will bring?

Read on! There's more.

Part II, "The Men Behind the Drills"

"Follow the ways of your ancestors" - Old Irish proverb

My previous story was about a family of dentists who have served our community, Clarksburg, West Virginia for four generations. The legacy began with Dr's. Dorsey and Claude Davis and continuing to this day with Dr. John Davis.

In 1968 Virginia Slims commercial stated, "You've come a long way baby." And dentistry has come a long way from Dorsey's $1.00 tooth extractions (1894) to Dr. John's acrylic composite fillings and digital x-rays (present-day).

Once again let's begin with **Dorsey and Claude**: Dorsey had a rather large farm in the Stealey section of Clarksburg, West Virginia where he raised cows, chickens and pigs. Dr. Robert Davis said the farm was located just past the West End Bridge by the Dollar Store. Remember, this was 1894.

In 1912, their partnership dissolved over the cost of an innovative machine, a machine Dorsey felt was necessary in this "new age" of dentistry. Dorsey wanted to spend $150 for an x-ray machine. Claude disagreed. Dorsey bought the machine anyway and Claude moved to Huntington. They never spoke again. After their breakup, Dorsey maintained his practice in a one-room office, using the hallway as a waiting room.

Dorsey embraced new science. He was instrumental in getting fluoride added to the public water system in Clarksburg. Although he had no anesthetics, he could legally administer cocaine for pain. Surprised! As a side-note, small amounts of cocaine were in the original formula for Coca Cola until the practice was discontinued in 1903.

Dorsey's son, **Dr. Robert H.** took over in 1929 and drew his own plans for an office, moving to the 5th floor (510) of the Goff Building two blocks away. It seems almost everyone in this family had a dental calling. I found out Robert's uncle, Dr. John B. Davis, was a Colonel in the Army Dental Corps and Robert B's sister was a dental hygienist.

In 1959, the family drill was passed to **Dr. Robert B. Davis.** Most of the information gathered for these stories came from Dr. Robert B. Davis. I found his ability to remember such long-ago facts fascinating.

At one point his story-telling led to dentures. I was surprised to hear that vulcanized rubber (vulcanite), developed by Charles Goodyear in the 1850's, was used as a base for early dentures. He cleared up one historical myth: George Washington didn't have wooden teeth! The base for his dentures were carved from hippopotamus ivory and fastened to his one remaining natural tooth, with the upper and lower hooked together with springs. That explains his stern look in paintings. And his teeth were a combination of gold, lead, animal and human teeth. His lower denture is on display at the National Museum of Dentistry in Baltimore.

Robert did share something personal. There was a time when he seriously considered becoming an English Literature teacher. If he had followed this calling, we would have lost one fine dentist, yet gained one first-rate teacher.

In 1988, Robert passed his drill to his son, **Dr. John B. Davis** (Dr. John). Earlier in his career he had a General Practice Residency at Ohio State University in Columbus, Ohio, plus a practice in Delaware, Ohio before joining his father in the late 1990's. Dr. John also volunteers his time and expertise treating patients at the Susan Dew Hoff Clinic in West Milford, West Virginia. By the way, his brother Paul is also a dentist.

The final piece to this story is not about another Dr. Davis, but about two very remarkable ladies, ladies who I'm sure are responsible for this smooth-running practice:

Betty Brandli began working with Dr. John's grandfather, then his father and is currently working with Dr. John. Perhaps in the future I will write a story titled, "Betty Brandli, Training Three Generations of Dentists."

And then there is Anne Davis, Robert's wife and Dr. John's mother. Together, these ladies run the office and keep their dentists on task. Truly a family practice.

Well there you have it. Four generations of service. The only remaining question is, "Will Dr. John's daughter be the fifth?" What about it Kierstin?

Special thanks to the entire Davis family for this warm and interesting story.

I was so lucky to find Dr. John. By the time I returned to Clarksburg, all the professional people I knew before I left were either dead or retired.

"Guess Who's Coming to Dinner?"

"Those who dream by day are cognizant of many things which escape those who dream only by night." Edgar Allan Poe

This story is about six people. People I have admired and the questions I would like to ask them, but never will. These six have interested, fascinated, and influenced me in many ways. Although impossible, as you shall see, I've even imagined a formal dinner party and you'll never "Guess who's coming to dinner" at our home.

Seated to my right is Ernest Hemmingway. Across from him is William Shakespeare. Beside Mr. Hemingway is Thomas Jefferson. The other three haven't arrived yet. I'll introduce them later. Different times. Different personalities. Different accomplishments. All brilliant. men gave the world so much.

Can you imagine having them all around one table? Remember, it's all right to dream. What my guests have given to the world is well documented. What I would like to say is, "Please, just talk among yourselves. I just want to listen. Tell me about your world. And where you feel ours is heading." Glancing toward Shakespeare: I see, who many consider, the greatest writer in the English language. His plays, sonnets, and poems have been translated into every major living language. I would apologize, for not taking his work seriously in high school, hoping he would understand and forgive me. "Much of one's youth is wasted on the young."

I would like to know about his private life, which little has been written. About his family, his fears, and regrets. Sitting beside him at the Globe Theatre in London for a performance of "Hamlet" would be beyond words. He was only 52 when he died.

Across the table is Ernest Hemingway. A man's man, or so it seemed. I read his many novels throughout the years. His characters were usually strong but had a certain grace about them. Such brilliance and such a tortured soul, battling demons we could never imagine. Funny though, he's one of the few artists who achieved fame within his lifetime. He won the Pulitzer Prize in 1953 for *The Old Man and the Sea* and the Nobel Prize for Literature in 1954.

I visited his home in Key West, Florid a few years ago. As I stood beside the desk where he penned many of his manuscripts, I imagined him handing me a draft of *For Whom the Bell Tolls* and saying, "Well, what do you think?" The descendants of his 6-toed cats still roam the property. When I was 12, he took his own life. He was only 62. He would have loved West Virginia. His memorial is inscribed with: "Best of all he loved the Fall. The leaves yellow on the cottonwoods. Leaves floating on the trout streams. And above the hills. The high blue windless skies. Now he will be part of them forever."

Sitting beside him is Thomas Jefferson the always thinking quiet one. I can see him jotting notes in that small notebook he always carried. How does one properly address him? Would it be Mr. President, Mr. Secretary (of State), Mr. Ambassador (to France), or simply...Mr. Jefferson. So much knowledge in one mind.

Beyond the obvious, he was an accomplished architect, inventor, archeologist, gardener and planter, musician, wine lover, and noted gourmet. Most of all, I would like to walk with him around Monticello (his Virginia home) and listen to him talk about his gardens and his beloved orchards. Listen to him talk about the future, including his hopes and dreams.

Years ago, as I stood beside his grave at Monticello, I read his epitaph, which he wrote:

"Here was buried Thomas Jefferson
Author of the Declaration of American Independence
Of the Statute of Virginia for Religious Freedom
And Father of the University of Virginia"

Such an understatement. But, that was Jefferson. He died in 1826... on July 4th. How appropriate, for a man who gave us so much.

Ah! I see my other guests haven't arrived yet. I hope you won't mind waiting a while.

When I began writing this story, I knew it had
to be continued. Please read on.

"Guess Who's (also) Coming to Dinner"

*"The world is so rich, simply throbbing with rich treasures,
beautiful souls, and interesting people."* – Henry Miller

Ah, I see my final three guests are arriving. If you missed the introductions in the previous story, I invited six people to dinner. These people have inspired me so much through the years. I just wanted to say, "Thank you. Thank you for making me think, question, seek answers, and sometimes, just laugh."

Already seated are William Shakespeare, Ernest Hemingway, and Thomas Jefferson. My next guest to arrive is President, John F. Kennedy. He and Mr. Jefferson should have much to talk about. President Kennedy, for many of us, who came of age during your presidency, Camelot was more than a fictional castle. It was hope! Hope we saw disappear in a flash. If that terrible day in Dallas could be erased, you would be 90 years old.

Yes, your flaws and accomplishments are well known, but you always seemed to have the ability to rise to the occasion. Even though you lived an unfinished life, you united and inspired...for that, you have my admiration and respect.

Please excuse me, my next guest has arrived. Gentlemen, may I introduce Ms. Katharine Hepburn. Don't bother; she won't talk about her four Oscars, an Emmy and two Tony Awards, or that she is ranked by the American Film Institute as the top female star of all time. By the way Mr. Shakespeare, did you know Ms. Hepburn played a leading role in your play, "As You Like It?"

To me, Katharine Hepburn epitomizes unconventional and straightforward. She was outspoken and intellectual, when many (if not most) of the Hollywood stars were, well just stars. Listening to her spar with Bogart in *The African Queen* is a classic example of strong and determined. Her 1967 performance in *Guess Who's Coming to Dinner* allowed us to look at racism, marriage, and love through different lenses.

How many of you remember her as Ethel Thayer in *On Golden Pond*? What a beautiful look at growing old...together. Oh, the strength one must summon when they see someone they love slipping away.

Through the years, she played women who were strong, fiercely independent, intelligent, brash, quick witted and just plain spunky. In those roles she wasn't acting. She was playing herself. For those reasons and so many more, I'm pleased to have her in our home.

I see our final guests have arrived. It is my pleasure to introduce Ms. Helen Keller and Anne Sullivan. Ms. Keller, if I may, some of my guests may not be familiar with your work and accomplishments. Please allow me a few minutes. Although you have experienced amazing fame and success, none of my other guests had to overcome the obstacles before you. At eighteen months old, an illness robbed you of your hearing and sight. For the next seven years, you lived in a dark and silent world.

Then, Anne Sullivan entered your world as your teacher and friend. The first word you learned was water. Anne spelled it in your hand by the water pump. On that memorable day, you were reborn into a world of words and beauty.

As the years went by, you learned to read and write in Braille and to speak. You graduated from college and wrote many books. You traveled the world, lectured, and continue to inspire everyone you met. When we face difficult times, we should remember your words, "Once I knew only darkness and stillness. My life was without past or future. But a little word from the fingers of another fell into my hand that clutched at emptiness, and my heart leaped at the rapture of living." Ms. Keller, thank you for coming.

Oh my, dinner is about to begin. I must go. I hope you have enjoyed meeting my guests. They have helped me become who I am. Perhaps someday, I hope you will have the opportunity share "Who's coming to dinner" with those at your home.

Remember, anything is possible…even if it's only in a dream.

When I reach Heaven, although many say "if",
I want to hold one "Grand" dinner party.

Thanks for Bringing Me Joy - Suzanne

"We cannot hold a torch to light another's path without brightening our own." – Ben Sweetland

It was June 1999. I was standing in a middle school cafeteria for the end of the year faculty meeting. I just completed 18 months as a middle school assistant principal. This was Phase 2 of my career after teaching twenty years. In a few short weeks, I would begin Phase 3, high school administration which was my comfort zone. For 15 of those first 20 years, I taught political science to 18- year-olds. After 20 years, I felt I needed a change and new challenges.

Sandra, my wife, warned me middle school was a different world. She spent 26 of her 30 years working with middle school teachers and children. Of course, I didn't heed her advice. For 15 years, my world was young adults and now, suddenly I was staring into the faces of 7th grade children with their mood swings, tempers, and irrational behavior. During those 18 months, I aged 10 years.

Yet, working with the teachers was rather easy. I tried to be accessible, supportive, and was learning how to be a good (better) listener. Through my 31 years of educational experience, I can comfortably say, "Teachers make great talkers but generally poor listeners.," However, I was trying to be a better listener. Trying to be there for the teachers and trying to survive 7th grade! In the end, I did survive…barely.

So, there I was, my final day in middle school. As the awards were winding down, I was recognized for my efforts and the fact I was moving on to high school. All I could think about was, "Let me out of here." As the meeting was concluding, a young reading teacher held up her hand and asked if she could present me with something she had done. She handed me a piece of rolled up parchment paper tied with a sky-blue ribbon. As I began to open it, I saw her look toward the floor. On the parchment was a beautiful hand painted beach scene. Puffy white clouds dotted the blue sky as it met the beige sand. Toward the bottom was a gold and white beach towel spread under a red and white stripped umbrella. A multi-colored beach ball was close by.

Written on the scene was this poem:

"Mike,
Stay loose, Learn to watch snails. Plant impossible gardens.
Invite someone dangerous to tea.

Make little signs that say 'Yes!' And post them all over the
house. Make friends with freedom and uncertainty.

Look forward to dreams. Cry during movies.

Swing as high as you can on a swing set by moonlight.
Cultivate moods. Refuse to be responsible. Do it for love.

Take lots of naps. Give money away. Do it now. The
money will follow.

Believe in magic. Laugh a lot. Celebrate every gorgeous
moment. Take moon baths.

Have wild imaginings, transformative dreams, and
perfect calm.

Draw on the walls. Read every day. Imagine yourself
magic. Giggle with children.

Listen to old people.

Open up. Dive in. Be free. Bless yourself. Drive away
fear. Play with everything.

Entertain your inner child.

You are innocent. Build a fort with blankets. Get wet.
Hug trees. Write love letters.

Thanks for bringing me joy,
Suzanne"

That day in June, she gave me much more than a beautiful poem. She allowed me to see life through her eyes...the importance of remembering those who help us, even when we're not aware. You see, I had taken over her class a few times when she was with her mother, who was dying. I listened to her talk about the childhood memories with her mother. At the time, little did I realize the importance of what I was doing.

Today, her poem hangs in our library. A constant reminder of the importance of being human and taking the time to listen.

For we never know why, how, or when we will make a difference in someone's life.

And if you're one of the lucky ones, as I was, maybe some day someone may brighten your path, as you did theirs, by saying, "Thanks for bringing me joy."

Suzanne, I hope you have found joy in your life.

The Barber Shop...Man's Last Frontier!

*"Good company upon the road is the shortest
cut" - Anonymous*

Yes, there are still a few places a man can go that will make him feel safe. It doesn't have to be fancy, but it must look familiar. In a world of constant change, men need security and familiarity. "The Barber Shop" provides such a place. It's much more than a place for a hair cut. It might possibly be "man's last frontier," a place where a man can be a man!

Let's take a hard look at why the barber shop is so important in the growth of "boy to man.

Starting with my earliest memories: My Dad always took me to Oscar's Barber Shop in Hartland, a neighborhood in my hometown of Clarksburg, West Virginia. It was a thing of beauty. I remember the long mirrors, the ornate cash register, the wooden bench, the smell of tonics and the booster seat. Dad always let me give Oscar the 50 cents for the hair cut – part of becoming a man! The final leap was when Oscar said; "Mike, you don't need this booster seat anymore." I was finally a man., at least I felt like a man.

I knew I was growing up when Mom and Dad let me go to Oscar's alone. However, going to the barber shop was more difficult for me than most. Understand, my Mother owned a beauty shop for over 44 years and constantly volunteered to cut my hair. I found every polite and respectful way to say n0. Remember, this was the 1950's and no near-man would have his hair cut in a beauty shop. That is why I always respected the name Barber Shop. It has a man's ring to it and it hasn't changed. Unlike women's shops... first known as beauty shops, then salons, then unisex salons and now...full service spas, offering nail services, tanning, facials, massages, and hair removal.

I am sure spas have their place butI just want a haircut without the stress of menu decision making. The only decision making in a barber shop is, "How do you want it today?"

Let's look at one barber shop in Clarksburg, West Virginia and its contribution to man-development! For years, this shop was in Traders Alley, a small cut through which separated two main streets. You could get your hair cut, walk down the back stairs and be in a pool room. Let's all pause and grunt like Tim Taylor of *Tool Time* fame. It doesn't get any better than an old-fashioned barbershop. The perfect barber shop: stripped barber pole, swivel chair, razor strap on the side, and the snap of the barber's cape! Oh Yea!

Neither the shop nor the pool room still stand, but the name still graces the window at its new location on Buckhannon Pike, in Clarksburg. I promised not to identify the owner or the shop so I will give him a code name - Nod (hold it in front of a mirror).

Nod has owned a shop for 31 years and still cuts every "Strand" of hair with the precision of a surgeon, even after standing 10 hours a day, It's what a barber shop is all about - man-development. Little boys no longer needing the booster seat, magazines about cars, football, and 'wrastlin,' friendships and conversation!

I went for a hair cut and 4 men were ahead of me (no appointments). I knew it would be a long wait...then Nod said, "Next" while looking at me. Two already got their cuts and stayed to talk. One just stopped to bring Nod coffee. And, one asked about a car for sale...only in a barber shop! A place for stories, gossip, informative political debate (gulp), hunting news, and car talk...man talk! A place where politicians, priests, police, teachers, judges, factory workers and candlestick makers all check their hats at the door.

Nod's barber shop – every barber shop...a foundation of manhood. May it always be there for us. Providing a safe and familiar shelter from the outside world. But wait...Nod, tell me it's not true! Tell me I didn't see one of 'them' in my chair! It wasn't really a girl was it?

Perhaps the barber shop is truly... "man's last frontier."

This was personal. Don (aka Nod) has been a friend since childhood. It really upset me when one of them (a girl) who is, let's just say, a very interesting person, started going to Nod for a $10 haircut as opposed to $30 at a salon. Think what you like.

Michael S. Lambiotte

The Godfather of Fitness

"Dying is easy. You've got to work at living"
– Jack LaLanne

This story is about a young delinquent who assaulted his brother and set his house on fire. At 15, he was a self-proclaimed addict. Addicted to sugar and junk food. However, with his mother's support, he turned his life around and became one of the most successful and influential people in his profession.

His defining moment came days after his mother forced him to attend a lecture by Paul Bragg, a noted health and nutritional expert. Shortly after Bragg's lecture, he joined the Berkeley, California YMCA, the first step toward a lifetime dedication to health and fitness.

At 18, he opened a health food bakery. In 1936, he opened his first gym, which welcomed and encouraged women, a first in the industry. From 1936 to 1985, he starred in his own television series. He has authored numerous books, designed exercise equipment, and continues to lecture. Now, at 94, he lifts weights for 90 minutes every day and walks or swims for 30 minutes. If you're old enough, you may remember him by his signature blue jumpsuit. The "Godfather of Fitness," Jack LaLanne.

An amazing man. He still holds the world record for pushups. At 42, he did 1,033 in 23 minutes. At 70, he swam 1.5 miles. Oh yes, I forgot to mention he was handcuffed, shackled, and towing 70 boats with 70 people?

He has and should be an inspiration to all of us. Granted, he takes health and fitness to a level few (if any) of us mere mortals could accomplish. In one interview, he stated, "Virtually anyone at any age can be fit and feel their best if they follow this simple plan: Exercise, eat right, and keep your mind challenged." "And keep your mind challenged." That one stood out for me.

Of course, he's in a class by himself. He made a commitment at an early age and stayed the course for the next 79 years. And he's still going strong…literally! Jack LaLanne is Jack LaLanne because of an extremely disciplined lifestyle, great genetics, and a life sprinkled with a lot of luck. But, he's right about the exercise thing: Exercise won't make you younger, but it will make you feel younger.

You don't have to be a committed gym rat, which is the perception of some.

However, if you're beyond 50 (like me) and can't remember 20 (like me), make sure your heart and muscles are on the same page. Also, for the inexperienced or those with neglected bodies, a personal trainer might be a wise choice. But remember...exercise is exercise! Let your dog take you for a walk. Rake leaves. Work in the garden. Ride that bike. Swim. Take a dance class. Just do something regularly besides sit and click the remote.

Eating right? That's a tough one for many of us. Only the totally committed adhere to a strict diet of twigs, berries, nuts, mountain water, fish, and dried grass. On the other hand, easing in a few more veggies, fruits, fish, and whole grains isn't that painful. It's like wading into a cold mountain stream for a swim. Slow and easy. Eventually it becomes invigorating.

I remember what LaLanne said about brain fitness, "An idle brain will deteriorate just as surly as unused legs." He made it sound like pushups for the brain. Makes sense, at any age. But, it's especially true for seniors. Exercising your brain is just as important as your biceps.

Too often, seniors that can do don't do! The TV becomes their shrine with the same thing day in and day out. I thought about some of the seniors I know who play bridge, travel, do crossword puzzles, join book clubs, take classes, or do volunteer work. They share common ground with activities that challenge the brain. Something else I noticed, "They're young before their years."

Yes, I'm right beside Jack LaLanne when he said, "I don't care how old I live; I just want to be living while I'm living."

And what's your plan?

Being healthy and strong is a choice.

Jack LaLanne died in 2011 at the age of 96,
four years after this story was written.

'THE' MOUNTAINEER

He or She is the mascot of the West Virginia
University Mountaineer's

"Walk quietly in any direction and taste the freedom of the mountaineer. Where each stone, each bend cries welcome to him." – John Muir

Not long ago, The Associated Press (AP) printed a list of the top 10 college mascots. As with any mascot, their job is to excite a crowd. Some make us laugh while others are fuzzy and frightening and a select few can symbolize the spirit and soul of an entire state.

Let's look at the AP's Top 10. And then spend some time talking about one very special mascot ranked number 8.

No.1 was Colorado's Ralphie the Buffalo. Yes, a 1,300-pound buffalo in full stride dragging five handlers the length of the field can be intimidating. Pretty scary way to begin a football game.

No. 2 was Georgia's Uga. Seeing an English bulldog in a red and black Georgia turtle neck might not be as intimidating as Ralphie., but it does prove that funny ears, sagging jowls, protruding teeth, a wide stance and narrow hips can be beautiful and endearing. Go Dawgs!

No. 3 was Florida State's Chief Osceola. Nothing like seeing a Seminole Chief in full war paint on a magnificent Appaloosa galloping across the field and then jamming a flaming spear into the 50-yard line to fire up a crowd.

No. 4 was Mike, LSU's tiger. How would you like coming out of the visitor's locker room and having to run past a roaring and snarling 700 pound Bengal tiger?

No. 5 was Auburn's War Eagle. Daunting to watch a golden eagle with an 8-foot wing span continually circle the stadium and eventually land on his handler's arm at the beginning of each home game.

No.6 is the Stanford Tree. Yes, Stanford's mascot is a tree. A student runs around in a big cardinal red leafy-tree costume. Their nickname is The Cardinals. Honestly, I don't have a clue about this one, other than dumb can be memorable.

No.7 is Bevo, Texas's burnt orange longhorn steer weighing 1,800 pounds with 72 inch horns. He doesn't charge the field or snarl from a cage. He doesn't have to. When you're this big, standing and staring is threatening enough.

Ranked No. 8 is West Virginia's own buckskinned clad, coonskin capped, musket toting West Virginia Mountaineer... "THE" Mountaineer! As Eric Hansen from *The South Bend Tribune* said, "The guy has a gun. Would you mess with him?" When my list is completed, there's more regarding our Mountaineer mascot, past and present.

No. 9 is Texas Tech's Masked Rider. Reminds me of Zorro galloping around the stadium on a black gelding. Impressive if I say so myself. Since 1974, the Masked Rider has been a woman. There is a message here: Don't mess with a masked woman in black!

No.10 is Sparty from Michigan State. One sports writer said Sparty looks like a Roman-attired Jay Leno on steroids. You be the judge.

That's college's best. Now, back to 'The' Mountaineer: West Virginia adopted the Mountaineer as its official mascot in 1890. In the 1920's and early 30's, unofficial mascots wore flannel shirts, bearskin capes and coonskin caps. In 1936, Boyd "Slim" Arnold became the first official buckskin-clad Mountaineer. Three local men, close to my hometown of Clarksburg, West Virginia, have been Mountaineers: John Stemple (1994), Andy Cogar (1996) and Michael Squires (2008). In 2009 Rebecca Durst served as our second female Mountaineer. The first being Natalie Tennant (1990), now serving as our Secretary of State.

Our current Mountaineer, when this story was written, is Brock Burwell from Harrisville, West Virginia. "Brock Burwell," the name just sounds 'Mountraineerish' - big and powerful! Being selected as "The" Mountaineer is quite an honor. For this person not only represents a university, he (or she) symbolizes the soul and spirit of an entire state.

When I see our Mountaineer, 'The' Mountaineer run onto the field with head held high and rifle higher, I think: "Montani Semper Liberi" (Mountaineers are always free, the state moto). I see a fiercely strong and independent man or woman who sees no mountain too high or odds too great.

When that rifles 'BOOMS,' sending plumes of smoke skyward, I think, "It's a good day to be a Mountaineer!"

Brock Burwell, from Harrisville, West
Virginia was "The" Mountaineer for
2010-2011

In West Virginia, being a "former" mountaineer mascot
elevates one to the status of a Rhodes Scholar.

The West Virginia State Flag
Symbols and Meanings

"Great things are done when men and mountains meet." -
William Blake

It flies from atop our state capital building, Charleston, West Virginia
and other state buildings. It's in our schools and our court rooms. Our
current state flag was adopted in 1929 and is one of the most prominent
symbols of our state. It gives us our individual identity. However, I fear
few could describe our flag and even fewer would truly understand its
symbolism. Ah, I see you disagree. Perhaps it's time for a test. Remember,
I'm a former teacher. It's like being a Marine: No ex-Marines, just former
Marines.

West Virginians: Have a pen and paper handy see how many of these
questions you get right.

#1 What are the two primary flag colors?

#2 Identify the three symbols in the center of the flag?

#3 What is inscribed above the symbols?

#4 What is inscribed below the symbols?

#5 What is "crossed" below the symbols?

#6 What article of clothing is below the center symbols?

#7 What flower encircles the symbols?

Answers: #1 Blue and white. #2 A farmer, a rock, and a miner. #3
State of West Virginia. #4 Montani Semper Liberi (Mountaineers are
Always Free). #5 Rifles. #6 Liberty Cap. #7 Rhododendron. If you got
all seven questions correct, I should ask the Governor to issue a special
Gubernatorial Patriotism Medal. If you got three or four right you're
probably above average...historically.

However, the real purpose of this story is not only to explain the
symbols that adorn our flag but to examine the values they represent.
Our state flag has a blue border with a pure white background. The blue
symbolizes vigilance, perseverance, and justice while the white denotes
purity...both borrowed from the U. S. flag.

In the center is our state seal. Incidentally, this seal was designed by the
renowned French artist Joseph H. Diss Debar who came to West Virginia

in 1846 and lived in West Union (Doddridge County). The seal is ringed with rhododendrons, our state flower. In the center of the seal is a large rock with June 20, 1863 inscribed. The date West Virginia became a state.

To the left of the rock is a farmer and to the right a miner. At their feet are two crossed rifles with a Liberty Cap. Inscribed above the seal is, "State of West Virginia" and below is "Montani Semper Liberi."

Diss Debar chose the farmer and miner because they were (and still are) central to the economy of our state. The rock symbolizes our stability and strength and our resilience to adversity. The two crossed rifles express the fact that West(ern) Virginia earned its liberty by fighting in a war that resulted in 620,000 casualties, more than all other American wars combined.

A Liberty Cap lies by the rifles. It resembles a woolen ski cap of today. Its origin comes from ancient times, when freed slaves were given this sort of cap to denote their freedom. In the eighteenth century, it symbolized freedom from oppressive governments. In our case, it was England.

When I look at the image of the farmer, I try to imagine how difficult it must have been...farming a state that is four-fifths covered by forests. Most of our state is hilly and rugged, yet these fiercely determined men and women cleared forests and moved boulders to create a better life from land far different from the vast agricultural areas in the south and midwest United States Our forefathers did it and we're still doing it...against all odds!

And I can only imagine the dangers, conditions and uncertainties the miners faced upon entering that first commercial coal mine which opened near Wheeling, West Virginia in 1910. As William O. Williams, who worked in the coal mines of West Virginia for 40 years said, "It's the meanest life in the world." Yet they did it and they continue to do it, despite today's risks and uncertainties. To me, our flag represents who we are. It represents beauty, strength, determination, sacrifice, and a willingness to stand together...strong and tall.

That's why, "Montani Semper Liberi," (Mountaineers are Always Free) and always will be.

Fly it with pride!

The West Virginia state flag

Take the time to learn the history behind your
state flag. You just might be surprised.

CHAPTER 5

Being a Man…It's Not Easy

Bigger – Stronger – Faster – Better

"Let no feeling of discouragement prey upon you, and in the end you are sure to succeed" – Abraham Lincoln

Male athletes are bigger, stronger, and faster, therefore they are better than female athletes. Before you begin to boil tar and rip open the feather pillows for a good old fashioned tarring and feathering, these are not my words, nor my feelings. But, I suspect they're the words and feelings of many. In most cases, I agree: Male athletes are bigger, stronger, and faster than female athletes – generally. However, they're not better, only bigger, stronger, and faster.

As a former player, coach and (now) team-sport spectator, it bothers me when women's sports are generally not given the respect and fan support they deserve. I'm sure the reason is deeply rooted in sociological stereotypes that only people with a closet full of degrees understand, but it still bothers me. Maybe some people are still stuck with the mind-set, "Me hunter. You clean cave."

Even when I was playing my 1967 football-style basketball in high school, the only high profile activity for girls was cheerleading or band. Although, we did have a Girls' Sport Team which played other schools in volleyball and basketball. However, they played after school or on Saturday mornings to a handful of fans and received little publicity. There was no softball, field hockey, soccer, track, tennis, swimming, tennis, cross country, or golf teams – in 1967.

But, in 1972, things changed. I wish I could say society (as a whole) stood up and said "It's time to leave the cave. It's not fair! Girls deserve choices." Unfortunately, it wasn't that way. On June 23, 1972, the United States enacted a law stating: "No person in the United States shall, on the basis of sex, be excluded from participation in, or denied benefits of, or be subjected to discrimination under any educational program or activity receiving federal assistance." They called it Title IX.

This law opened the door for women in sports a door forced open! For even today, there are those who still oppose Title IX…behind closed doors. Although the reach of Title IX goes way beyond high school and college sports, you may breathe easy. I have no intention of turning this into a college-level lecture class.

Let's focus on women's sports. In a span of 36 years, girls' basketball went from Saturday morning with few fans to prime-time college women's basketball. However, women still did not receive the respect and fan support they deserve, regardless of the level or sport.

This is just wrong and we are to blame, certainly not the press. Look at the local and national coverage men and women receive and then look at the attendance figures. Especially WVU (West Virginia University) basketball. Per a recent poll (2010), the men aren't even in the top 25 nationally, yet average attendance is around 10,000. Yet, the women are ranked 14th nationally and average only 2,600 fans.

The men are not better…just bigger, stronger, and faster. High school attendance is similar. Football stadiums and gyms are packed for the boys. Yet, a much smaller number attend girl's basketball and even fewer for girls' soccer and softball. The women work just as hard as the men and in many cases, harder because they are up against discrimination, discouragement, stereotypes and sexism. something few male athletes have faced, at least since 1972.

Seeing our boys come off the field or court tired, sweaty, and dirty is accepted because they are boys! Perhaps it is time for society as a whole to accept seeing our girls come off the field or court tired, sweaty, and dirty because they're girls, learning to be leaders just like the boys.

In 1972, the courts opened the door for equality. It's time we treat our female athletes with equal respect and give them the support they deserve. Think: That tired, sweaty, red-faced girl coming off the court or the field may be our next President, Nobel Prize winner, judge, jet pilot, teacher, or nurse. For today, she is learning lessons her grandmother never had the opportunity to learn.

Show up and cheer!

You disagree. Get a couple of your middle-aged pot-bellied buddies and volunteer to go one-on-one with your local girl's high school basketball team for a half.

Have rescue waiting!

Clarksburg Needs More Street Walkers

If you think this story is about the world's oldest
profession, perhaps you should consider why you
thought this.
"I dream of hiking into my old age" – Marilyn Doan

While driving down my hometown's Main Street the other evening, I saw a few street walkers. As I started down the hill from 3rd Street, a few more were visible. Even as I started up Quality Hill, as it was called in another day and time, more were present. None of them looked the same, dressed the same, waved the same, or spoke the same way. Some were in pairs, but most were alone. There were all shapes and sizes. However, there was one characteristic they all seemed to share...they were enjoying what they were doing! Clarksburg, West Virginia needs many more street walkers like the ones I observed.

Now, take a deep breath, pull in your claws and smooth those hackles. I was not observing or referring to prostitutes. What I saw were plain ordinary law-biding people just enjoying the beauty of being alive, the companionship of a special person or friend, just being alone, or the more focused – power walking.

For so many years, I took for granted how wonderful it is to peacefully walk the Clarksburg streets and not look over my shoulder or have one hand on a self-defense device. Where I previously lived, walking the streets was not always pleasant, relaxing, or an escape from the pressures of the day. In fact, it was more of a test of your survival skills. Even going to the board walk, in Virginia Beach, Virginia and looking at the ever-changing ocean was not always pleasant. Seeing people dressed to shock or intimidate is not my idea of relaxation.

Recently, my wife Sandra was walking with a friend who was visiting from Virginia. They were walking in our sweet Goff Plaza neighborhood (as Sandra calls it), as a jogger approached my wife's friend, she tensed up and started to move into the street. The jogger smiled and said, "Hello ladies isn't it a beautiful evening." He then moved into the street so they could pass. Sandra's friend looked at her with a sad puzzled look. Sandra looked at her and said, "Yes Linda, people in Clarksburg actually smile and speak".

Therefore, in my opinion: Clarksburg needs more street walkers, for many reasons. It is amazing what you can see, smell, hear, and feel while walking our neighborhoods. Fall is a beautiful time of the year – a time to get out and become a walker. Who knows, you might even improve your health and not realize it. Having fun is like that.

Soak up the fall flowers, look at the beautiful architecture which abounds throughout the city, let your dog gather all the information he or she wants from the fireplug, the fence post, or the neighbor's tree or watch in amazement as they play with a butterfly.

When walking with that special person, take their hand and just smile. Sometimes a smile can say so much. Invite your neighbor for a walk and talk. It doesn't matter what you talk about. What matters is that you are sharing time and life. As you become or continue to be a street walker, don't be afraid to talk with a stranger. Everyone you know was a stranger at one time.

As you walk through your neighborhood or through some of our beautiful parks, I hope a few of these words will come to mind, "Use your eyes as if tomorrow you would be stricken blind…Hear the music of voices, the song of the bird, the mighty strains of the orchestra, as if you would be stricken deaf tomorrow."

"Touch each object as if tomorrow your tactile sense would fail. Smell the perfume of the flowers, taste with relish each morsel, as if tomorrow you could never smell and taste again. Make the most of every sense; glory in all the facets of pleasure and beauty which the world reveals to you." – Helen Keller

Exercise – soap for the soul.

Drop and Give Me 20!

Both tears and sweat are salty, but they render a different result. Tears will get you sympathy; sweat will get you change – Jesse Jackson

Veterans, what are your memories regarding the title? Sorry to bring back boot camp, but you were probably in the best shape of your life. Have you tried on that uniform lately? If so, scary huh! Bulging buttons and a belt that shrunk.

Soon, "Drop and give me 20" will have a whole new meaning, for more than veterans. It will be New Years Eve and you will bring out your 'Resolution List.' No doubt, somewhere in the failure category is, "This year, I'm going to get in shape." Be honest! It's there and I know it. So, what happened? Let me guess: You lacked commitment, a goal, and a plan.

Let me help this year. Let us begin with your commitment to getting in shape., also known as, "I want to get up as easily as I get down and not be out of breath when I tie my shoes." Caution, before you begin, get a physical and be honest with your doctor and take the honesty part very seriously.

Your goal is to look in the mirror and say Yes, instead of blaming the mirror for distortions. On the mirror thing: Next time you get out of the shower, stand in front of the mirror. Nothing more needs said. Be realistic. Looking like Arnold in his prime or Jenny Lynn (2006 Ms. Figure Olympia) probably isn't in the cards, but liking what you see in the mirror is!

Your plan is to visit the local gyms or health clubs around our city and talk with the managers and trainers. I know, you say you can do it at home…quit lying! Home workouts do no work, for most. Look at the rusty weights and dusty tread mill in the basement.

Next, because you probably haven't been in a gym since high school, let's set some things straight. Yes, there are gyms that remind me of an old *Rocky* movie with loud grunting and plenty of sweat. Then, there are designer gyms where people wear $400 outfits, never sweat, make up never runs, and love the mirrors.

Funny, the ones I visited in Clarksburg and Bridgeport, West Virginia are neither of these. The one I joined is up on the hill was the YMCA. Look beyond the treadmills and barbells and you will see something truly remarkable: People of all ages, shapes and sizes sharing one thing - a love for life. For them, it's more than a place to get in shape. It's a place to develop new friendships, continue old ones, to remember when, argue, joke, and share life.

You'll see people with oxygen tanks, in wheel chairs, the elderly, and the young. all exercising and improving their life. No one cares who you are, how much money you make, where you work, or who your father is. Most of the time, you never get past first names. One special group at the gym on the hill is the Old Fart Clu, as they are known. You must be 65 to join with the oldest is in his 80's. One of them said, "If I quit exercising, my arms and legs would fall off." Oh, do they ever love life.

You see, going to a gym is about more then getting into shape. Just ask the Old Fart Club. To them, exercising can't stop the clock, but it can slow it down. I know, some people just dislike the gym environment, like my wife Sandra. She will work in the garden until she is covered with dirt, shirt soaked with perspiration (girls don't sweat), and every muscle aches, but that's not exercise (for her), its masquerading as fun. She would rather endure open heart surgery without anesthetic than go to a gym. Her garden is her gym and that is fine, for her. But, what about you! When I was a personal trainer, my philosophy was, "I will take you from where you are, to where you want to be, to where you never thought you could be."

This New Years Eve, have a commitment, a goal, and a plan...for a better quality of life. Think about where you want to be!

Happy New Year...Now, drop and give me 20!

Note: As you can tell, I wrote this story shortly after Christmas. A few years back.

Everyone should find their own path to a healthier life.
It makes us forget about the years behind us.

Golf...Through Her Eyes

"Keep your sense of humor. There's enough stress in the rest of your life to let bad shots ruin a game you're supposed to enjoy." – Amy Alcott

The Chinese invented it during the 11ᵗʰ century. The Dutch invented it in 1297. The Scotts invented it in 1465,Who really knows who invented it.? However, most agree the modern worldwide "Home of Golf" is located at St. Andrews, Fife, Scotland. Right now, you're probably thinking, "Who cares. I just enjoy playing." Others say, "Who cares. It's a stupid game. " I 'm the former and Sandra, my wife, is the later.

I just thought it might be interesting to take a few minutes and look at 'Golf Through Her Eyes.' Although I've played on and off for years, Sandra never embraced the game. Her exact words are, "It's stupid." Here's her evaluation of golf, or as it was once called G (gentlemen) O (only) L (ladies) F (forbidden).

In Sandra's words:

First: It's stupid. You hit a little ball, chase it, hit it again, chase it, and then try to put it in a little hole. Why not just hit it, pick it up and drop it in the hole and go home?

Second: It makes you hot, sweaty, and irritable. Who wants to walk for miles in 90-degree heat or when it's freezing?

Third: A tee time should be 'tea' time. A hot cup of Earl Gray tea is the ultimate tea time.

Fourth: If you're going to play the stupid game, at least ride in heated and air conditioned carts.

Fifth: No game should take all day. It's ridiculous!

Sixth: At every tee, there should be a "tea" stand, serving the traditional southern drink – sweet tea. Never cigars and beer!

Seventh: It costs too much. Is it necessary to have the latest toy such as monster clubs, high-tech uranium infused balls, and range finders? If you're good, you don't need them. If you're bad...you're bad!

Eighth: Temper tantrums are for 2-year- old's. Why throw or break those expensive toys. It's only a game. It's supposed to be fun. Relax and enjoy the stupid game.

Ninth: If you're going to come home tired, sweaty, and cranky…go to work!

Tenth: It's a stupid game, but I might enjoy spending a Saturday or Sunday with you. I could drive the cart. No jokes! I'll bring my tea and your whatever. Maybe we could have an early dinner and just maybe… I know boys like to be with boys and do boy things, but occasionally, just occasionally, it might be nice to do a 'we' tee or tea.

Well, there it is. Sandra's 10 reasons golf is stupid. If Sandra gave the game a chance, she might not view it as stupid. She might elevate it to just dumb. However, I have an ace in the hole to win her over. I know she'll never be a player but I'm shooting for, "It's not bad." My biggest challenge is to get her on a course. Not as a caddy (not that crazy) but as my cart driver, towel person, and personal assistant.

For me, golf was (is) always about enjoying the beauty of the course and good friendship. She's my best friend and she loves beauty…flowers, trees, wild life, well-manicured lawns, and wide-open green spaces. Doesn't this describe a golf course?

When we talked about her Top 10 list, I assured her No. 7, 8, 9 will never apply to me. I have the same clubs my parents gave me in 1968. You guessed it. I'm not very good and I know it, therefore, I can sit back, swing, watch the ball go wherever, and laugh at myself.

No. 10…well, it just might be fun. The 19th hole could take on a whole different meaning. No. 1-4 might present a challenge. But, I love challenges. No. 5 doesn't matter when you're having fun with your best friend and friends. No. 6, I'll bring some for her and whatever for me.

If you're not a golfer – I make no apologies for this story. Because, it wasn't really about golf…was it?

Sandra will never embrace the game.
My best hope: She can offer advice on the landscaping.

Golf...Through My Eyes

My personal philosophy: If you can't play good – at least look good.

"If you've had a good time playing the game, you're a winner even if you lose." – Malcolm Forbes

In 2007, I wrote *Golf through Her Eyes*, my wife Sandra's totally biased opinion about the esteemed game of golf. She said, "It's stupid. You hit a little ball, chase it, hit again, chase it and then try to put it in a little hole. Why not just hit it, pick it up, drop it in the hole and go home?"

She just doesn't understand the many life-lessons golf teaches. That is why this story is titled, *Golf...Through My Eyes* (AKA) "Lessons from a little white ball." First, always **Dress for Success:** If you can't play good, at least look good. Dressing properly for golf may not make you play better, but you'll look good when you hit a dribbler, a shot that only goes a few feet. Remember tennis star Andre Agassi's saying, "Image is everything."

Having the **Right Equipment** can improve your golf score, your performance in the board room or in the classroom. After taking up the game (again) after a 30-year hiatus, I realized my 1968 Marty Furgol Northwestern club technology was just a little bit outdated. I purchase new clubs in 2013

Of course, the right equipment in the wrong hands can produce disastrous results, which brings me to **Practice.** Remember this quote? "Practice doesn't make perfect. Perfect practice makes perfect." When I returned to golf last year, I took a few lessons from a local club pro. After hitting some range balls, he said, "Not bad Mike! Except for your grip, stance, shoulder position, flexibility, hip rotation and weight shift." We both laughed and immediately began a corrective action plan, " Practicing the right way with the right equipment." Good life-advice.

Golf also teaches**, Don't Over Think** a problem. As the Nike slogan says, "Just Do It." Evaluate your situation, execute good fundamentals and just hit the ball! Good for the golfer, butcher, baker and candlestick maker.

Another valuable golf lesson is, **Learn to Laugh at Yourself.** Life's way too short to take it so seriously. If my divot (grass clump) goes farther than my ball (a frequent event) I think, "What the hell happened?" I laugh, try to figure it out, but move on.

I move on to developing **Short Term Memory**. Don't dwell on the past. Carrying bad shot baggage to the next tee (or project) clouds thinking and interferes with the many shots ahead and putts waiting to be made.

Golfers frequently learn **Humility.** Just when we think we have the game figured out, then comes the 'round from hell.' One of my favorite golf sayings is, "Great shot...I love this game! Bad shot...I hate this game!"

Playing golf also teaches us to **Take Chances.** Don't be afraid to ask yourself, "What if?" There's a big difference between calculated risk and stupid. At a local golf course, I decided to attempt to carry the water - for the first time. It wasn't the distance. It was the water that frightened me. My shot went straight, high and four feet short of the bank. Splash! Yet, given the same circumstances next time, it's bombs away - again. Risk, yes. Stupid, no.

Moreover, golf helps us **Deal with the Unexpected,** the highs and lows: Wind gusts. Sudden thunderstorms. Partner heckling. Cigar ashes in your eye. A flock of geese landing on the green. Sometimes, on the course and in life, "stuff" just happens. You must learn to deal with it.

Another golf lesson is, **Thoroughly Evaluate** every situation before acting. Before attempting that birdie putt, check your lie from every angle, calculate the break, ball speed, and condition of the green. Take a couple of practice swings, a deep breath and let it out slowly. And, if you play like I play, ask for divine guidance. Then, strike the ball. If you evaluated and executed properly, the next sound you hear is 'kerplunk.' the sound of hitting the bottom of the cup. Life is good!

Above all, the one lesson to always remember is **Have Fun.** Enjoy the beauty of the course, fellowship among friends, a friendly wager, and a salute to a great teacher from the 19th hole.

Golf teaches you to laugh at yourself.
For if you don't laugh, you will cry your eyes dry.

How I Saved 1,500 Minutes

"Organizing is what you do before you do something, so that when you do it, it's not all mixed up." — A.A Milne, creator of Winnie-the-Pooh

By my calculations, if I stay on my present course, I will have saved 1,500 minutes by the end of the year. That amounts to 30 minutes a week. Two hours a month. 25 hours a year. This means I can set aside two full days of self-indulgent fun sometime during the year. And this incredible feat was accomplished by simply being organized. I call it 'time management.' Sandra, my wife, calls it something unprintable.

The motivation behind this time-saving effort is simple, "Frustration and my feet hurt." Let me explain: Sandra and I have never been a couple who says, "This is a man's job" or "This is a women's job." In our home, there are just jobs. We clean. We do yard work. We cook. We grocery shop. However, there is one exception to the we rule. She does the laundry unless I have written instructions or proper supervision. My laundry gaffes are what legends are made of.

Let's go back to groceries, which is the heart and soul of this story. One day last year I said, "Why don't you let me do most of the grocery shopping? That way you'd have more time to do other things." Don't laugh, I am a pretty good cook and I enjoy grocery shopping. Between mom, dad, and Sandra, I've been well-schooled in the fine art of food buying. However, I was not prepared for what lay ahead?

As I soon found out, shopping a super-sized all-in-one grocery, hardware, clothing, automotive, and garden center store can beat you down, physically and emotionally. Every Thursday (list in hand) I walked that enormous store: north, south, east and west, back and forth. Ninety minutes later, frustrated and with aching feet, I was in the checkout line. "There's got to be a better way. A more efficient way," I thought. Then it dawned on me, "Why not organize the grocery list by section and by isle." When I mentioned this to Sandra, her look said, "Idiot," but her words were, "Whatever works"

To me, it made perfect sense because I function better with list: A yard list. House list. Errand list. Phone call list. Check it off when it's done list!

When you have a 4-item brain and a 6-item day, lists are mandatory. So, the next day I made a special trip to the super store for strategic planning. 'Operation Time Saver' was in motion. By the following Thursday my plan was mapped out and placed on a chart by section and isle.

Under each category I would write the items needed: Section 1: Pharmacy and Toiletries. Other items in that end of the store were also included. Section 2 - Dog Food and Cleaning Supplies. Section 3 - Dairy Products. Aisle 13 - Beer and Wine. Aisle 12 – Soda and Chips and so on. This process continued until I got to Aisle 1 - Ice Cream. Then a sweep through the Meat and Cheese Section, ending with Fresh Vegetables and Deli.

With my system, there was no back-tracking and no wasted time. No browsing allowed. Stay focused! Not on the chart, not in my cart. As I crossed the finish line, I mean standing in the checkout line, I looked at my watch. I shaved 30 minutes off my previous time. My only obstacles to an even better score were middle of the aisle 'chatter boxes,' terrified small children and mothers as I slid through the corners, and equipment malfunction (a wobbly front cart wheel).

This, my friends, is how I will accumulate two full days (and one hour) of self-indulgent fun by the end of the year. Quality boy time! Maybe I will invest in some golf lessons to improve my last score of 64…for nine holes.

Yet all this was accomplished by being (ODF): Organized. Disciplined. Focused. Ok. Maybe I went a bit overboard. But if you think about it, doesn't every successful endeavor depend upon being ODF.

My system was working fine until the store reorganized their isles and shelves to combat shoppers like me.

Just a Little Bit More

"Enough is abundance to the wise." – Euripides

Let's see: The recipe calls for olive oil, red wine, oregano, sun dried tomatoes, and one clove of garlic. Maybe I should add one more clove of garlic. 'Just a little bit more' will make it better. As I was about to add the extra garlic, I felt my arm being pulled back. It was the strangest of feelings.

One of Dad's culinary calamities came to mind. He was a very good cook, but prone to excesses, something I inherited honestly. The directions on the tenderizer package said, "Soak meat for 15 minutes." Of course, 30 minutes would be better, according to dad. Being only 12-years-old, I wholeheartedly agreed. As the timer struck 30, Dad tried' to remove our steak from the tenderizer, which had turned to mush.

As I held that clove of garlic over the bowl, perhaps Dad was telling me, "Uh, remember the mush." Why are most (valuable) lessons learned the hard way or through mistakes or failures? What ever happened to the easy way? Nevertheless, I think I'm beginning to get it, after all these years.

But, it's been a long bumpy road. For instance: For the New Year's Day football games (before cable and remotes), Dad would have the stereo tuned to one game, his transistor radio tuned to another, while I switched the old Philco (TV) between games. More football was always better! Or so we thought, back in 1961. What Mom wanted never crossed our minds.

And there was a time when I would always add a little bit more when mixing the lawn chemicals. Surly more would kill the bugs and weeds faster, always ignoring the dizziness, headaches, and blurred vision. A small price to pay for a dark green weed and bug free lawn. It just soaks in anyway. Or so we thought...back then.

Why do we think more is better? Contrary to the opinion of a large percentage of our female population, real men do read directions. We just chose to ignore them! Even my years and experience at the gym does not exempt my ego from 'more is better.' Not long ago, I was bench pressing a lot of weight. Feeling very good, I said to myself, "Just one more rep." I forgot to consult my shoulder. There I was, with a lot of weight stuck on my chest. Fortunately, others came to my rescue. Obviously, more was too much - that time.

Being fair, it isn't always easy resisting the tempting pressures of a society geared toward big and more. How many pairs of shoes do we really need? Buy one, get the second half price! Final Sale! And most men will agree, a bigger steak always tastes better.

I'm sure you have heard this, "And sir, would you like to super-size that...?" When I was a teenager, a 16 oz. Coke was the ultimate. Today, a 42-oz. drink is common. Before tipping the cup, notice the calories, sugar, and caffeine. Then, map out the restroom locations as you leave the drive through.

How many times have you said, "I would be much happier if I had a better job and made more money." In 1966, Paul McCartney was asked to reveal the true meaning of the song, *Can't Buy Me Love*. He said, "The idea behind it was that material possessions are very well, but they won't buy me what I really want."

And what is it we really want? Or think we want? Just a little bit more! And that will make it better. At one time, perhaps, but now I think Sir Paul was right. Unfortunately, it took years and many mistakes before I began resisting. Oh, the temptation is still there. But I'm resisting because I remember the mush!

One of the many encouraging characteristics of getting older, although many are discouraging, is, "As the vision fails...we begin to see many things more clearly." Plus, a little voice keeps encouraging me by saying, "Less is more and just a little bit more is too much!"

Simplicity. Simplicity.

If only the young could see...

As hard as I try, and as many times Sandra reminds
me, I must add just a touch more.

Man & His Land

"Do what thy manhood bids thee do."
– Sir Richard Burton

Throughout history, man's success has been judged or measured in a variety of ways. Perhaps by the number of goats or cattle he possessed, by his number of wives, or by the amount of land, he owned.

Let's look at today, and ask ourselves, "How does man judge himself?" Is it by that prestigious job and that European luxury car, or is it by the success of his children? Perhaps he looks at the number of years he has been married or the quality of his man cave - that private retreat where a man can be a man! It could be a workshop or an old hunting cabin.

I think today's man judges his success by the size and quality of his 'Man Land,' also referred to as a man cave. My retreat it located in the basement, which is not any old basement. It's finished with a large fireplace, a wide screen television with a monstrous Bose sound system - my retirement gift to myself. This entertainment area is truly a crank it up, window bulging, lamp shaking measure of a man...this man.

Add a reclining over-stuffed chair and a sofa big enough to double as a bed and you have the ultimate "Man Land." I know. Most women don't understand these primal needs. But, men just need their space.. We need a place to scratch and not get yelled at. A place where it's ok to use your t-shirt as a bib. A place where jeans can double as a napkin and we're not afraid to unbuckle after eating too many hot wings. A place where a little popcorn on the floor or a beverage mark on the table is OK!

Of course, women can enter Man Land but they must understand the rules: No yelling. No criticism. No adjusting the volume. Remember, this is our private retreat. A place where friends gather to cheer our favorite teams (anyone who plays Michigan or Pitt). Remember, this a place where we can become *Rambo* or win the Daytona 500, if only for a short while.

Probably, this man stuff goes back to pre-historic times, a time when man ruled the cave. Or so he was led to believe. As we evolved, this need for a man-place also evolved.

How many guys remember building forts or tree houses and posting signs that read, "No Girls Allowed." You were simply cultivating seeds that would later grow into Man Land.

Strange as it seems, my intense study of this phenomena has uncovered something very interesting: Man, is not alone in his desire to have a private retreat. Women also need a special place. 'Woman Land' just doesn't have the same ring, so I'll just call it 'The Quiet Room.' This is a room where she can safely remove the many hats most women wear. A special place where she can retreat. The Quiet Room…a place for reading and reflecting. A place to get away from the madness of life.

Her room that reflects who she is, or who she wants to become. It is a place to write a letter to a childhood friend now living far away, or a place to carefully turn the pages of a family album, which has turned yellow with age and memories. It can be a place where she can enter a world of make-believe, as she did as a child. As Alexandra Stoddard wrote, everyone needs, "A Room of One's Own." Inside every woman is a little girl. A little girl who grows up too quickly. She needs a place to surround herself with pretty and quiet.

Inside every man is a little boy. A little boy who never forgets how much fun it was building that fort. He also needs his place. A place where big boys can act like little boys.

However, a truly smart man will fluff up the pillows, run the sweeper, dust the tables, light a few candles, turn down the Bose, insert a DVD of *"To Have and Have Not" (Bogart and Bacall)*, and invite her to join him in Man Land.

Because you never know, eventually he might be invited to join her in "The Quiet Room."

The need for an adult Man Land goes back
to the sign beneath the tree house,
"No Girls Allowed"

Men Are Different from Women

"If there is to be any peace it will have to come through being, not having." – Henry Miller

Christmas is the setting for this story.

Yes, it's true. The holidays bring out many differences. None greater than the differences between men and women when it comes to shopping. It took a marketing teacher in 1995 to help me fully understand these differences. She was having a difficult time deciding what gifts to buy her husband, children, and other family members for Christmas.

Not known for my sensitivity and timing, I chimed in, "Not me, I did all mine in two days." Bought. Wrapped. Under the tree. This was one of my better examples of "Boys say stupid things." She just glared and said, "Mike, you don't understand. Women shop. Men buy." Of course, to me shopping and buying were the same thing and I loudly said so. Immediately, I was given a crash course in Marketing 101.

You know what, when she finished it made sense. A lot of things made sense. It is true...men buy! When we leave the house, we have either a mental or written list (checking it twice) of the must have items. We know the stores we're visiting (and the order) and where the items are located. If it's not there, we're off to the next store. No substitutes or looking around. Browsing is for girls!

Sometimes, if there's uncertainty, we'll show the clerk a picture. When buying clothes for the female members of our family, we often sneak to the closet and look at sizes. Real men don't ask! Smart men don't guess! On the flip side, it's true, women shop. Women may have mental or written lists but they're open to alternatives. If this isn't exactly what I want, let me look at this, or let me try that. Women are more flexible when it comes to choices and colors because they are prone to browsing, "This isn't exactly what I want, but it looks good. It looks better than what I was looking for. I'll take it!"

All this takes time., time most men would rather spend looking for the remote. When Marketing 101 was over, many things made sense, beyond the obvious. I now understood why dad and I 'bought' while mom was the Lone Ranger. And why, as a small child, my grandfather took me to the movies in Wheeling, West Virginia while the women shopped. Today, when Sandra and I go to the mall, we synchronize our watches and meet in front of a girl store.

Yes, men and woman are different, But, as you head toward the malls this holiday season, notice the similarity: Arms will be loaded and cars will be packed with those must have gifts, all the results of shopping and buying. Perhaps we should stop and think, "What is a 'must have' gift? How do we decide and what is the determining factor? It is so easy to become overwhelmed and lose focus, especially when all we hear is, "I want," Final Sale, and Only 3 days left.

Perhaps we need to take a deep breath, slow down and think. A long time ag in a far-off land, the birth of a child was the greatest gift we would ever receive. The smell of hay, the sound of sheep bleating, a donkey swishing his tail, and the look in the eyes of Mary and Joseph as they knelt by their son - the perfect gift to the world.

Close by was Caspar holding the gift of myrrh and beside him was Balthazar with the gift of frankincense. Kneeling opposite Mary and Joseph was Melchior, placing the gift of gold beside the manger of this very special child.

Each brought only one gift. Gold to symbolize kingship on earth. Frankincense, an aromatic resin, symbolizing the child's divine nature and role. Myrrh, a sweet-smelling anointing plant oil, symbolizing suffering and sacrifice. How did Caspar know what the years would bring? They did not shower this child with 'must haves.' Each gave only one gift...a symbol of their love and respect.

As we shop or buy this season, remember what we are celebrating... the greatest gift we would ever receive!

Sandra and I found the secret to "spousal and partner shopping" – synchronize watches, divide, and meet at the coffee shop.

Pass the Salt Pills and Aspirin

"The world hates change, yet it is the only thing that has brought progress." – Charles Kettering

This was written as a tribute to high school football.

"Pass the salt pills and aspirin," it is fall and it is high school football season. This story is dedicated to those who played high school football in the 1960's. Judging by today's training, medical knowledge, and equipment, most of us should have died on those hot and humid August practice fields. But we survived to tell our sagas of 'then and now.' And, there is so much more to this story than football.

This tale is also dedicated to those who still believe, "No change is the best change." A phrase all too often used by those who do not really understand change. Let's set our time machine for August 15, 1964. The first day of high school football practice for us in North Central West Virginia. No pre-season conditioning. It was full pads: helmet, shoulder pads, hip pads, knee pads, and cleats. Full contact from day one! At the end of each day, death would have been welcomed, but you hurt too much to die.

Fortunately, by 1966, the starting date was moved to August 10, requiring five days of conditioning before full contact. During the conditioning period, only helmets, shorts and cleats were allowed before the head banging began. We practiced twice a day, at 8am and 2pm. Two and a half hours each practice with heat and humidity totally ignored and water breaks were forbidden. Coaching philosophy back than said, "Water was for sissies and fish."

However, as players, we did have a way to go around the moisture ban. We hid lemon slices in our helmet ear hole and would suck on them while in the huddle or when the coaches were not looking. In desperate times, we would soak a (small) towel in water and wrap it around our neck and suck on it for moisture. Unfortunately, it got a bit salty by the end of practice. Don't laugh or be repulsed. Desperate times call for desperate measures.

The training philosophy was, "The more you sweat... swallow more salt pills."

During tackling drills, when your head hurt so bad you wanted to cut it off, managers dispensed aspirin. Both given out like M & M's at a chocolate convention, without water. No sissies or fish allowed.

Our closest thing to an athletic trainer was a senior (student-manager) who wanted to be a doctor when he grew up. Our training table was an old picnic table in the attic of the locker room at Hite Field. In Clarksburg, West Virginia. With all these negatives, you know what, I loved every minute of it. Well, not every minute, but I did love the entire experience. For it was the best we had to offer...in 1966. But change was on the horizon!

Now, set your time machine for August 30, 2008. I've just returned from visiting two high school football programs in Harrison County, West Virginia. How's this for change: They have weight lifting year-round, three weeks of conditioning in early summer, four days of conditioning in August, and two days with pads before beginning contact. They still practice twice a day, but at 9am and 7pm. One team practices on artificial turf with a mist machine blowing water into the air.

They also have certified Athletic Trainers and completely equipped training rooms that resemble ER's (hospital emergency rooms). The trainers monitor player's weight outside, heat and humidity, and adjust practice times accordingly. Water breaks are given every 15 minutes, salt tablets and aspirin are now forbidden. Both teams I visited have team physicians and one has a physical therapist on call. The slightest cuts and injuries are immediately tended. Don't even get me started on the advances in equipment, because my jealousy boils over!

However, I have always embraced change. I remember my father talking about playing in a leather helmet with no face mask. I played wearing what we called a suspension helmet - nylon straps kept your head from contacting the plastic outer shell, most of the time. Today, your son plays with an inflatable rubber liner inside his helmet. Forty years of progress.

However, I wonder, "If someone finds this story in a book in 2048 (folded and yellow), what will the game of 'futball' look like? What will the world be like? I hope there will still be coaches coaching. Young men and women dreaming. Friday night lights and cheering crowds. Old guys in the stands talking about bygone days. And the phrase, "No change is the best change" has long been forgotten.

> Every generation provides the very best technology
> available – even leather helmets.

The Dumb Boy Gene

Love and respect women. Look to her not only for comfort,
but for strength and inspiration. Blot out from your mind
any idea of superiority; you have none." – Giuseppe Mazzini

Being a dumb boy and being around dumb boys most of my life, I'm convinced that we are born with a gene that make us say and do dumb things. You remember learning about genes (DNA) from your science classes. They are those inherited traits we get from our parents and grandparents, like height, weight, eye and hair color and body structure.

Today, scientists are using genetic research to determine treatments for all types of diseases and physical ailments. However, not much is being done about the dumb boy gene. Nonetheless, I truly believe boys are born with this gene and of course, the gene's influence on behavior varies from very mild to off-the-scale insane. For me, nothing else explains why boys do and say dumb things.

Let's do a very unscientific examination of typical boy behavior from very young to very old boys - boys like me. By age 11, we generally know the basics: Right from wrong, please and thank you and lying is bad. Nonetheless, we still do dumb things like climbing that tree we were forbidden to climb, resulting in broken arms and various abrasions. "Look Mom, no hands!" as we're riding our bicycle down the alley, moments before we flew over the handle bars. "No Dad, I didn't hit the baseball that broke the neighbor's window. I don't care what the other nine kids said." It's the dumb boy gene. What other explanation could there be?

When we get to middle school the dumb boy gene really makes us crazy. Impressing girls becomes the center of our universe. This gene encourages us to lie to Nancy about Susan when we know it will get back to Cindy, although we really want Mary to find out. And we don't care about their' feelings because it's all about me, me and more me. It's the 'dumb boy gene.' What other explanation could there be?

As soon as we reach high school we learn the Peacock Strut,' as the dumb boy gene continues to mature. Dating becomes serious. We attempt to make everything perfect. Perfect clothes. Perfect manners. Mr. Polite at his best. Tell her what she wants to hear. Then our chest-thumping ego forces us to brag about exploits that never happened. Look at me! As the peacock struts the hallowed halls of high school. It's the dumb boy gene. What other explanation could there be?

When we become fully feathered working adults, the dumb boy gene is peaking.

While dating, it's always the best restaurant, finest wine, right music, and a romantic

Movie. What she wants she gets. Impress! Impress! Compliment! Compliment!

Unfortunately, many times marriage or long-term commitments allow the dumb boy gene to peak. Over time we forget how to shave and bathe regularly. Our chest falls closer to our waist. Then, an exciting evening means boxer shorts, a beer and the remote.

That dumb boy gene makes us forget about consideration, kindness and tenderness. It erases the memory of the behavior that got us where we are. Too much me, and not enough we.

He criticizes the few (many) pounds she's put on, ignoring the multiple births and hormonal changes. Look in the mirror Pillsbury Dough Boy!" In the most severe cases, the peacock, even though he's lost some feathers and his colors have faded, he will still strut to see what is on the other side of the fence. "Ah, the grass is so much greener over there," he thinks. Many a dumb peacock has jumped the fence, only to learn that poison ivy and thistle are also dark green. It's the dumb boy gene. What other explanation could there be?

The dumb boy gene may never be identified or isolated by the geneticists, but that doesn't mean it doesn't exist. However, its effects can be controlled with a simple pill called 'Respect.' Take one every day. That way you will never forget who you brought to the dance.

We can't help it, we're just born girl-dumb!
And age doesn't make it any better.
But we try!

Michael S. Lambiotte

Why Do Baseball Coaches Wear Uniforms?

"If you want to make enemies, try to change something." –
Woodrow Wilson

I spend a lot of time wondering why things are the way they are. For instance: Why are male birds colorful and females drab? In the human world, it's the opposite.

Another puzzler: During the 17ᵗʰ century, wealthy men wore heavy makeup, as did women. Today, men don't (at least most don't) and women spend hours painting, brushing, curling, and plucking.

Nonetheless, some change is good, at least through these eyes. Give me 30 minutes and I'm ready for the fanciest holiday ball, fishing, or the beach. Sandra, well let's just say it takes her longer than 30 minutes. I'm just thankful this is the 21ˢᵗ century.

Another life mystery: Why do many female spiders eat the males after mating? Talk about being used. Oh yes: Why is the female mosquito the one who feeds on blood why males eat nectar and other sweetness? Finally: Why is the female honey bee the one who stings? The male is 'stingerless,' defenseless, and unable to feed himself. After mating, males are driven out of the hive and die. I'm sure there's a moral here, but some things are better left for another day.

Now, the all-time mystery. Why are baseball coaches (managers) required to wear the team uniform? No other sport, at least none I 'm aware of has this requirement. The answer will be uncovered later. But for now, close your eyes and try to imagine what these sidelines would look like if they followed baseball..

Football: It's September 28ᵗʰ and Robert C. Byrd High School in Clarksburg, West Virginia is playing arch-rival Bridgeport High School from neighboring Bridgeport, West Virginia. You look to the side lines and see that both coaches are in tight football pants, knee socks, shoulder pads, jerseys with number 1, and earphones over their helmets.

Basketball: Could you imagine Mike Krzyzewski of Duke in Blue Devil blue baggy pants and a sleeveless jersey? Do you really think Pat Riley of the Miami Heat would give up his finely tailored Armani suits and hair gel? Gymnastics: Beside the uneven bars, giving instructions to the U. S. Women's team is Bela Karolyi – in leotards! Cheerleading: Use your imagination with this one. Even I'm not that bold. Wrestling: You're at the state tournament and your team's coach runs toward the scorer's table - in a wrestling singlet. Finally, swimming: As much as I would like to give examples, not in a million years.

If these images are somewhere between ridiculous and frightening, let's look back at baseball. I'm not sure, but I think I know why baseball still requires its managers to wear the complete uniform. Seeing Alex Rodriquez, Derek Jeter, or Johan Santana in a baseball uniform does the sport proud. They're current players, super stars, and fit.

Do you really think legendary mangers such as Lou Pinella, Don Zimmer, or Tommy Lasorda look forward to putting on skin tight stretch pants, or pants with stirrups, knee socks, team jerseys, cleats, and a baseball cap? After talking with a few old-time umpires and players, they told me that back when they were kids, many managers were also players. One old baseball junkie thought Pete Rose was the last one to wear both hats (manager/player) and that was 1986.

Finally, I believe I have solved the mystery. It's because of tradition, a tradition over 100 years old. Nevertheless, it seems baseball is holding on to a tradition that (at times) is rather embarrassing. Good grief it is time for a change! Look at many of the current managers, as they walk to the mound. Thank goodness other sports didn't follow their lead...remember the examples!

However, boys will be boys, at any age. There are probably a few managers that like wearing the uniform. These same men probably think they look good in their military uniform from the Korean War. Personally, I would rather see manager's in team colors, wearing a pullover with the team logo, sneakers, and regular pants...long pants please!

Some of you are thinking, who cares! And, that's OK.

A few weeks ago, as I was watching the Red Sox, I was just wondering – Why?

Bottom line: Baseball coaches are a little weird
anyway. That probably explains it.

CHAPTER 6

My Home Sweet Home

Comfort and Convenience

"Growing up, I absorbed the Southern obsession with place,
and place can seem to me somehow an extension of self." -
Frances Mayes

In, January 2008, I wrote a story titled "Man and His Land." It was about that private retreat. That special place where man can be a man! It goes by various names. For me it's simply known as Man Land. Well friends, as you read this, Man Land is getting an extension.

Sandra is the architect of this renovation, but I decided to refer to it as my "Man Kitchen. When we bought our home in 2005, it had a full basement divided into four rooms, three of which were finished. Man Land is one of the three. The fourth was used as a laundry room by a previous owner and as pretty Spartan-like - lock walls, water hookups, concrete floor and cupboards that didn't match.

From the very beginning we (especially Sandra) had the idea of turning it into a galley kitchen. It's a very small L-shaped space. After hundreds of trips from Man Land to the upstairs kitchen for man-snacks and man-beverages, I finally said, "It's time for the Man Kitchen! Just a basic fridge, sink, some counter and cabinet space."

Sandra looked at me and said, "Excuse me! If we're going to spend the money, it's not going to be just a Man Kitchen. It's going to be bright and cheery. Functional and tastefully designed. A kitchen we can both use, enjoy and is appropriate to our home"

I stood my ground. Folded my arms. Looked her straight in the eye and said, "OK. We'll do it your way," which is the mark of a well-seasoned husband. A few weeks later, after working on the design and selecting a company to do the work, the trucks began to appear. With the trucks came the expected confusion, chaos, dust and noise that goes with any renovation.

I just casually mentioned to a friend at the gym what we were doing and he said, "Why do you need two kitchens? You'll never get your money out of it." I looked at him and said, "You're right. I don't need two kitchens. I want two kitchens." We continued to exchange friendly boy-barbs until we got bored and the conversation turned to NASCAR.

However, on the way home I thought about what he said, "You'll never get your money out of it." And he was right. We probably won't. But I don't plan on ever moving (again) and quite frankly, I don't care about getting my money out of it. What I care about is the "Comfort and Convenience" that spending the money will bring me right now and in the years to come. With each passing year, steps become steeper and increase in number.

My philosophy is: If you want it, can afford it, then do it. Quit waiting for the right time. If we wait for the right time, we'll spend most of our life waiting. If we worry about getting our money out of the things, we will never enjoy that long-awaited sun room or new garage. We'll never buy that summer home that hard work and careful planning through the years has made possible. When you put in that pool and your neighbor says, "What a waste of money." Wave to him when its 90 degrees, while on your pool float with a Cohiba (Cuban cigar) in one hand and a Corona (Mexican beer) in the other.

Go ahead; enjoy that room addition, new porch or patio. Who cares if you'll get your money out of it? When you buy a new car, you know you'll never get your money out of it, but buy it anyway and enjoy it! Life's way too short as is. Too short to put a price tag on "Comfort and Convenience," at least it is for me.

If you want something and can afford it, I say, "Why not!" Remember, tomorrow never comes. In my opinion, far too many people live their lives as is, content with what was, and never enjoy what could be.

The right time is now!

This was personal. Did you ever know someone who reached a certain life-plateau and quit? I do. They were unhappy and didn't know why.

Everything Is Too Inconvenient

Teach us delight in simple things. – Rudyard Kipling

Since my return to Clarksburg, West Virginia in 2005, I have realized getting where I want to be, buying what I need (or want), and seeing who I need to see is just too inconvenient!

Let's begin with the Health Department (flu shot). We chose to go to the First Methodist Church in the center of Clarksburg – how inconvenient! Starting time was 9:00 a.m. Knowing this was an advertising ploy, we planned to go early, find a parking spot, wait in line to register, and then remain among the masses for the opening bell.

We arrived 30 minutes early, parked by the side door, and followed the well-marked signs to the place of reckoning. I couldn't believe it, five people were ahead of us! I was ready to voice my displeasure but the person in front had a gun – he was a Deputy Sheriff. Therefore, silence was the better part of valor!

They began administering shots 10 minutes early. As I approached the nurse, I asked, "Do I get a sucker if I don't cry?" Apparently, she failed to appreciate my humor and immediately produced an icy-cold stare. Lesson learned: Do not make jokes when someone is about to stick a long-pointed object into your arm!

The inconvenience of the experience was overwhelming. The location was in the center of the city, parking was easy, there was no line, and the hit was administered in a professional way by an RN! By the way, she was great and it didn't hurt. I did make the sucker joke but she just ignored me and said, "Next".

While I am on a roll, let me talk about our city agencies. I went to the Court House to see where I needed to go to pay my taxes, register my cars, get a dog license, research a property deed, register to vote, and get a building permit. Yes, I needed to do them all. After going through security, I asked a deputy for directions to the needed buildings. He smiled and pointed straight, left, right, and up. I thought he was giving compass directions but he was pointing to rooms and floors, all in the same building.

However, I had my chance. He told me I had to go to another building for the building permit. With a sarcastic smile, I said, "And how far is that?" He pointed, this time across the street. Way too inconvenient! Everything in one building, but one.

As months passed, I realized many more Clarksburg inconveniences. Parking a block from the main parade route or festival location is way too much for any civilized person to tolerate. Standing at Third and Main Street, I saw three banks and knew a fourth was around the corner – way too inconvenient for my banking needs.

Another thing, going out to dinner is such a chore. With all the nice restaurants, making a choice and the long drive (1-2 miles) keeps us home… too inconvenient. However, Sandra has talked me into driving all the way to Bridgeport, West Virginia for a special occasion. It is just too far to go, for someone who lives in Goff Plaza (neighborhood). If I am rested, I will make the half mile journey to our favorite steak house on old Bridgeport Hill.

Another nuisance is the lack of (and variety) grocery stores. My Father taught me that grocery shopping is an event which includes visiting several stores before completing the list – it's a Belgian thing! I am very proud of my Belgian heritage. Having seven grocery stores and one big warehouse store with in four miles of my home is just not convenient enough! Even having a local pharmacy that still delivers, at no extra charge (with out expecting tips), is intolerable! Imagine the audacity of these people! Expecting someone to open their door for meds when the weather is frightful

Suddenly, something happened, I began to realize how much I really LOVE these inconveniences, or should I say conveniences - small city conveniences! Trust me, everything I have talked about is a Clarksburg convenience and there is so much more. Having lived in a large city for 32 years taught me what real inconvenience is: traffic, parking congestion, road rage, over-priced restaurants, rude city officials, pollution, and… "the beat goes on"!

So, next time you have negative thoughts about your small city, I hope you will remember at least one of these (in)conveniences…take a deep breath and keep in mind, "Everything is just so convenient…in a small town…in your town!"

True, living in a small-town means giving up
a lot. But, look at what you gain.

In Search of... 'Old Dog & Top Dog'

"Never eat more than you can lift." – Miss Piggy

Before moving back to Clarksburg, West Virginia in 2005, we always looked forward to returning a few times a year to visit family and friends. Prior to leaving for Virginia, we stocked up on Italian olives and Italian bread., something we could not purchase in southern Virginia

However, there's one culinary delight I could not stock. For me, it is an American icon as patriotic as apple pie and fried chicken. It is the all American Hot Dog. Not just any old dog. A (West Virginia) mountain dog with everything! To any foreigner (non-West Virginian) a dog with everything can be scary. "What do ya mean everything!" Of course, everything (to a West Virginian) means: mustard, chili, and onions. Although, it is acceptable to eliminate the onions for sissies and people returning to work.

While visiting, Dad and I would seek out some of the 'Old Dog' houses. Chain and new houses didn't count, although some are good. We went for memories and stories. With a couple of dogs and a frosty beverage, we talked about old days and old places, always disagreeing about which place deserved "Top Dog" honors. Over the years, we may have missed a few, but very few.

With each passing year, there were fewer favorite places. One summer, I came home and Lowell's on Main Street and (now) E.B. Saunders Way was gone. Dad just said Lowell probably got too old and closed. Who knows? A couple years later, another Grand Dame of hot dog excellence vanished – The Strand Pool Room on Pike Street. As a child, I would occasionally accompany dad for Saturday errands. The Strand had wonderful dogs plus dad could catch up on his sports. But, I always had to promise, "Don't tell Mom." It was the pool room thing.

But all was not lost during my years in Virginia. I found one good substitute dog house...Lester's A combination of tasty dogs and owner charisma. The owner (Lester) was a retired Navy chief who treated everyone like the "Soup Nazi" on *Seinfeld*. He abused everyone equally. But the food was great. His walls were decorated with pictures of him with presidents, movie stars, politicians, sport greats, and the guys from the neighborhood.

Lester's kept me going until my return to Clarksburg in 2005. However, by then very few of the old dog houses remained. While driving around, I thought of a Beatles song *"There Are Places I Remember."* It went like this: "There are places I remember all my life, though some have changed. Some forever. Some have gone and some remain. All these places have their moments. Some are dead and some living."

I know I'll often stop and think about them. Like Mrs. Webb's in Hartland, my childhood neighborhood. She served such grand dogs, but oh so slow. But we "love you still." Another grand dog that stands out is the ones served by the football mother's clubs at Hite Field, the field where I played high school football. Today, only one concession stand remains. Sad. There is something about football, fall evenings, and dogs.

Three other "Places I Remember:" The Sanitary and Coney Island on Pike Street. And the Stonewall on Third Street. "Gimme two with everything and a coke." All gone.

With only two of our old haunts remaining and with dad's passing in 1999, the responsibility sits squarely on my shoulders. Who will be crowned "Old Dog & Top Dog, at least in my opinion.?

One is located by the Robinson Grand Theatre in Clarksburg. It's small but still a pretty ritzy place, called The Ritzy Lunch. The sauce has a unique smoky flavor and they offer 'Devil Dust' to heat it up a little. The wooden booths date back to the 1930's

The other dog house is in Nutter For, West Virginia by the bridge that no longer exists. Dad would stop on his way home from the Pittsburgh Plate Glass Company where he worked for 36 years, say hello to Thelma, bring home the dogs, and share her stories.

Both family owned (still). If you are in Clarksburg area, try them out and let me know what you think. Remember, it's for "Old Dog & Top Dog" honors. But don't go alone. Some things are meant to be shared. A couple of hot dogs plus a cold drink = a lifetime of memories.

But, remember what Miss Piggy said!

Hot dogs are a state treasure in West Virginia – unhealthy, but still a treasure. Debating the best are what feuds are made of.

And West Virginians know something about feuds.

Little Security at Local Football Game

Through these eyes, one of the simple pleasures I have enjoyed since my return in 2005 to Clarksburg, West Virginia is attending some of the local high school football games. My first visit was to Robert C. Byrd High School (RCB) to watch the Eagles play Liberty High School.

Immediately, I was disturbed and concerned over the lack of school security and police presence. Looking around the stadium, I only saw two police officers. I kept looking for more but that was all I saw. As I continued to look around, I suddenly realized why there was little security.

Before we go further, let me explain why I was so concerned. In my previous life, while living in Virginia, I was a high school administrator who oversaw the school athletic program and security, just to name few of my responsibilities. For each football game, I hired 17 police officers, the mounted unit (4 riders and horses), and had my six security guards on duty. Everyone was evenly dispersed throughout the crowd with walkie-talkies and one on the roof of the school with binoculars. The police and security were constantly on the look for groups of thug wannabees flashing hand signs or making threats. Oh yes, I might add that these signs were not saying, Eagles Fly High" or "Liberty Rules".

Everyone who entered the stadium was searched with a metal detector. All bags were searched and even mothers had to take their babies out of the strollers so they could be searched. Even after the game, the police were in the communities keeping people moving out of the parking lots and away from the school. Tragically, this was as important as game security because an innocent person was murdered in our parking lot a few years ago in a gang-related initiation.

This was not Friday night football in Beirut or Baghdad. This was just a typical high school Friday night in the big city south of the Mason-Dixon. Now you see why I thought there was too little security at this Clarksburg game. My 32 years away from Clarksburg made me temporarily forget about a kinder gentler place.

Let's go back to that first game at RCB. There were groups of young people gathering in groups, laughing, talking and trying to be noticed but not noticed by certain boys or girls. Parents greeted one another, not with a suspicious eye, but with a handshake, hug or pat on the back. Fans supported their teams and were respectful of the opponents. There were even a large number students cheering along with the cheerleaders, what a novel idea!

The teens I saw were respectful and dressed appropriately even though they may have battled with their parents earlier…some things never change! The biggest problem I had was preventing a nosebleed from the top bleachers, straightening out the "not 17 anymore" back when the game was over, and waiting for the band to march out. The police were right in the middle of it all, talking with friends, parents, and students. Although, I did notice that they were always keeping a watchful and professional eye on the surroundings. This may not be Beirut but it also isn't Camelot.

I suddenly realized why there was so little security…it was simply not needed. However, Clarksburg must keep a watchful eye on changes from within and influences from the outside. I ask all fathers, mothers, elected leaders, churches, and all citizens of small towns everywhere to do everything humanly possible to keep Friday night football just like it is, in your home town. It reflects who you are. Finally, always remember to support our men and women in "Blue".

What have we become when security at a high
school event rivals that of a military base.

These Eyes Can See Clearly Now

"It's not the honor that you take with you, but the heritage you leave behind." – Branch Rickey

In an earlier story, I talked about emotional walls, hillbilly jokes, my home town of Clarksburg and how difficult it was (at times) being from West Virginia. As a native of Clarksburg who lived in the South for the past 32 years, you can imagine (or maybe you can't) what it is like to be the brunt of jokes and movie references.

At times, I would even go along with the jokes or even enhance them. Yes, making fun of West Virginia has made the career of some comics, at our expense. Although I rarely showed my anger toward these jokes to anyone but my wife (who is also a Clarksburg native), I really got tired of being asked, "Is the state flower actually the satellite dish. Remember when they were the size of the television station transmitters?

Since I was an only child, I had an easy out when asked how many times I out ran my sister. Although, I could out run most of the girls on Liberty Avenue, my home street. Spending 30 years in education, I was constantly asked state political questions. I lost track of the times I said, "No, the governor's mansion did not burn all the way to the axle. I would simple say axle(s). It was a doublewide with new vinyl windows."

These quick-witted answers would usually quiet my southern colleagues. However, there were always some who would delight in showing their ignorance time and time again with shoeless and one leg longer than the other jokes.

The quickest way to prevent ignorant ridicule is to head it off at the pass. I always made it a point to show off my new black Converse high tops and to show them that one heel was not built up for hill walking. I have now graduated to designer sneakers and I must admit that I am 'gellen.', with both shoes the same height. Funny though, those Converse shoes are not as comfortable as they were 40 years ago. The quality must be in decline.

As my years in the South multiplied, I slowly regained my appreciation for the internal and external beauty of West Virginia, Harrison County, and Clarksburg. Oh yes, now I remember, this is called Mountaineer

Spirit. Earlier, I had talked about how Hollywood hasn't been kind to our state in many ways. Movies like *Coal Miners Daughter* (I know, it was about Kentucky), and *Deliverance*.

When I think of *Coal Miners Daughter*, my heart swells with pride and my eyes tear. For I think of the hard, dangerous, necessary work these men and women perform. Their sense of family and work ethics could teach my former colleagues much about life and much more about living. I also think of one little girl's dream of success and the struggles she overcame… AKA Mountaineer Spirit.

When I watch *Deliverance*, I think of many scenes, but one I will always remember is where the young boy, sitting on his porch, is playing the banjo and duels with the guitar player, hence the song "Dueling Banjos". I remember the look in the young boy's eyes when he out-played the outsider. A look that said, "Come on back when you want some more… AKA "Mountaineer Spirit".

So, my fellow West Virginians and Clarksburgians (sic), when we are joked about the mountain state and our city and Hollywood is unkind to us and comedians launch their careers at our expense, show your Mountaineer Spirit and pride and say, "Yes, I am from West Virginia. I do dangerous work, necessary work, provide for my family, look out for my neighbor, raise my children (just don't let them grow up), love life and living in West Virginia. Now, come on back when you want some more!"

Through these eyes, after returning home, I can see so much more clearly now!

Regardless of where you live, find something to be
proud of – like it or not, it is your heritage.

CHAPTER 7

In My Garden

Bird Man and Garden Lady

*"One of the deep secrets of life is that all that is really worth
the doing is what we do for others" — Lewis Carroll*

Welcome! I'm Dick Clark and I will be your host for this star-
studded gala, honoring two unselfish and deserving Harrison County
West Virginia residents. We are in the beautifully restored Waldo Hotel
n downtown Clarksburg for the first "Really Special People Awards." For
security reasons, our guests were escorted into the hotel through a series
of tunnels that have also been restored.

With no further ado, let me introduce our first presenters. Please
welcome Mike Lambiotte and Jennifer Lopez (my story, my fantasy).
Thanks Dick! May we have the envelope please? In the category for
"Unselfish devotion to wildlife and beauty," the award goes to....Bird
Man and Garden Lady.

Before they join us, let's take a quick look at this video. Please direct
your attention to the large screen. Each time I would drive to the YMCA
on Lowndes Hill, I would watch (and stop) for the wildlife. Not the type
I experienced in high school. I mean the deer, squirrels, and songbirds. I
found myself stopping to enjoy the sounds and sights of nature. The deer
would look at me and say, "Excuse me, I'm having breakfast."

The several bird feeders that line the road were always a flurry of
activity. Cardinals, goldfinches, and nuthatches, all competing for food.

The squirrels, like gymnasts, mastered the art of labor division. One would hang upside down (while eating) and shake seed to the others waiting below.

Once, I saw a doe eating from a feeder while her fawn picked tasty morsels off the ground. I made a point to thank the Y staff for hanging the feeders. They said, "Oh, we're not responsible. Some man who lives over the hill takes care of them." They didn't know his name, so I respectively call him 'Bird Man'. As the months passed, I would see him park his car and fill the feeders. Even take the damaged feeders home for repair. I thanked him one day and told him how much I appreciate his kindness. Certainly, the squirrels and birds thank him, they play for food. He just smiled and said, "I counted as many as seven cardinals in one tree, impatiently waiting their turn." The Bird Man on the Hill…quietly doing for others and expecting nothing in return.

Now Dick, could we please have the next video? Outside the Y you see a garden filled with beautiful flowers. Again, not being shy, I asked which staff member is responsible for this striking garden. I just wanted to compliment and thank them. Their answer was, "A lady just came in one day and asked if she could take care of the gardens." Months later, I was walking through the Y parking lot and saw an open trunk. Not unusual at a gym. Probably someone late for a class or absent minded (like me). What was unusual, it was full of plants. Then, behind me, I heard a shovel break the dirt. As I turned, I saw her…"Garden Lady on the Hill." I introduced myself and thanked her for creating such beauty.

Leaning on her shovel and pulling her hair back from her face she said, "Well, it's not as good as I like, but it was just a patch of weeds when I started. As we walked around the garden, she gave me the Latin and common names for many of her plants. Not your average week-end gardener. She was special, quietly doing for others and expecting nothing in return. As I drove away, they both reminded me of an old Chinese proverb," One joy scatters a hundred griefs."

Oh yes, there is much more to their stories, but we're running out of time. So Dick, we are very happy to present this "Really Special People Award," for unselfish dedication to wildlife, beauty, and balance. And now, please welcome this year's recipients to the Ball Room of the beautiful Waldo Hotel…Bird Man and Garden Lady

A silly story about two incredibly unselfish people.

"Kill da Wabbit"

"Most of us need to be humbled more often, to be reminded that nature is not only more complex than we think, it's more complex than we can think." – Gary Paul Nabhan

Thanks to years of watching Elmer Fudd pursue Bugs Bunny, I now share Elmer's frustration. We have bunnies in our gardens. Unlike Elmer, I refused to be outsmarted. Ok, I admit, they're cute, but not while eating our plants.

When Sandra, my wife, and I lived in Virginia, we had many gardens, really big gardens with plenty everyone…people, deer, rabbits, birds, and snakes. We shared and no one was greedy. Now, since being 'citified,' our gardens are tiny by comparison. Sandra gives me a tiny rectangle in the back yard, where I grow food. Flowers are more important, as every well-married man knows. But, let us get back to "Bunnies in the Garden"

It was early spring. The tulips were first emerging and Sandra was inspecting each plant. Then, I heard a scream! The plants had been snipped off like they had been cut with pinking shear (aka bunny nibbles). Never fear, I said, "Lambo-Rambo," Sylvester Stallone style was on it. As Elmer said, "Kill da Wabbit."

I found my tree stand, camouflage clothes, shotgun, face paint, and headband. Then, Sandra yelled, "We live on East Main Street., in the middle of town you idiot!" Oh yea! Better go to plan B., which included motion sensors, lasers, air horns, and sirens. She also nixed this idea.

Plan C. Merry (our Labrador retriever), could become a beagle, a dog that is a self-propelled nose. Early one morning, I saw a small bunny nestled among the flowers. On command, Merry bolted out the door. My heart stopped! What if she got into the flowers chasing the bunny? Sandra would hurt me in ways I could never imagine. I was saved! Merry was sniffing everything but the bunny. It was nestled tight to the ground in a typical 'bunny freeze,' even though Merry and I were only inches away. Even a honeybee almost landing on its nose, didn't make Bugs flinch.

Suddenly, I stopped hearing the man-made sounds around me. It was just me, the bunny, and the bee. It was then I thought of the mysterious deaths of thousands of bee colonies throughout the country. Nature…what is she trying to say about balance. I thought of Mr. Love, an old friend in Virginia who taught me about keeping bees. He never used insecticides. His words were so clear, "Mike, always remember, if it will kill bees, it will eventually kill man."

It was as if he was standing behind me. As the bee flew away, it was just me and Bugs, eye-to-eye. Merry was stalking a leaf. I remembered how we would watch the bunnies, in our Virginia orchard, play bunny tag. Watching was what I called 'Old people recreation.' The hawks would watch too, but for a different purpose. .

Then, the siren of a fire truck brought me back to the sounds of man. Merry was killing a stick, so I said, "Bugs, go away," which didn't work. A gentle nudge convinced him to join his friends in our neighbor's yard. I realized I was a failure (like Elmer) when it came to bunny control. But, it was Sandra to the rescue.

In one of her many garden books, she read about using cayenne pepper on 'wabbits.' Rest easy, the pepper was not for seasoning, it goes on the plants. However, handle with care and never stand down wind when applying. Yes, I learned the hard way. The pepper doesn't harm the plant and will keep Bugs and his buddies away. It must make them sneeze or have mild heart burn, but regardless, they stopped eating the plants.

So, Merry and I, hanging our heads in defeat, retreated to the back yard. As nighttime approached, it was show time. I could see the chimney swifts diving and dancing. A bat just intercepted a moth. A red squirrel was heading home, using the telephone line as a tree limb. Bugs was probably in his nest, sneezing. And the bees were in their hives…hopefully!

Again, I heard, "Mike, Remember, if it kills bees, it will eventually kill man."

Is anybody listening?

I know rabbits are God's creatures. But can they go eat someplace else.

When the Lilacs Bloom

"More than anything I must have flowers. Always. Always." - *Claude Monet*

Spring – "You know it's here or getting near, when the lilacs bloom." Put the boots away. Hang up the snow shovel. Tie up the salt bags. Because… spring is about to spring. Spring is my new best friend. Of course, every season is my new best friend. One of the many reasons I love living in West Virginia. I can always tell when spring and garden season is about to pop because there is a tinge of pink on the tree tips, a cool breeze, and warm sun.

But, the telltale sign is when 'they' come out of hibernation. You know the ones.

You see them early in the morning, still in their bath robes or in old clothes and scruffy shoes…scratching in the dirt to see any sign of a peony bud or daffodil or tulip leaf. They are the ones who wait (impatiently) for every mail carrier's love…garden catalogues. Once out of their winter habitat, they wait for God's splendor – the first flower of spring. They are simply called… gardeners.

The really special one's garden for the pleasure of others, more than their own. Over the years, I have been able to place gardeners into two classifications. One type grows things to eat and the other grows things that smell good and look pretty. I am the former and Sandra, my wife, is the latter. There is a warning here. Smell good and look pretty can be contagious, as I have found out. I admit, I am beginning to like 'pretty' as well as 'taste good." Damn you Sandra!

Yes, there I was early one morning scratching around in the mulch trying to be the first to find a bud. Remember, I'm very competitive. And there it was, the first red peony bud of spring. Being the modest person I am, I yelled for Sandra to come outside. As I was strutting around the yard like George Jefferson with a perfect head bob, I kept yelling, "I found it first…I found it first… nana nana boo boo!"

Sandra witnessed the advanced stages of 'gardeners love. I originally caught it from Dad (taste good stuff) but Sandra is responsible for the advanced stages consisting of color appreciation, design, and a love for composted manure. She is teaching me that gardeners love is a life-time affliction and spreads like ripples cast by a stone thrown into a lake. This ripple effect begins with one person, one vision, and one beautiful flower.

It spreads from one home, to one neighbor, to one neighborhood, and eventually... to one city. It can start with a beautiful basket of flowers on your porch. Watch out! What eventually happens is ...community beauty.

Learn to spread the beauty. Help your child plant daffodil bulbs in the fall and let them smell the earth. Show them an earthworm and explain how important they are. Watch their eyes as their garden blooms in the spring. Plant a peony in memory of one you loved and still love. As it multiplies over the years, consider dividing and sharing its beauty with a friend.

Friendships formed around flowers and sharing become something special. Dad taught me that a garden can satisfy your hunger. Sandra is teaching me that a garden also feeds and helps satisfy the soul. Even souls that appear lost. There is one such soul that frequently walks by our home. His clothes are wrinkled and soiled. His stride is stiff and unsteady, never looking our way or speaking. One day last spring, Sandra was in the front yard gardens with Merry (our Lab). The man stopped, looked around and said in a soft slow voice, "Gee lady, those sure are pretty flowers." The only time he has ever spoken.

For a few brief moments, a soul was fed...by the smell and sights of spring flowers.

As you rise this this beautiful spring morning remember, "Where flowers bloom, so does hope." – Lady Bird Johnson

I saw many lilacs before meeting Sandra. Now, I smell them.

CHAPTER 8

Sitting in A Tree...K I S S I N G

A Very Creative Love Affair

"Anyone can look for fashion in a boutique or history in a museum. The creative explorer looks for history in a hardware store and fashion in an airport." – Robert Wieder

This was a most unusual love affair. It was not on the *New York Times* Best Seller List. It was not splashed across the front page of the tabloids, nor discussed on the many television talk shows. But it had the makings for these. Michael and the lady met by chance, exchanging flirtatious looks and a few suggestive comments.

They met again at a dinner party and immediately knew there was something special happening. They shared several romantic dinners. One evening, he hinted at the possibility of her staying the night. She declined. Their romance included ex-girlfriends, ex-husbands and a mysterious younger man. It had an international flavor with visits to Milan, London and New York. She even considers ending their romance because they're so different. He loves jazz, she enjoys opera. He sells modern art. She despises it.

Michael's jealousy results in an embarrassing scene at a London restaurant when he sees her with another man. Later, she is furious and asks, "What made you act that way?" Their eyes meet and he says, "Because I love you." Yes, this was a most unusual love story. Especially because it was a series of commercials airing from 1987-93 in England and from 1991-97 in the U.S. The versions are a little different but the story-line is the same. Remember the "Gold Blend/Taster's Choice" coffee commercials? Each episode was a cliffhanger: Sexy, a bit suggestive, entertaining, romantic and above all, very creative.

These commercials were much different from the usual insulting mindless commercials we've come to expect from much of the media. Perhaps you sense: I usually use commercial breaks to visit the restroom or re-stock my emergency food supply in Man Land. However, I became fascinated by these commercials, anxiously awaiting the next installment, like a very classy soap opera.

They were brilliantly written and acted, incorporating seductive looks, well-timed pauses, classic music and romantic dialogue. Creativity was alive. And to think, they were simply selling coffee! Instant coffee at that.

Creativity (in any form) always attracts my attention! It can be a renewed appreciation for art, the brilliance of a newly designed football defense, or a golf course focusing its design to accommodate and encourage the physically challenged. I applaud the restaurant, coffee shop, or bakery which employs the moderately mentally challenged as wait staff and greeters. I have always been attracted to the unique, such as shrubbery trimmed in non-traditional forms like the ones in front of a veterinary clinic where we once lived. They were trimmed to look like different animals (topiaries).

I remember so well, reading about a hotel which trains, employs, and provides shelter free-of-charge for a few homeless people. The creativity of a city government which models its own program for providing jobs to the unemployed after the CCC (Civilian Conservation Corp) camps of the 1930's.

Risk-takers, not necessarily. To me, they are creative thinkers willing to do something a little different. And this type of creative thinking usually provides positive results. For Nescafe, their sales went up 10% during their 'Romantic' commercial run.

All this got me thinking, perhaps it's time we apply the "Taster's Choice" approach (Creativity and Innovation) to the many local issues before us: Preserving our historic buildings. Other cities like ours are doing it, so, why aren't we? Reversing the wide-spread apathy toward our civic responsibilities. We need a creative way to help people think beyond 'me.'

Hunger and homelessness. It's our problem, not just theirs. Every person is just one bad decision or one business failure away from being homeless.

We also need to unleash our creativity on generating community cooperation instead of competition. We need to learn how to play well together! And the silent majority needs to wake up and speak up. You can make a difference! To our civic leaders: Find a creative way to shed the tentacles of the past. As Frank Tyger said, "Discoveries are often made by not following instructions, by going off the main road, by trying the untried.

Creativity, it gets results…

By the way, you can view the Gold Blend commercials by Googling "Nescafe Gold Blend Adverts 1980's." Enjoy a romantic cup of coffee.

For those too young to remember – creativity was alive and well!

For When I'm Gone

"I love it, I love it; and who shall dare to chide me for loving that old arm chair?" – Eliza Cook

Norman was quietly sitting in his favorite chair on the porch. Ethel, his wife of 62 years, was putting the house back together after celebrating Norman's 80th birthday. "Ethel," he yelled, "Hurry up! Get out here before the air gets too damp." "In a minute Norman, the ice cream is melting. Hold on to your suspenders," she shouted.

Patience was never one of his virtues. However, he waited and rocked as the stars twinkled overhead and the hooting of an owl could be heard in the distance. Norman looked around the porch smiling and thought, "Someday, just think. I'm going to have to leave all this. I hope it's not tomorrow."

And then Ethel opened the screen door and said, "Come on you old fool, let's go to bed. It's almost 10 o'clock. You're going to get a chill and get sick. Then I'll have to nurse you back to health...again." Looking over his shoulder, he saw her smile and say, "Happy birthday Norman."

He wasn't sure if it was his knees or the chair creaking, but he got up slowly, making sure all his parts were working. He hated to go in, but he knew she was right, still he grumbled out loud. Just loud enough for her to hear. As Norman walked toward the living room, he stopped and looked around at 62 years of life and love. He was 18 and she 17 the day they wed.

So many memories. So many stories. He thought, "When we're gone, who will remember? Who will remember the history behind our treasures? At least they're treasures to us." He looked at the tea table that belonged to his great grandmother and the. her sterling silver loose-leaf tea spoon infuser sitting to one side.

Then he heard the clock strike 10. The same grandfather clock he bought Ethel for Christmas many years ago. It was made in England in 1796. As Norman made his way into the dining room, he looked up and saw the pedestal punchbowl that belonged to Ethel's grandmother. Walking past the china closet, Norman stopped. It was as if he could hear their wedding glasses clink together. Looking around, there they were, together, side by side. He just shook his head and thought, "Damn hearing aide, it must be the batteries," but he was smiling as he entered the kitchen.

A glass of milk and a pinch of Ethel's homemade birthday cake were in order, knowing she would disapprove., but Norman thought to himself, "A man's gota do what a man's gota do… especially on his birthday." As he slowly walked up the stairs, he realized he had a mission to accomplish.

For the next several days, Norman walked around secretly scribbling in an old notebook and every evening he went into the library and closed the door. On the seventh day, he demanded to know where his trusty Kodak Duaflex camera was. "Norman, they stopped making them in 1960. Even if I could find it, there's no film, let alone flashbulbs," said Ethel.

Norman barked, "Well then woman, someone's gota go to town. I need a camera!"

Since he couldn't drive anymore, he meant Ethel had to go to town. Two weeks later, Norman announced, "Well old woman, if I die tonight, you need to put this in a safe place."

Norman presented her with a book of pictures with a hand-written history for each one. "Also, behind every painting and picture throughout their home was a letter explaining what it was and where it came from," he said. He just turned and walked toward the porch. Sitting in her favorite chair, Ethel saw pictures of her grandfather's old store keeper's clock, Norman's old pocket watch, and his great grandmother's milk pitcher with the cat handle. And so much more. She saw a lifetime of memories. Painstakingly preserved by a man who had trouble remembering to take his medicine.

As Ethel opened the screen door, Norman looked up at her and said, "Just something for when I'm gone I love you old woman."

We should all chronicle our cherished heirlooms – hoping that some day, someone will pick one of them up and smile.

Especially, when one is gone and the other can still smile.

The Journal

*"My memory is certainly in my hands. I can remember things
only if I have pen and write with it and I can play with it."* –
Dame Rebecca West

Entry date: **April 7, 2005**. Move in day. I was walking toward Hardees
as the moving van turned down East Main Street. Excited, I rushed back to
our new home. My enthusiasm was slightly overshadowed by the thoughts
of 'Unpacking!' Thirty-two years of our life was heading toward me.

By the end of the day, all had gone well, except for my blue hand-made
(by me) cupboard which had to be disassembled to fit in "Man Land."
Exhaustion reigned at the end of the day. Within minutes we (I) devoured
a good portion of the turkey my mother-in-law provided. Finally, there
was peace.

Entry date: **April 7, 2006**. This concludes my account of the first
year in our new home. To celebrate, we went to Blackwater Falls and
Dolly Sods. Merry (our Lab) enjoyed the ride, sniffs, and walks, but slept
most of the way home. When we got home, we celebrated with pizza
and champagne. Merry was too tired to eat. She got a big drink and
crashed. No more boxes. Sandra deserves a Medal of Valor, with a cluster
of happiness and peace. I am certain there will be a garden of peonies in
heaven with her name over the entrance.

What you just read was the first and last entry of something very
special, at least to me. Without Sandra's knowledge, I kept a daily journal
of the first year in our new home.

On the first anniversary of moving in, I presented it to her. My version
of Ralph Edwards' *This Is Your Life*, a very popular television program in
the 50's.

Since then, we periodically open the journal to a current date (like
today) and relive those special moments. Without writing, many of these
memories would have been lost in life. Thinking back, there were many
firsts I wish I had recorded. I always had the best of intentions, but just
never followed through - until that special day in April. Through the
years, little voices kept saying, "Write it down. Write every day. Today's
unimportance is tomorrow's smiles."

In 1971, I was sitting in a college convocation listening to a young English professor (PhD at 31) talking about his latest book. A book about his younger years (imagine that) as a high school English teacher in Cincinnati. His journal was now a best seller. All I could think about was, "It's Friday!"

Even after years of teaching and my long-term association with G. William Whitehurst, a Virginia U. S. Congressman for 18 years, I still failed to see the need for putting pen in hand for memories. Every year the Congressman was a guest in my class and time after time he referred to his daily journal and his years on The Hill.' His book, "The Diary of a Congressman" is now in its 4th edition.

During my 31 years in public education, keeping a journal was only a fleeting thought. I was always too busy, or so I thought at the time. Now, most of those memories are buried too deep for retrieval, with only an occasional tragic or heartwarming event surfacing. Not until near the end of my career did I realize the importance of the beginning.

How ironic: There was a time when I felt I didn't have the time to write. Now, I feel there isn't enough time to write everything I want to write, for now I now understand the words of a congressman and a young professor: "Write every day. Write about your feelings and daily events. What you remember today will be the memories of tomorrow."

As a new father, mother, husband or wife, write about that first year. Your child's first birthday or year in school. Write about that special vacation. Write for your children and your grandchildren, for they will always be with you. Imagine...thirty years at any job. What you've seen, smelled, heard, and accomplished.

Your thoughts may never become a book. But they will become a wonderful gift. A gift of forever.

Every once and a while, I pull this journal from the book shelf, pick today's date and Sandra and I share a special time.

The Smiling Heart

"My heart leaps up when I behold a rainbow in the sky." –
William Wordsworth

There we were, headed for a beautiful Caribbean island. My thoughts were of scuba diving, exotic food, and steel drums. Sandra was engulfed with a book, no doubt thinking about relaxing, sleeping late, and taking in the tropical landscape. We were leaving our world behind and about to enter a tropical paradise. Little did we know what was in store? As the days raced by, our senses were stimulated beyond words. For me it was excitement and adventure. For Sandra, it was beauty and calmness.

However, it was one simple and unplanned event that made our hearts smile. On our first night, as the heat and humidity turned into a cool evening breeze, we noticed everyone quietly walking toward the beach. To satisfy our curiosity, we joined them. We saw locals and guests, young couples. families with children, older couples holding hands sitting in beach chairs, on blankets, and on the sand.

The only sounds were an occasional soft whisper or the clink of toasting wine glasses. For we were enjoying one of God's wondrous events - a beautiful orange sun slipping below the horizon. As a sailboat passed in front of the half-departed sun, its silhouette made everyone gasp.

When the final flicker of orange disappeared, everyone applauded, a kiss or two were exchanged, children giggled., and a few weathered hands were clasped a little tighter. Then, as quietly as we came together, we went our separate ways. Later we learned, this was the island way of paying respect and enjoying one of life's simple pleasures. Every evening, strangers became friends. We learned something very special that week…how little it takes to make a heart smile.

The image of that sunset is as strong today as that first night, years ago. Funny though, it took a trip of 1380 miles to help us appreciate the beauty in our own back yard.

Beauty such as sitting on my patio at dusk and looking at the pink, orange, and purple brush strokes above the tree tops. Or, driving through our West Virginia mountains at day break after an ice storm, and watching the rays of the sun dance through the tree branches. How wonderful it is to feel the sun warm the day or stop beside a rippling stream and listen to nature's song.

More simple pleasures: Watching a deer eat from a bird feeder. Carefully and quietly, you part the blinds to get a better look. The doe suddenly turns her head and looks straight at you. She appears to nod a thank you and continues to eat. Walking the river bank, you knew as a child as a flock of geese begin their graceful landing, soon joined by joined by a mother and five fuzzy goslings.

This was so special: A peaceful walk in the park with Merry (our Lab) and being rudely interrupted by a red squirrel scurrying across our path and up the closest tree. For the squirrel, a routine game of hide and seek. For Merry, it's all about retrieving that bushy tailed critter. She keeps circling and sniffing...while the squirrel is three trees away leaping, laughing and twitching its tail. Little did we know this walk in the park would end by taking a deep breath of happiness because we could recognize life's simple pleasures.

Sandra and I still talk about the little green tree frog which entertained us late one night on a warm summer evening years past. As we went to turn out the kitchen lights, we noticed him in the middle of the window, motionless, except for those small revolving eyes. With only the light above the sink, we spent several minutes watching him capture his dinner with precision, grace, and lightening quickness.

For me, it all began with a trip to a far-off island. It was then my eyes were opened to how little it takes to make my heart smile...right in my own back yard!

As Peter Magargee Brown once said, "The moments we call life are the moments when we see."

I hope you see your sunset.

Why do we always seem to be chasing rainbows –
when the gold is right beneath our feet?

CHAPTER 9

Holidays – Time to Dream

And they Knelt in Prayer

"An open home, an open heart, here grows a bountiful harvest." – Judy Hand

Take a trip with me to the Berkeley Plantation, on the banks of the James River in the colony of Virginia. It is December 4, 1619. Capt. John Woodlief and 37 other settlers are holding hands and kneeling in prayer as this proclamation is read: "Wee ordaine that the day of our ships arrival at the place assigned for plantacon in the land of Virginia shall be yearly and perpetually kept holy as a day of thanksgiving to Almighty God."

They were giving thanks for their safe arrival after a two-and-a- half- month voyage from Bristol, England. To this day, each first Sunday in November a Thanksgiving Festival is held on the grounds of Berkeley Plantation.

Now, let us travel up the coast to Plymouth, Massachusetts. It is 1621. The Plymouth colonists and Wampanoag Indians are sharing an autumn harvest feast. The colonists are not celebrating their arrival, they are celebrating their survival. The survival of a long and brutal winter in 'New' England. Of the 102 settlers, 18 were adult women, with only 4 surviving the winter.

So, on that autumn day in 1691, 53 colonists and 90 Native Americans sat together in celebration and cooperation, for thankful they were. For the colonists, they knelt in prayer, giving thanks for their survival. For the Wampanoag's, it was their tradition to celebrate the harvest and give thanks for a bountiful growing season. Together, they dined on venison, fowl, clams, oysters, Indian corn, leeks, pumpkin, chestnuts, acorns, onions, parsnips, and dried currants.

And now, it is nearly November 27, 2008 – Thanksgiving Day. As you read this story, millions of Americans will be traveling from near and far to be with their families for Thanksgiving. Just what does it mean for you? It is a day to thank God for life, love, and joy as it was for the colonists in 1619? Or has it become Turkey Day" football, and Christmas kickoff?

Nevertheless, the turkey will be in the oven. The smell of (oyster) dressing will swirl around the house with cranberry sauce, mashed potatoes, and gravy waiting patiently on the stove. I, like many of you, will join hands with family and friends and bow our heads in prayer. We will ask God to bless our food, remember and take care of those who are no longer with us, thank God life, love, and the joy of family, and keep those around our table safe and healthy.

However, this year my prayers will include many other thoughts: I will take time to remember the sacrifices of those early colonists. I will remember not all tables will be as bountiful as mine. And pledge to share my bounty in the years to come so others may smile on Thanksgiving. I will give thanks to be living in a country that can elect a leader whose historical ancestors were slaves of that same country, only 140 years ago.

The next time I walk into a bookstore, I will stop and look around and think, "Freedom is at my very fingertips." Even as I write my stories, I never fail to give thanks for I can write my mind and feelings without fear of government censorship. Furthermore, on my next trip to a Veterans Administration Hospital, I will make a point to shake as many hands as possible and say, "Thank you. Thank you for your sacrifices."

For your life has been ever changed, so mine can stay the same."

The next time I visit a National Cemetery, whether it is in Grafton, West Virginia or Arlington, Virginia, I will kneel among the thousands of white headstones and say, "Thank you, for what you gave, so my life can stay the same." Lastly, this special prayer will be said for the thousands of men and women around the world defending what some of us take for granted, "Almighty God, protect and guide them home safely, for there is an empty chair at the table, waiting to be filled."

I just had a friend buried in a National
Cemetery. He is with his comrades.
People like him have allowed me to write the stories I have written.

Thanks and Giving

Love – the more you share with others, the more you have. -
Mother Theresa

As this holiday approaches, let us take (perhaps) a different look at "Thanks and Giving." Travel with me to December 11, 1620. A group of English settlers (Pilgrims) were looking for a better life and settled near Cape Cod. Sorry, Plymouth Rock was only a short stop.

It seems the natives were not friendly so the English moved further south to establish a colony. Perhaps it was because the natives made fun of their hats and shoes or maybe the move was the result of a premonition about the brutal New England winters. Nevertheless, by spring half had perished and those who survived owed their survival to friendlier natives.

When fall arrived, natives and settlers celebrated survival, family, and friendship.

The celebration-feast didn't consist of turkey, dressing, cranberry sauce, or mashed potatoes. It was deer meat, duck, seafood, cabbage, onions, corn and squash. By some accounts, the feast lasted a week and they didn't call it "leftovers".

Following the meal(s) there were games, singing, smoking, and giving thanks. We still have that tradition today. Today, we call it football, MTV, a good Cuban cigar (or a bad domestic), and a late afternoon nap. What had happened to thanks and giving?

Over the years, I have thought about how thankful and blessed I was growing up in a *Father Knows Best* and *Leave It to Beaver* family. I was surrounded by loving parents, grandparents, and great grandparents. Then, something called life happened – I started to grow up. My family started to shrink, as some of them were having Thanksgiving with God. I got married and moved away. In few short years, my table went from 12 relatives to four,.

Suddenly, I became very thankful for the memories of those holidays. I will always smell mom's turkey, dressing, mashed potatoes, and deserts. Yes, memories can make you cry happy tears. Our first Thanksgiving, after returning to Clarksburg, West Virginia brought back those happy tears. As we gave thanks, with only our mothers seated beside us, I felt the presence of my entire family.

Later, I thought about how thankful I was for my health, my family, how wonderful it is to live in Clarksburg again, and the beauty of this state. I am thankful for the sacrifices of our men and women in uniform. We take freedom for granted, until it is lost! Take a few moments and think about the reasons you must be thankful. For starters, you are breathing! It is better than the alternative. As a friend at the gym said, "I would rather look at the green grass than the roots"!

As we approach our second home-coming Thanksgiving, my thoughts reach toward the giving in Thanksgiving. Giving is what is important. I thought about the friend Sandra invited to Thanksgiving when we were living in Virginia. Her family was in the mid-west and her health prevented her from traveling. I thought about the principal of Sandra's school, who anonymously placed a round- trip ticket on the desk of a first-year teacher who could not afford to travel home for Thanksgiving. She was sending money home to help support her family in Kentucky.

It seems easier to open our hearts and our homes during the holidays. But why not try opening and giving all year – what a novel idea! There are many ways to give back to our community. The easiest, give your time! Give your time to the soup kitchen your church charities, the humane society, shelters that assist battered spouses, the Salvation Army, our schools…the list goes on and on!

Time is precious and if you feel you cannot spare some of yours, there is always the check book! Your time and/or money will never be turned away, I guarantee it! They never have too much of either. Give a food or clothing basket (anonymously) to a needy family. "We should not forget to entertain strangers, lest we entertain angels unaware." – Hebrews 13:2

So, as the holiday approaches, give thanks for who we are, where we are, what we have and the beauty that surrounds us. Most of the world is not as fortunate. Take time to give some of what we have to those in need. Oh yes, don't forget about football. How appropriate if the Redskins were to play the Patriots!

Happy thanks and giving. For the travelers – Be safe!

As the years go by, my family circle is shrinking – my thanks
still grows and my giving increases in importance.

But Mommy, It Wasn't a Dream!

"If you can't accept anything on faith, you are doomed to a life dominated by doubt." – Kris Kringle, Miracle on 34th Street

This story may not be grammatically correct, but someone very special said that was OK.

Mary, turn off the lights and say your prayers. Ok mommy. Kneeling by her bed, Mary recited, "Now I lay me down to sleep, I pray the Lord my soul to keep, Should I die before I wake, I pray the Lord my soul to take. God bless mommy, daddy, and even my little 'dorky' brother."

Why are boys so gross? God, when daddy said, *I'll Be Home for Christmas,* I know he probably won't, but please keep him safe. One last thing, could you ask Santa to stop by? I really need to talk with him before *Christmas Time Is Here.*

And then Mary closed her eyes thinking, *It Wouldn't Be Christmas Without You* daddy. A short time later, she felt something touch her shoulder. "Mommy, it can't be morning yet," she said. As Mary opened her eyes, she gasped with excitement. Santa, is it really you!

Yes Mary, its *Jolly Old Saint Nicholas.* Santa to you. I was told you really needed to speak with me. We mustn't wake your mother. So, speak very softly. Tell me what's on your mind. Well Santa, is it too late to change my Christmas list? Well of course not. But you still want *The Christmas Shoes* don't you? Only if daddy is here to see me dance on Christmas morning. Oh Mary, I can't promise you he'll be home for Christmas. But I'll ask my angel friends to do their best to watch over him.

Santa, about my little brother. When he wrote, *All I Want for Christmas is My Two Front Teeth* and *I Want a Hippopotamus for Christmas,* and a drum. Please! No hippo or drum. Hippos are gross...like him. And the last thing I need outside my bedroom is *A Little Drummer Boy.* But he could use the teeth. They'd keep him from talking funny. If daddy can't be *Home For the Holidays,* could you see he has a *White Christmas*? Please, *"Let It Snow!"*

Oh Mary, that's going to be awfully difficult. You know it's very warm where he is. But, we'll see. One last thing Santa, *The Night before Christmas,* please make mommy smile again. Then Santa placed his hands over her eyes and said, "We'll see. Just listen for the bells."

Slowly, Mary's eyes became heavy and she drifted back to sleep. The next morning, she jumped out of bed and raced downstairs. Mommy Mommy, she yelled, Santa came and talked with me last night! Stop it Mary, her mother shouted. The last thing your brother needs is more holiday nonsense. Christmas is still two days away. But mommy, it wasn't a dream! Mary, that's enough! Go up stairs and get dressed.

For Mary, the next two days were filled with dreams of snow and Christmas morning. She thought, If only I wish hard enough. As she lay in bed on Christmas Eve, she felt a tug on her blanket. She knew it couldn't be Santa, he was way too busy. Then her little brother whispered, *I Saw Mommy Kissing Santa Claus.* Go to bed dork. But then she heard the bells. She looked at him and said, *Do You Hear What I Hear?*

Quickly, she got out of bed and peeked over the upstairs railing. And sure enough, there was Santa holding mommy in front of the Christmas tree. Mary could hear him say, *Merry Christmas Darling.* She was crying and smiling at the same time. Then Santa knelt, placing something under the tree.

As they walked toward the hearth, there they were...a pair of white satin dancing shoes. And then her dorky brother whispered, "Why is Santa wearing daddy's Army boots?" Mary smiled at him and said, "Never mind dork. I'll explain it later. Now hurry back to bed!"

When she came into her room, there was snow beside her bed and a note on her pillow saying, " Never lose faith, Love Kris."

Isn't it a shame children have to grow up and become adults

Dear Santa, It Really Wasn't My Fault!

And so happy Christmas, I hope you have fun, The near and the dear ones, The old and the young. – John Lennon

December 16, 1957: Dear Santa, Honest, it really wasn't my fault. All the bad things I did this year, the older boys (Jimmy, Bobby, and Johnny), made me do them. It's tough being 8. About teasing Barbara and pulling her pig tails: It was a dare. Some days, I think she is kinda cute, but don't tell anyone. Anyway, the older boys tell me you are getting old and forgetful. So, I'm making a list and checking it twice. Remember... the bad stuff wasn't my fault!

So, here is what I want for Christmas this year:

- A saucer sled...Karen, Janis and I crashed my old one.
- A Roy Rogers lunch box... I threw my old one at Jimmy and it went into the river.
- A new 26" bike. That's what the older boys ride... a Schwinn Black Phantom with baseball cards and balloons in the spokes for engine noise!
- A new dart gun. This time I promise not to target the lamps or Chester, my pet goose.
- Swim fins...I am tired of Janis out-swimming me.
- A Lash LaRue bull whip...Let's leave that one alone...OK!

Mom said I could only ask for 6 things. But, if you have any left-overs, there is always room for more on Liberty Ave. That's 163 Liberty Avenue, Clarksburg, West Virginia.

December 16, 2006: Well Santa, I saw you at the Christmas parade and you still look great. Red and white are your colors. But, back off the fudge. Rudolph (red nose and all) and the boys are not as young as they use to be.

Funny how quickly time passes. In 1957, I couldn't wait to grow up. But as 2006 winds down, I'm still a child (at heart) when I hear you yell "ho ho ho" and wave at us big kids. love a parade! Guess what, I am still a list-maker. Some things never change. Remember the one in 1957? I know, it was selfish, but what did you expect, I was only 8.

I will always believe... so here is my 2006 list:

Dear Santa:

- Please watch over Mom and don't let her fall into the shrubbery putting up Christmas lights. Airplanes are already buzzing the house trying to land.
- Please give our local, state and national leaders the wisdom to make the right decisions, not just the popular ones.
- Watch over all children and help them grow into adults.
- Guide the homeless toward shelter and give them hope so one day, homeless will become a forgotten word.
- Help us embrace and appreciate cultural differences and learn from one another, not fear one another.
- Convince our children that education will not only open doors but pull them through.
- Clarksburg, West Virginia, my hometown can rise from the ashes. I have seen it done in other places with a lot less than what we have. Right decisions take courage!
- Let us learn from the ones that give us unconditional love – our pets. May we always provide them a warm bed and plenty of food.
- Teach me to forgive as quickly as I want others to forgive me.
- Good health for my family, friends, and neighbors.
- Keep our service men and women safe. Bring'em home soon!
- In your travels, remember; don't tell anyone about West Virginia... it is a secret!

Well Santa, how have I done so far? Quite a change, isn't it? Little boys do grow up...well, in some ways.

Now, back to selfish: If a Harley-Davidson Fat Boy appears in my garage, I'll tell my wife Sandra it was your personal summer ride. That way, she won't make me return it. Oh yes, 'Big Guy', can I order a really DEEP snow? Sledding, snowball fights, and making snow angels were so much fun (in 1957). I know, I'll call the old gang…oops better not. We are senior citizens now – or almost.

Maybe we better just go to the park and watch the children and remember when. Finally, Santa: Be safe. Flying can be dangerous. And, "Have yourself a merry little Christmas."

Isn't it amazing how big boy toys become so complex,
although there is a little boy always inside.

December 23...two more days and I will be born.

What was Jesus thinking right before he was born?

Yes, babies waiting to be born think, have feelings, talk, and do a lot of moving around. Every expecting mother knows this. However, I wonder what baby Jesus was thinking? Like most babies, he probably wasn't too anxious to come into the world. He probably said to himself, "What's the hurry. I'm in a warm comfortable place, plenty of food, room for exercise. What's the rush?"

But, baby Jesus was different, as the world was about to find out. Not only did he have an earthly Mother and Father who were anxiously waiting his birth, he also had a Heavenly Father. This Heavenly Father knew where the world was heading and made the decision to give his only son to Mary and Joseph. He had a plan.

This Father knew what was ahead for his son. Thus, he told this tiny child, still in his Mother's womb, that his birth would bring such joy to Mary and Joseph and joy to the world. He also told him, "As you grow into a man, you will nurture friendships and love." What he didn't tell him was that he would also become the victim of hate, treachery, and betrayal. Little did he know, only two days before his birth, the enormous pain and suffering he would endure during his final days on earth.

Despite all this, on December 23 (a very long time ago), a small child began to kick and squirm deep inside his Mother. He was telling her, "Mom, I think it is time." Also, in a far-off place, three Kings saw a star high in the sky. They didn't know what it meant but they did know this, "We must follow this star." And follow it they did. Upon arriving at their destination, they knew they were witnessing a miracle, a miracle that would save the world – the birth of the Christ child.

It was now December 25. This infant, who Mary and Joseph called Jesus, took his first breath and greeted the world. Like most newborns, he must have thought, "Woo, what happened? Where am I? What am I doing here? Can I go back?" But, he adjusted to his new world and walked where no man had ever walked before. Did you ever wonder what it would be like to walk the hills, valleys and streets where Jesus walked? Climb the steps that Jesus climbed, carrying the cross on which he would later die.

I wonder what he is thinking today (December 23) two days before his birth? In two days we will celebrate a birth that brought hope and love into the hearts of so many. As you awake this December 25, think about that small child. Think about what his Heavenly Father sent him to earth to accomplish. Feel the love that Mary and Joseph felt for each other. Think about friendships and forgiveness and never lose sight of hope.

Many times, I begin my stories with a quote. However, this time, I would like to end with one. From Sandra and me to you on this December 25, 2006: *"To cherish peace and good will, to be plenteous in mercy, is to have the real spirit of Christmas. If we think on these things, there will be born in us a savior and over us will shine a star, sending its gleam of hope to the world."* – Calvin Coolidge, December 25, 1927.

Don't be afraid to follow your shining star!

There is so much about the life of Jesus we do not know. Where was his childhood home? Who were his childhood friends? Where was his favorite place to go when he wanted to be alone? When did he first realize, he was different from others. Did he ever fall in love?

Jesus, the man we often forget. But he never forgets us.

December 25, 1927

My wife has always kept my ship sailing straight and into the wind – especially when I have chosen to veer off course – she is my navigator. - Michael Lambiotte

On September 23, 2006, I began writing my stories. I must say, picking a topic and determining a title has been easy. I have so much to say and so little time to say it. Of course, that is because I am new, naive, and inexperienced in the world of journalism. But, it is fun. I hope I never lose the fun feeling.

However, I have reached a major dilemma...my first writers block! I guess it is all right that I use that term now that I have three months' experience as a published writer. With Christmas so close, I wanted this story to be a journalistic masterpiece. However, all my ideas (so far) have ended up as little balls of paper being batted around the floor by the cats.

However, my wife Sandra keeps me grounded and focused. When I suggested the masterpiece goal, she just took off her glasses, gave me 'the look' and said, "KISS" – keep it simple stupid! Because she is my chief research assistant, quote finder, proof reader, and major critic, I decided to ask her to help me through this writers block.

Here are some of my top journalistic masterpiece ideas for my next story. I considered re-writing *Twas the Night Before Christmas* with a Caribbean theme, using iguanas instead of mice. Next came the idea of taking *Rudolph the Red Nose Reindeer* and write it as a rap song. Then, there was the idea of taking *I saw Mommy Kissing Santa Claus* and turning it into a romance novel/short story. My final attempt at breaking the block was to do a re-make (with a twist) of *It's a Wonderful Life* with Rush Limbaugh and Madonna in the lead roles.

Nothing was working, so I went to Sandra for help, She looked at my topics and notes, took off her glasses, and was brutally honest. When she was finished with her constructive criticism, she simply pointed to the computer. Without saying a word, I dropped my head and slowly returned to my desk.

For several minutes, I could feel her eyes burning into the back of my head and then I heard her chair move. As she stepped beside my chair, I saw a magazine in her hand and I thought, "Was I going to get whacked or what?" To my surprise, she kissed me on the neck, reached over my shoulder, and laid a magazine in front of me, opened to a beautiful quote. As I read the quote, I realized this would be my next story and our Christmas gift to you and yours:

"To cherish peace and good will, to be plenteous in mercy, is to have the real spirit of Christmas. If we think on these things, there will be born in us a Savior and over us will shine a star, sending its gleam of hope to the world." – *Calvin Coolidge, December 25, 1927.*

In Sandra's own subtle way, she was telling me to be true to myself. She has often said, "You have your own style and way of telling a story. Just write what is in your heart and be true to that style."

I wanted to write a story that would be one for all ages – for children, parents and grandparents, and men as well as women. My mother was born in 1927 and I wondered what her first Christmas was like in that drafty old farm house near Jacktown, Pennsylvania. Then, my thoughts turned to December 25 and I could smell fresh hay, hear the bleating of sheep, and see one flickering candle as its light reflected off the face of a very special child.

My story was already written, many years ago. Wishing peace, health, and happiness to all… near and far.

I have always tried to give Sandra the credit she deserves. To support her in her many activities. And sadly, I have failed too often.

Michael S. Lambiotte

Reindeer Training Camp

"Faith goes up the stairs that love has built and looks out the window which hope has opened." – Charles Spurgeon

This story is for the children, young and old who still believe. Recently, I was privileged to attend the North Pole Reindeer Training Camp. On December 1st, Santa has all his reindeer report for camp. No, they don't live with Santa all year long. As he called role, each raised his hoof or replied 'here' with a snort: Dasher, Dancer, Prancer, Vixen, Comet, Cupid, Donner, and Blitzen. Rudolph, just "blinked" his nose.

Their contracts required them to weigh no more than 350 pounds. Apparently, Dasher, impressed with his performance last year, spent way too much time at the moss and grass buffet. He weighed a pudgy 475. When Vixen got on the scales, the other reindeer gasped! Last year he was a slim 275. This year he was ripped and cut, weighing a rock-hard 350 pounds. Rumors of performance enhancing moss swirled.

At dinner, one of the elves, Bushy Evergreen, told me some facts not generally known about Rudolph. His father is Donner and his nickname is Rudy. And it was Donner who suggested his son take the lead to light the way on that one foggy Christmas Eve. Without that glowing red beacon, Christmas might have been cancelled and that night Rudy secured his place in history.

At precisely 5:00 a.m. the next morning, elf Wunhorse Openslae rousted the reindeer for breakfast. While most dined on carrots, oatmeal flavored grass, and succulent moss, Dasher was placed on a special low cal diet of dried leaves and birch bark. After breakfast, for endurance, Rudy led the mighty seven on a 50-mile trot through the snow.

Dasher was confined to a treadmill under the supervision of elf Alabaster Snowball.

After the run, they (including Dasher) lifted weights, under the direction of elf Shinny Upatree. Each reindeer was required to pull a 500-pound Yule log 400 yards from the toy shop to the reindeer barn, and back.

The agility training was designed to perfect rooftop landings and takeoffs. Elf Pepper Minstix had them sprint 10 yards and stop, shuffle

156

right then left, and sprint 10 yards, a total of 200 yards. Moving 36 hooves and 9 massive antlers in one direction was no easy chore, but one they had to master. Surprising to no one, Vixen won all the strength and agility drills, adding to the rumors of performance enhancing moss.

The first week ended with its share of injuries. Dasher had turf hoof and Dancer strained his knee. Their trainer, elf Sugarplum Mary, immediately iced it down in a snow bank. Blitzen received a concussion when the harness on his Yule log broke and he ran head first into the mailroom. However, they all recovered quickly because they knew their big night was approaching.

During breakfast on day 7:00 a.m., Santa's mandatory drug testing results were revealed. With all eyes fixed on Vixen, Sugarplum announced, "All tests negative!" And the room erupted with clicking hooves and Rudy's nose blinking wildly. Vixen was proof, "Extraordinary results can be achieved by ordinary hard work and dedication." The second week of training camp began with intense harness work. It was magical to see all nine reindeer working as one.

On my last day, I was treated to a sight seen by few – Reindeer Dress Rehearsal. There they were, dressed in their finest and shiniest Christmas harnesses, impatiently pawing the snow. As Santa settled in his sleigh and tightened the reigns, Wunorse grabbed my arm and said, "Better stand back or you'll get covered with snow!" In a bellowing voice, Santa yelled, "Ready Rudolph! Now Dasher! Now Dancer! Now Prancer and Vixen! On Comet! On Cupid! On Donner and Blitzen. To the top of the porch. To the top of the wall! Now dash away! Dash away all!"

And the magic of Christmas was before me. As I was leaving, Shinny whispered in my ear, "We hope you'll share this story with the children... young and old." When I got home, I found this note in my jacket, "If only more people would believe. Love, Sugarplum."

Try to imagine a buff Rudolph. Even reindeer need to work out.

Thanks For The Memories.....

Moments big as years — John Keats

As Frank Sinatra once sang, "Thanks for the memories of things I can't forget," the song makes me think of Clarksburg, West Virginia, my home town, and I think "Thanks for the many holiday memories ...some 30 years old". Bear with me, while I share some of my fondest memories of this holiday...near and far. The Christmas parade in Clarksburg: The glitter, marching bands, and the gleam in children's eyes as Santa approached... and in my own eyes.

The elegance of the Holly Ball, a charity event to benefit the local hospital: Women looking so beautiful and gentlemen in their finest tuxedos. The decorations sparkled like diamonds on black velvet. Oh, what a worthy cause. May the tradition always continue.

Taking my Mother to see the Christmas lights...how special! As we drove through Goff Plaza, Stealey, Hill n' Dale, the Clarksburg Country Club neighborhoods, and neighboring Bridgeport, West Virginia, the hills were aglow. How special, just sharing time together.

The memories of driving down Old Bridgeport Hill and looking at the city lights, remembering why Clarksburg is called the Champagne City, with lights twinkling in the shape of a champagne glass. Seeing Santa's (rein) deer grazing on the lawn of my Mother-in-laws apartment in the Riverbend neighborhood. They must be bulking up for their big night. I counted 15 der on the front lawn. All simple pleasures in the city where I grew up.

More small town simple pleasures and memories: Total strangers saying, "Merry Christmas," as I did my shopping. The elderly lady who held the door for me as I left one store with arms full. Seeing the swans on Liberty Avenue, the street where I lived as a child, as I was going to my Mother's home Christmas Eve: The swans were bedded down on the bank facing each other, their necks forming the familiar heart shape. I stopped to say hello and they honked ...it sounded like, "Merry Christmas."

I remember Santa, in the rain in front of the Court House waving at each passing car with his trademark smile and belly jiggle. The candle light service at my church. The Community Christmas Dinner at the First United Methodist Church, bringing people together: some with families some without, bankers and the homeless, the elderly and the young – together as one!

Imagine what it would be like if we could extend this unity for two days or…

Memories from the past…walking down Main Street in Clarksburg on Christmas Eve, last minute crowds, Salvation Army bell ringers, and the beauty of the Court House Christmas tree. Hustling in and out of the stores looking for that final just right gift: Oh, how I want to re-live those memories. Santa, help make Clarksburg "sparkle" again!

Shopping the day after Christmas: Never Again! I did it once several years ago when I lived in Virginia. I am still scarred from the trauma of competing for the last parking space on the planet. Plus, there was the fear of facing two shoppers, carts loaded, side-by-side in the aisle, eyes focused on the last great deal of the century, something no man should face alone.

Such memories of dear friends: My old friends, my new friends, and my special friend that helped me gain a greater appreciation for my Belgian heritage. Thanks Vicki!

Never forget New Years Eve: This year, my wife Sandra and I still partied, but with old friends Patti and Don, sharing memories, laughs, and hopes. Also, we didn't have to set the alarm for the 11:50 p.m. Champagne toast.

As we begin 2007, let me leave you with one last thought. I have been informed that there is a new gang in town. It goes by the initials SES. It stands for, Secret Elf Society. It is rumored to have been started by two old women who anonymously delivered a Christmas tree, decorations, clothes, toys, and food to a single Mom and her infant child for Christmas. My sources say they will recruit two more members each year. Very Secretive! It is believed the SES will become a major force in our city – What a beautiful idea! Watch out, for old ladies dressed as elves!

So, Clarksburg, "Thanks for the Memories", memories I will never forget. You created beautiful memories for me as a child and even more beautiful recollections this year. Please, everyone, take a few minutes to add to your memory chest.

This Christmas, sit around the fire and share what
no one can take away from you – memories.

The Elf That Said, "I Quit!"

"Hope is the thing with feathers that perches in the soul, and sings the tune without the words. And never stops at all." - Emily Dickinson

A special story about, "The elf that said, I quit!" On December 12, Santa called an elf meeting. With only 13 days left, he wanted a progress report. Alabaster Snowball, the administrator of the Naughty & Nice list went first. "Santa, all is well. The naughty pile is much smaller this year. I'm forwarding the nice list to the toy factory."

Looking at Bushy Evergreen, inventor of the magic toy-making machine, Santa said, "Bushy, can you and your assistants handle the additional orders?" "No problem Boss. We're ahead of schedule." Pepper Minstix, head of village security, whose duty is to keep the location of Santa's Christmas village secret was next. "Not to worry Santa. The toy-part supply line has gone unnoticed. No one's been able to track any reindeer training."

Then, Shinny Upatree, the oldest elf and cofounder of the secret village said, "Santa, the remodeling of the reindeer barn was completed on time and the weather station upgrades are up and running." Now it was Sugarplum Mary's turn, chief kitchen assistant to Mrs. Claus. "Santa," she said, "The fruit cakes are wrapped, the reindeer treats will be ready Christmas Eve, Mrs. Claus has planned your goodie sack and we won't forget your thermos of hot chocolate this year…promise!"

"And how about you Wunorse Openslae," Santa asked. Wunorse is Santa's sleigh designer and chief maintenance engineer. "The rails have been reinforced. A new harness is ready for Rudolph. And I replaced your brakes. We can't afford any more roof sliding accidents." The last to report was Makit Kumtru. He's responsible for processing and sorting the children's requests into categories based on what they want; toys, clothes and miscellaneous.

Next, Makit spoke about the child who wants what Santa can't give. Makit looked at Santa and said, "Listen to these letters: " Dear Santa: Keep mommy safe. She's in the desert protecting me and daddy. She's a Marine.

Daddy tries, but I miss mommy." "Dear Santa: Please make daddy stop drinking and hitting mom. She cries almost every night."

"Dear Santa: My little brother just went to heaven. Can you send him back? Mom and Dad are so sad. And I miss him too." "Dear Santa: Help daddy get a job. He's driving mom crazy. He alphabetized the spice rack last night."

Makit handed these letters to Santa and said, "There's thousands more like these in the mail room. I just can't stand it any more. I quit!" As he was leaving the room, he turned and said, "Toys won't make these children smile." After walking for almost an hour he decided to rest under one of the hemlock trees behind the reindeer barn. High in the tree, their resident squirrel Fuzzy Tail was shelling nuts. In another tree Saw Whet, Pepper's pet owl, was patiently calling "SwEE," waiting for her husband to return with a tasty mouse for dinner.

Then, Blizzard, a backup reindeer came over and lay beside Makit, sheltering him from the wind and light snow that began to fall. Looking at Blizzard he said, "Big guy, I just can't do it anymore. They're not asking for toys...only hope. I can't process the impossible." As Blizzard nuzzled him under his arm his massive antlers hit one of the hemlock branches, causing a light dusting of snow to fall on their heads. He looked at Blizzard and saw a twinkle in his large brown eyes.

Makit got up and ran back to the main house as fast as his little legs could carry him shouting, "I un-quit. I have the answer." Santa looked at him and said, "Makit Kumtru have you been in the special eggnog again?" But then he whispered to Santa, "Get Bushy to make a special dust. We'll call it 'Hope Dust.' Just sprinkle it so it falls on every child and adult. Hope is never impossible. Everyone needs to believe in something." Santa looked down at him said, "Big little guy, I'll see what I can do."

As the sun rose on Christmas morning, there was a light snow covering every roof top – some called it 'Hope Dust."

I can't imagine life without fantasies. This was a truly fun story to write.

Michael S. Lambiotte

The Magic Wrap

"Love never dies as long as there is someone to remember." –
Leo Buscaglia

It was December 1, 2030. The sun was beginning to shine through the bedroom window. Slowly...very slowly, he got out of bed. Every day, becomes harder and he moves slower. Nevertheless, he makes his way toward the kitchen. A few minutes later, he hears his wife coming down the stairs. As always, he's waiting with her morning coffee. For 58 years, a simple labor of love. She asks him if he knew what day it was. It's Saturday, he said. No, it is Saturday, December 1st. Beginning with the first year they were married, she always gave him a gift on December 1st.

A simple labor of love which also meant, "Let the decorating begin!" His job was to put up the tree, string the lights, and place the candles in every window. The ornaments were her job. Every piece had story or special meaning and she could recall every one. Funny though, he had trouble remembering what day it was, let alone who gave them a decoration 58 years ago.

However, he could remember one special decoration, a small furry racoon they named Rocky. She bought Rocky the first year they were married and was always placed near the top of the tree. Recently, he noticed some of Rocky's fur coming off. Very appropriate because he was also losing some of his fur. They were both getting older.

When they were finished decorating, every door had a magnificent wreath and a treasured sled was on the front porch. For weeks, the aromas of holiday baking swirled throughout the house. Only now, most of the treats became gifts. Although, he always delighted in sneaking one or two pieces of fudge and a small slice of fruit cake. Sneaked treats always tasted better.

Long gone are the days of frantic shopping and buying. Now, all they want is to share beautiful memories and one more Christmas...together. Oh, a few old friends still come by to visit and share egg nog. Their younger friends, well they're younger. They have their parties and 'must go to' affairs.

Through the years, it always amazed him how she could remember what goes where and with what., especially the Christmas table...always elegant, set with their beautiful wedding china and cloth napkins folded like stars. Her fingers don't bend like they use too, but the napkins are still perfect. Add the crystal and sterling silver with multiple forks and spoons (which he still can't figure out) and elegance is redefined, at their table. Since the beginning, he teases, sometimes too much. But deep down, he can't imagine the table any other way.

She pays attention to every detail. He waits for Christmas Eve, with a child-like gleam in his eyes. Then, it is finally here - Christmas Eve. Now, they celebrate on the sofa by the fireplace. Waiting. Waiting to hear the church bells at midnight. As the bells fade, he looks at her and says; Well, we made it one more Christmas. After their traditional toast, it's off to bed. But this year, he said he just wanted to sit a few minutes and look at the tree.

When she got up, she took her wrap and placed it around his shoulders. Don't sit here long, you'll get a chill. He looked at the tree, with all its beauty and suddenly felt sad. Someday ...all too soon, only one of them would hear the bells on Christmas Eve. Feeling the warmth from her wrap, his sadness turned to joy...as if it was magic. What a wonderful life they shared. What beautiful memories. The warmth he felt: God was telling him they would always be together. They would always hear the bells on Christmas Eve. For He knew their love would never die. As he slowly walked past their Christmas tree, he swears he saw Rocky wink at him.

This Christmas, as you reflect on your life and the days ahead - treasure every day. Especially treasure the ones you love. For all too soon, you too will be sitting on the sofa, waiting to hear the bells on Christmas Eve.

Wishing you magical Christmas season.

I can't imagine a Christmas morning without my wife
Sandra. We've gone from silly teenagers to silly old
people – together. I hope we leave together.

My New Year Gnomes

"To help all created things, that is the measure of our responsibility; to be helped by all, that is the measure of our hope." – Gerald Vann

In a desperate attempt to steer the New Year in the right direction, I contacted some old friends. Although small, their power and cleverness are often described as superhuman. They're called Gnomes. If you ever meet one, the "G" is silent, so it sounds like 'Nome.' Although many consider them a mythological creature primarily living in the woods, many have moved into our gardens and homes. To me, they are real and very much needed, especially today and around my neighborhood.

For the benefit of those unfamiliar with gnomes, folklore says they originated in Scandinavia, migrating to Germany, then throughout Europe, and later to North America.

Most people have never seen one. They're extremely shy and only come out at night.

They're very small (6" tall), but appear a little taller because of their pointed red hats.

They usually dress in solid colors such as blue, red, or green. The males generally have a long white beard. They're considered fierce guardians of the earth and protectors of all wildlife.

I contacted the garden and home gnomes because they have the personalities and intelligence of humans (some believe wiser). They also have exceptional vision, not just eye sight, but the ability to see things as they should be, not as they are. Gnomes have come to symbolize integrity, honesty, modesty, and hard work. And they pride themselves in aiding all living things. Keep this in mind.

My first encounter came this past fall. Merry, our Labrador Retriever, was stalking something in the back yard. She suddenly stopped, jumped back, ears at attention, forehead wrinkled, and head tilted to one side. When I went to investigate, I saw something move under a peony leaf. I lifted the leaf with a stick, thinking it was probably a toad, Merry's arch enemy. Suddenly I heard, "Hey buddy, watch the stick! And call the mutt off before I punch her in the nose!" Gnomes can be a bit feisty when threatened.

That was my first, but not my last encounter. The first is the ice breaker. Over the next few months I was introduced to most of the neighborhood gnomes. By mid-December I was convinced they could help with some issues that have troubled me these last few years. Remember their characteristics? I was impressed with how cleverly they provide aid and guidance to humans and we don't have a clue! They're so tiny and are everywhere.

After winning their trust, this is what I asked, "Please assist our city lawmakers and policy makers in placing the good of the whole before the good of one or the few. Give them eyes that see. Not just where we are or where we want to be, but where we never thought we could be. See what can be accomplished when the goal is bigger than any one player."

To the gnomes inhabiting our historic buildings, "Help the powers to be see the importance of such a magnificent part of our history. Many need a lot of work. Look around to see what a cancer called neglect can do."

To the gnomes gathering in the abandoned Robinson Grand Theatre late at night, "Keep applauding. The right person will hear the music. This grand dame of yesteryear is worth saving." And finally, to the gnomes who roam our airport and old office buildings, "Assist the competing groups to see by compromising, we all win."

When I had finished, the gnomes all huddled together. Their leader then approached me and said, "Hey big guy, lean down." I can't tell you what he said. That's part of the deal. But I can say, "Never estimate the power of a gnome."

So, the next time, late at night, when a leaf moves in your garden, it might not be a toad or the wind.

'Little' people. Enormous knowledge.

Michael S. Lambiotte

Cinders, Salt, and Snow Shovels

*Announced by all the trumpets of the sky, arrives the snow. -
Ralph Waldo Emerson*

Do you know where you left your snow shovel? If not, you better find it. The teaser snow we experienced recently was just a reminder that cinder, salt, and snow shoveling season is upon us.

I remember shoveling snow as a teen but for the past 32 years I lived on the coast of Virginia, where it seldom snows. However, the winter that my wife Sandra and I moved there (1972), we experienced our first southern snow. It began on a Sunday evening and snowed all night. By morning, the snow was 3" deep. School was closed for a week! Yes, a whole week – no snow plows, salt, or cinders... let alone snow shovels.

For 32 years, I never owned a snow shovel or boots. Returning to Clarksburg, West Virginia, changed everything. Last winter reminded me that I was grossly unprepared in the fine art of shoveling. Therefore, I have decided to write a short manual on shoveling preparedness. I am calling it, "Cinders, Salt and Snow Shovels" or possibly, "How to Finance the College Education of Your Chiropractor's Child".

Chapter One – Motivation! Everyone needs motivation! Therefore, I visited the Division of Highways in Gore West Virginia. Standing outside the chain link fence and peering through the tiny square holes, I saw beauty. Shinny snow plows assembled like soldiers. Huge mountains of cinders were pointing to the sky, just begging to be scaled. Garages were piled high with salt, waiting to turn glaciers to puddles. The trucks that would soon push the plows were lined by the gas pumps. It looked like the Daytona 500.

Chapter Two – Equipment! If you don't have a shovel or it has disappeared, purchasing a new one is not always easy. The new aerodynamic shapes and sizes may be confusing, many with crooked handles designed to save your back. Be a real man (or woman), buy a standard straight-handle shovel. Remember your chiropractor's child!

Or, you could do what I did. I went to my mother's house. She has every size and shape made from 1950 to present. It is a museum of snow shovels. If you still have old faithful, pound it flat, brush off the rust, and make sure the handle is smooth.

Chapter Three – Get in Shape! If you are a baby boomer like me, the mind says, "Bring it on (snow)"! But wait, the heart and back are saying, "Maybe we should talk."

You could join a gym or do 100 squat-thrusts a day (ask an old guy what they are). If you are brave and confident, you could hold your newly purchased or reconditioned shovel in front of you (at arm's length) and duck-walk around the neighborhood but make sure to not make eye contact with any neighbors. Remember, "Snow's a comin!"

Chapter Four - The Final Chapter! Now, for the serious side. Make sure this winter is not your final chapter. Snow shoveling can be dangerous and can kill, regardless of your age or physical condition. Stupidity strikes at any age. When the snow comes (and it will), take it easy and slow. Be smart. Wear appropriate clothes, shoes with good traction, gloves, and stay away from the wet stuff. It is heavy!

Of course, you could always follow my father-in-law's advice which was, "I can wade through it a lot easier than I can shovel it." Your neighbor's might not agree but it is a thought. Oh yes, don't forget about the eager person who (for a small fee) will do it for you.

For the snow studs that are in pretty good shape and have mastered the fine art of shoveling, remember random acts of kindness. We all have neighbors who can't (for a variety of reasons) do their own walks. Do their walks early and deny ever doing it. It is amazing how good it will make you feel.

The theme behind this manual "Cinders, Salt and Snow Shovels" is to let the Department of Highways handle the cinders and salt and be careful so you can live to shovel another winter! Just a thought before you shovel. Take a few minutes to look at the beauty God has created. Watch your cat take its paw and try to capture a flake as it passes the window. Take your dog for a walk and watch them leap for a flake or try to imitate a plow. It will make you smile.

Oh yes, don't forget the beauty of creating a snow angel. Make a snowman with a child. Memories can never melt!

I truly try to forget when shoveling snow was fun.
And, it's working!

Michael S. Lambiotte

They're Out There and They're All Loose!

"Common courtesy costs no one anything." – Louise Ogden

On a recent chilly January afternoon, I decided to shovel the remaining snow from my sidewalk. Shoveling was never a favorite past time, but a friend informed me shortly after my return to West Virginia about some obscure ordnance requiring shoveling. It must be true because at the first sign of a snowflake, he is armed and ready with shovel and broom.

Wanting to be a good citizen, I complied by not only shoveling the newly fallen snow but also what the snow plow deposited on my walk. Snow plow snow is a short coming of living on a main road. The temperature had warmed a bit so the snow was melting, creating a small river of salt, snow, and ice. I affectionately call it "brown slush."

My game plan was rather limited due to a 4' fence, a variety of spring bulbs, and flowering shrubs. I was trained fast and well, "No brown slush on the green stuff." My only option was to carefully shovel toward the street. Generally, the approaching cars either slowed or moved toward the center lane. When finished, my brown slush was piled just over the curb, the entire length of my sidewalk. It was an architectural masterpiece with breaks for drainage and a trough between the pile and curb.

And then I heard the distinctive sound of an approaching snow plow, every 'walk shovelers' nightmare. He slowed and swerved as best he could but the results were like a giant wave destroying a sandcastle. Not easily discouraged, I re-shoveled and rebuilt. As I was admiring my handiwork, an old pickup truck was approaching and swerving toward me. With no where to run or hide, I was soaked with brown slush from bald spot to boots. I immediately 'saluted' him properly and in a very loud voice thanked him for such a kind act.

My wife Sandra, hearing the commotion, opened the front door and said, "Mike, we have neighbors now. What in the world…?" She stopped in mid-sentence. It was obvious I had been 'slushed.' At least she did ask if I was all right. "Certainly" I said. "Except for the invigorating feeling of slush sliding down my neck and salt in my eyes, I feel wonderful."

I quickly went inside and straight to the laundry room. She began taking the wet clothes and putting them in the washer. I felt like a

12-year-old who had just come inside after a day of snow ball fights and sledding - minus the fun.

By this time, she knew all the details of my near drowning experience at the hands of 'pickup boy.' She then looked at me and said, "They're out there and they're all loose." A phrase she often used to describe people who were rude, crude, and/or unreasonable, a phrase first used by a middle school principal she worked with when she was an office manager. As one out-of-control parent left her principal's office following a pathetic attempt to defend the behavior of her out-of-control child, he looked at Sandra and said, "They're out there and they're all loose."

Over the years, we have used it to describe several people and situations and it certainly applied to my assailant...pick up boy!

In the weeks following my slushing, I've often wondered, "What makes people do mean, rude, or crude acts. What joy is there in creating discomfort? Vandalism? Hurtful situations?" I like to think we were all taught basic manners and courtesy, right from wrong, blended with a healthy dose of common sense. But when I see people like the driver of the pickup who destroyed my sandcastle, I'm not so sure.

Or, when I hear a driver blowing their horn or yelling something obscene from their window just to scare someone for the 'fun of it,' I'm not so sure. When I read about someone throwing an object from a highway overpass, just to see what they can hit or at least scare someone, I'm not so sure.

What I am sure of is, "They're out there and they're all loose." Perhaps they need to be on the receiving end...just once.

To the 'perp' who slushed me:

If you ever find a shovel full of snow on your car hood – it was me!

Also:

Mean people just need to go away.

CHAPTER 10

My Community Soap Box

I've learned so much from my successes, but,
I've learned so much more from my failures.

3 Monkeys

"Nothing of worthy or weight can be achieved with half a mind, with a faint heart, and with a lame endeavor." – Isaac Barrow

Thank you for coming to our monthly meeting. Where are John and Debbie? Did they call or leave a message with anyone? I guess not. Regardless, congratulations on reaching a consensus and approving this new project. Yes, it's ambitious, but everyone agrees… the community will benefit. Now, we need volunteers to join me on a committee to get this started.

Enter the "3 Monkeys."

Looking around, I saw people with their hands over their eyes, ears, and/or mouth. Welcome to the first edition of "Mike's Pet Peeves" Not a new reality show, but reality.

If you are (or have been) a member of a club, board, or organization, you know them well. They are the ones that say, "You can count on me." Or, "Don't worry, I'll be there." The ones that seldom (if ever) show up and when they do, go monkey when there's work to be done. They are always armed with excuses, "I'm just too busy right now." "My daughter has travel soccer." "My spouse works nights." "I must cut my grass every Saturday." "My dog just had puppies." The list is endless. What they have going on is called Life.

There is a special place in my heart for the ones who show up, after missing several meetings, and say, "What's that about, fill me in?" Thirty minutes later, the meeting agenda is finally addressed. In case you haven't noticed, this is high on my "Pet Peeves" list. It's also very disappointing when people join a group and then do nothing but add the group's name to their resume. If you can't contribute or find that life has taken some unexpected twists and turns, step aside. Step aside for the good of the group.

Yes, I've missed my share of meetings over the years, but there is a wrong and right approach. Recently (over Memorial Day), my home air conditioning stopped working.

Three days with no air! Yes, we are a spoiled society. Tuesday morning, I said to my wife Sandra, "It wasn't really that hot last night, was it?" I failed to notice her splotchy perspiring face. Man dumb!

By now, it was 11:45 a.m. Sandra was gone and I was leaving for a 12:00 p.m. meeting. The technician called and said he was on his way. Dilemma! Cancel the repair man or miss the meeting. Remembering her splotchy face, I notified a board member that I would not be able to attend. . This time, I had my priorities straight. Splotchy face over meeting.

Yes, emergencies and life's speed bumps can complicate our lives. We are all busy, everyone has priorities, and we all have a lot on our plates. Unfortunately, some plates are constantly overflowing, resulting in quite a mess. Thirty-one years of education committees, political campaigns, and community organizations taught me well.

Commitment. Involvement. Without one, you can never have the other. When I was a very young teacher and being recruited for a curriculum committee, the chairperson pulled me aside and said, "Mike, there are three kinds of people: One makes things happen. One watches what happened. One wonders, what happened? If you not in the first category, don't come aboard." He was a retired Navy Commander.

Through the years, the image of the 3 monkeys and the Commander's words keep coming back. As I look around our communities, I clearly see what has been accomplished by our city offices and various organizations. I also see what remains to be achieved. I would like to ask our elected leaders, city and county officials, commissions, boards, and private organizations these questions: "Do you make things happen? Do you watch? Or do you wonder, what happened? Or, are you one of the "3 Monkeys?"

In every group and organization, we need only the first category. People who are true to their word. People who make things happen! If you're not in this group, please step aside or don't come aboard. The group or organization deserves your full attention. In the words of Napoleon Bonaparte, "If you start to take Vienna, take Vienna."

If you can't keep them locked up, at least avoid them at all cost. Or, perhaps recommend a good animal sanctuary.

I came, I saw, I forgot

"I know of no more encouraging fact than the unquestionable ability of man to elevate his life by a conscious endeavor."
Henry David Thoreau

In 47 BC Julius Caesar sent a short but profound message to the Roman senate describing a swift and total victory over Pharnaces II in the city of Tokat, located in what is now Turkey. The message said, "Veni, vidi, vici." Translated it simply says, "I came, I saw, I conquered." With that in mind, this story is about success and what it takes to be successful.

I present "I came, I saw, I forgot." They came from near and far to enjoy what many perceived as a once in a life time event. They came from all walks of life, sharing a common interest. When the curtain closed, they left fulfilled and inspired and little did they know a very small handful of people were responsible for the event.

Some said it couldn't be done because no one cared, but what began as one person's vision became reality, proving the 'naysayers' wrong. Those responsible heard, "Wow, what a great idea. This is just what the community needs. Let's do it again. I've never seen anything like it. Let me know what I can do to help."

With these statements still echoing in their minds, the organizers also felt inspired, "Maybe we should do it again? But we're going to need more help. This was too much for a couple of people." So, at their next meeting they presented some future ideas, ideas which were met with enthusiasm, that is until someone uttered these immortal words, "And now, who wants to volunteer to help!"

It was like another ice age. Everyone was frozen, eyes dropped toward the ground, vocal cords became paralyzed. You see, unlike Caesar who came, saw and conquered, most of them came, saw and forgot. They came to the events. They saw and enjoyed what was offered. But they forgot things just don't happen by themselves. People make them happen. Wishing and wanting never led to success. As the Swahili proverb says, "The prayer of the chicken hawk does not get him the chicken." The moral of this story is, "Good things happen when good people ban together."

There's probably not a person out there who wouldn't like to see new, different, and inspiring events within their community. Begin a lecture series with noteworthy speakers. Have regularly scheduled concerts featuring local talent mixed in with a "star" or two. A symphony performance more than once a year would be good. Arrange for a traveling art or historical display to visit your community.

How about creating a public children's garden? Let the children plant and help maintain it with the assistance of qualified adults. Teach them to have reverence for beauty and nature. Begin or expand adult education programs with classes ranging from teaching adults to read to computers. Or classes in sign language, nutrition, creative writing, photography, landscaping, or money management. How about a second language? Can't forget about languages!

Regular demonstrations by some local and guest chefs would be nice. A gourmet cooking school would be even nicer. Bring back the Harlem Globetrotters! Although I'm not a great fan of opera or ballet, I'm sure there are many in our community who travel great distances to enjoy these performances. But these events don't happen by wanting and wishing. It takes good people coming together.

Now it's time for some irritating clichés: People who'll stand up and be counted. People who will step up to the plate. People who think outside the box. People who believe, "Where there's a will there's a way."

My point is: To make new, different, and inspiring things happen takes work. Work by many people, not just a few. So, if you're going to volunteer or join a club or organization, be prepared to take ownership in the organization. Do your part!

Remember, "Good things happen when good people come together."

Nothing can be more powerful than like-minded
people with a purpose and a direction.

Pizza Economics

"Once the 'what' is decided, the 'how' always follows. We must not make the 'how' an excuse for not facing and accepting the 'what.'" – Pearl Buck

Being a successful teacher requires many skills, beyond the obvious (knowledge). Also required is superb acting ability and a little trickery. For Instance: As a high school political science teacher, I devoted Friday's to debating the events of the week. It was always a challenge keeping my students focused, especially late on a Friday afternoon.

However, one Friday, I ordered an unsliced 16"pizza for my last bell economics class. Shortly after class began, there was a knock at the door! The aroma of cheese and pepperoni quickly awakened their senses. I told them this was my treat for their outstanding efforts this week.

Now I had their attention! "How do we divide it up," some said. "Ah, that's your decision," as I produced a pizza cutter borrowed from the cafeteria. One young lady yelled, "We need a pizza cutting committee. I volunteer." Within seconds, a committee and chairperson were elected. Hungry teenagers make quick decisions. They decided to divide it equally. A 16" pizza divided by 28 (students) makes 28 very small slices. Nevertheless, they were appreciative, in a hungry 'sorta' way.

Before class ended, some asked, "Can we do pizza next week?" "Sure, if we have a good week, but you're paying for this one," I said. Our committee chair said, "No problem Mr. L. We'll take up a collection on Thursday. But, can we order a larger pizza or maybe two?" My response was, "Your money. Your decision."

When Thursday arrived, only 24 students were present. Some contributed and some didn't. The trap was set! On pizza Friday, they had some difficult decisions, considering all 28 were present. However, they decided to divide the pizza equally. I knew harmony would not last much longer. With each passing week, the drums of discontent became louder... as planned!

The committee was overwhelmed with, "He was absent when we collected money, why should he get any. My piece is still too small. I gave the most so I should get a larger piece. Yea, but I gave all I had while you still had money in your purse. I'm not paying any more. It's not fair!"

Eventually, they looked to me for guidance. Dodging a bullet, I said, "This is your problem, not mine." The pizza committee wanted to step outside to discuss the situation.

Before the committee chair closed the door, she turned around and gave me the look. I quickly turned away. I think she smelled a rat.

When they returned, she said, "We have a peaceful solution but first, we have to ask you something?" I knew my plot had been exposed. In a firm voice she said, "You set us up, didn't you? How could you! How could you turn pizza into an economics lesson? That's not fair." A teenager's favorite words. I responded, "Well of course I set you up, but how was the pizza?" After a calming period, I began my lecture: A pizza is just like a budget - any budget. Yours. Your family's. A city, state, or federal government. Any way you slice it; a 16" pizza is still a 16" pizza. That is, unless you add more dough ($). As expected, the dough reference brought multiple moans and groans.

I looked at a young man up front and said, "You have a choice; work longer hours, get a second job, or scale back your needs and wants. Sell your car. Forget about the new iPod. Every choice is a slice of pizza. For a government, it's about raising/cutting taxes, cutting/increasing services, or slicing the existing budget (pizza) differently. Everyone wants a bigger slice. Cut their project. Not mine! Make my piece bigger. Tough choices, no matter who it applies to: you, your family, a city, state, Congress, or a President-Elect.

I was interrupted by, "Can we tell you our pizza solution?" In the end, they came up with a logical solution to a difficult situation...peacefully. Because, they agreed on goal.

Thinking back on that lesson, perhaps I should now send a pizza to..."

Adding more dough is not always the best
solution. But, adding smart dough is!

Promise Me Nothing!

"I believe every right implies a responsibility; every opportunity an obligation, every possession, a duty." – Nelson Rockefeller

Woodrow Wilson promised to keep the United States out of World War I.

Herbert Hoover's campaign slogan promised "a chicken in every pot and two cars in every garage." Franklin Roosevelt promised to keep the U. S. out of World War II. Lyndon B. Johnson promised to "win the war on poverty." Richard Nixon promised to "quickly resolve the Vietnam War." George Herbert W. Bush said, "Read my lips, no new taxes!"

Sincere statements, or were they just saying what they thought we wanted to hear?

George H.W. Bush made the (in)famous "Read my lips" statement at the Republican National Convention in 1988. Was he sincere or just telling us what we wanted to hear, "No new taxes." Two years later, after being elected President, he entered into a budget agreement with Congress which eventually raised several taxes.

Nonetheless, whenever elections are upon us as they are right now, it makes me think of one of my father's favorite sayings, "Once, just once I wish a politician would stand up and say, 'I promise you nothing!'"

If any of you remember my father (Jean) who passed away in 1999 and knew him reasonably well, I think you would agree he was very opinionated and never hesitated to share his opinions. Come to think of it, there are probably few of you left who remember him. He would have been 89 this July.

Anyhow, he loved sports and politics and would argue/debate either with anyone, anytime and anyplace. He certainly had a polarizing effect on people - either you were in his corner or you couldn't wait to meet him in the center of the ring.

Several years ago, dad and I met one of his old buddies at the Food Court at the mall in Bridgeport, West Virginia. John said, "Mike, your dad almost created a riot last week. You shoulda been there. It was the best city government argument we've had in a long time. You gotta give him credit…he knows the facts."

For the unfamiliar, The Food Court at the Mall is where many of the retired glass workers (the few left) meet each morning to argue and debate everything from 'piece work' (an old glass workers term) and high school sports, to city government. During election time dad would get so angry at what some of the local politicians were (or not) saying he would shout, "One day, these guys are going to cause me to have "The Big One" (heart attack), a favorite saying by George Sanford of *Sanford and Son* fame Out of pure frustration Dad would frequently say, "Surly there's at least one politician out there who will stand up and 'Promise me nothing.'

Idle promises are just that...idle. We're not all idiots, just some of us. With our local elections only three days away, I would like to share dad's timeless philosophy regarding elections and politicians, "Promise me nothing! But if I vote for you, here's my expectation: Work hard and smart. Work for what's right, not what's easy."

"Never let me question your honesty. Really listen to what I must say... talk with me, not down to me. And never give me simple lip service. Resist temptation and political pressure. Remember, your vote and my faith is not for sale. Never betray that faith.

Be available and accessible. When I call, I want to talk with you, not all the people around you. Be visible in the community and not just during your election campaign!"

"And bear in mind, I have selected you to represent me and I am relying on your industry and your good judgment. Remember your roots. My vote put you in office and it can take you out as well." I think Dad borrowed the last phrase from the comedian Bill Cosby.

Dad saw the world in black and white. For him, the color gray did not exist. That's the way politics should be. Through the years his "Promise me nothing" has remained a cornerstone of my own political beliefs.

Someday, I would like to run for office with the platform,
"I Will Promise You Nothing." Dad would be proud.

Punch 1, Punch 2, Punch 3

"All the modern inconveniences" — Mark Twain

You just received an over-due notice about a credit card you don't have. You dial the 800 number and you hear an electronic menu consisting of a 'gazillion' choices, none of which help. The second time through, a miracle…one is close. Halleluiah Brother! Damn, I forgot the number. The third time, you write it down. Finally, a human voice. Then it happens, "Can you hold…click," and then the music begins. Unfortunately, it resembles the mating calls of the nearly extinct Central American bull frog.

Moments later, the phone goes dead. You were disconnected. Immediately, your head explodes, ripping out you last remaining hair. Sound familiar. This is a disease that has quietly invaded our lives. It's called "DCI" - Driving Customers Insane. It is everywhere, just waiting to pluck your last nerve.

Somewhere, back in time, in some small dingy corporate think-tank, a group of well-meaning 'brainiacs' devised this Punch 1 system. No doubt, they felt it would increase efficiency and ultimately save money. "Electronic answering is the way of the future," they said! But which way?

These same companies preach and teach customer service, throughout their food chain. I wonder, have those toward the top of the food chain ever tried using their own system! Somehow, I seriously doubt they have. Nonetheless, I am about to offer a solution. offer a solution. But not quite yet. Please read on. .

For a few minutes, let's talk about what customer service should be and who are the customers. First, everyone is a customer. You're a customer and I'm a custom. If I call you about an issue, I expect you to do your very best to help me resolve it. You could be having the worst possible day, with chaos and incompetence all around. But all I know is, "I need your full attention and I am depending on you."

When my wife Sandra was in Human Resources, she would receive 150 to 180 e-mails a day and close to 75 phone calls regarding employment issues. Do you really think e-mailer # 131 cares we had a busted water pipe or we were up most of the night mopping water? He cares about his missing pay check!

Caller # 24 has no idea that an irate employee is in the office demanding to see the Director, who is out of the building. She cares about being docked three sick days and has not missed a day in four years. All # 131 and # 24 cared about is Sandra helping them and that is how it should be.

When a customer needs assistance, the last thing they need to hear is a computer-generated voice made to sound human saying, "I see, I think I can help. Please answer…"

Enough already! Don't get me wrong, I embrace technology as tightly as the "Geek Squad." But, I feel customer service needs reinvention. Electronic answering can be scary. I have this terrible fear that some day I will call 911 and hear, "Please hold: Punch 1 if robbed, 2 if choking, 3 for heart attack, 4 for……."

Now, the time has come: My solution for reinventing customer service. Very simple… the old-time switchboard. Remember the 1950's movies, with the operator pulling and pushing dozens of wires, as calls came in? Meet the new version. Remember my credit card example? Now, you call the company and a "human" answers the phone. You tell her/him your concern. They enter the issue into their computer (no pulling wires) and 'whalla,' you are immediately transferred to the needed department. Oh yes, another human answers.

By chance, if I am put on hold, give me a news report or a comedy routine. Not elevator music! I lean toward the words of Elbert Hubbard, "One machine can do the work of fifty men. No machine can do the work of one extraordinary man."

The technology is there. But where are the people who really care about the customer…you, me, and them.

I wonder: Do the people who actually create
these "press" systems ever use them?

The Opinion Box

"The man who never alters his opinion is like standing water,
and breeds reptiles of the mind." William Blake (1757-1827)
British poet and painter.

Long ago, there was a young teacher who challenged his students to "gather your facts, think and then formulate an opinion. And never, never be afraid to speak your mind!" He even went so far as to reject a student's essay when he answered one question by saying, "I really don't have an opinion on this issue," even though they had been discussing the topic for three days.

The teacher wrote in bold red, "Well, it's time you have one! You're 18 and eligible to vote. Re-submit this after you've gathered your facts and formulated an opinion." Angry, he showed his mother what the teacher had written, "Can you believe this?" Looking up at her son, she simply said, "Yes."

A few years later, the mother approached the teacher's wife and introduced herself.

She told her the story about the red-penned paper, "Please tell your husband what he wrote on my son's paper was one of the best things a teacher had ever said to my son."

"Thank you," she said. "And what's your son doing now," she asked. "He just received his commission as an officer in the United States Navy."

Yes, having an educated opinion and being free to express that opinion is one of the many great things about this country. Along with this comes the opportunity to change that opinion based on new information and/ or personal reflection.

Take myself for an example: Over the years I have been a staunch opponent and advocate of capital punishment. However, new information and personal reflection have caused my opinion to drastically change. Today, I support capital punishment, but only in cases where the state is 100% certain the accused is guilty – no question, no doubt. During the 60's and 70's I was 100% opposed to capital punishment. What brought about this change – time and new information.

I also have strong opinions regarding abortion, gun control, military intervention and locally, the direction of our city. Many times, my opinions have changed for the same reasons – new information and personal reflection. However, to be well informed we must know the facts and to know the facts, we depend on our "Opinion Box.," that box we all possess which includes the information we rely on to formulate our opinions. What really scares me is a person whose box is empty or filled with biased or misinformation.

Now, ask yourself, "What's in my box?" Does it contain a variety of sources – newspaper, television, magazines and books? Are your sources biased (leaning one way or the other) or are they fair and accurate – that's what you're looking for. Do your sources provide a variety of editorial comments and 'Letters to the Editor?' Selective suppression results in unfair and incomplete information.

Is there diversity within your source? I would personally question the credibility of an all white Anglo-Saxon panel discussing issues which affect a Latino community. Does your source display double standards - holding some people to one standard while using a different standard for other groups?

I'm personally offended when a 62-year-old burglary suspect is referred to as a former Vietnam veteran. Why doesn't the same source refer to the 58-year-old female arrested for embezzlement as a recovering alcoholic or a former Girl Scout den mother?

As you see, I'm rather passionate about what's in my large "opinion box." As I grow older, I become less tolerant of those whose opinions are based on inaccuracies, misinformation, or pure emotion.

I don't care whether it's about abortion, military intervention or a local school bond.

Give me the facts. Give me both sides. And then, let me formulate an educated opinion. Also, understand, my opinion may change next week, next month or next year. And that's okay. But rest assured, the change was brought about by new information and/or personal reflection. Not the result of some narrow-minded article published on the third rock from Venus or gossip heard in the barbershop.

But, this is just my opinion!

To me, a person without an opinion is wasting my time.

Two Men & a Truck

"Opportunity is missed by most people because it is dressed in overalls, and looks like work." – Thomas A. Edison

While still in high school, brothers Brig and Jon came up with a plan to make some extra money. After school and on the weekends, they would move furniture or anything people wanted moved. They already had a truck, a 15-year-old 1967 green Ford pickup. Although barely passing inspection, it was their pride and joy.

Now, all they had to do was convince their mother, Mary Ellen, they could still do their household tasks and keep up their grades. Mom said, "It's your truck. Your backs. Your time. But if your chores or grades slip, your little business is history." She also said, "Remember, this is a small town and everybody knows our name. Be honest and fair. Work hard and remember 'The Grandma Rule' - Treat everyone the way you would want your Grandma to be treated. Keep in mind, everything you move is special, to someone. Respect is key!"

She even designed an ad logo for the weekly community newspaper. It was two stick figures sitting in a truck. The ad said, "Men At Work Movers...Two men and a truck to move your belongings." They even painted the logo on the doors of that old green truck.

At first business was slow first but picked up after a few weeks. By their senior year, they worked almost every afternoon and weekend. Whether it was one chair or a room of furniture, it made no difference. If it would fit in the bed of the green machine, it was handled with TLC (tender loving care).

All too soon for mom, the boys graduated high school and were off to college. Their little venture certainly did pay off. They had tuition money for the first year, helped with family expenses, and had a little spending money in the bank.

However, even though the boys were gone, Mary Ellen continued to receive calls for their services. Not wanting to disappoint old customers or turn down new ones, she decided to purchase a 14-foot panel truck for $350 and hire two movers. During the following year while the boys were gone, Mary Ellen made a whopping $1,000 from her son's moving business. Although she could have used the money, she decided to give $100 donations to10 different local charities.

The more I thought about this story the more I realized the many lessons we could learn from Brig, Jon, and Mary Ellen. The boys had a need and a plan to satisfy that need. They were not afraid of hard work or long hours., and they were providing a much-needed service within the community.

They knew the obstacles facing them (mom), yet presented their plan in a way which answered many of mom's questions before she even asked. Mary Ellen showed support and encouragement for her son's business venture, but established guidelines and insisted on certain core values from the very beginning.

The boys even established their own mission statement while still in high school, "To continuously strive to exceed our customer's expectations in value and high standard of satisfaction." Even after they left for college, Mary Ellen found a way to maintain a service that was not only appreciated but needed in their small town. It was to no one's surprise, Mary Ellen donated her first year's profits ($1,000). She spent her entire life volunteering and giving of her own time to help better other people's lives.

This story doesn't end here. After college and trying their wings, Brig and Jon returned home to help their mother with the business they started and she kept alive.

That was 20 years ago. Today, "Two Men and A Truck" is the nation's largest franchised local moving company. They have a fleet of more than 1,300 trucks with more than 200 locations worldwide, with offices in 32 states, Canada, and Ireland. Last year, their annual revenue was $193.3 million.

And it all started with an idea, a plan, a set of values, a determined work ethic and a 1967 green Ford pickup.

From a single acorn grows a giant oak tree!

Unfortunately, many of our good-intended social programs
have created a crippled, dependent society.

Want to be successful? Hire a beekeeper!

"Coming together is a beginning; keeping together is progress; working together is success." - Henry Ford

As the honeybee landed on one of my tomato plants, I noticed the pollen baskets on her hind legs were full. Yet, she continued her mission, I watched her float from bloom to bloom and then I flashed back to one of my former lives - a beekeeper. Years ago, my interest in bees was stirred by my uncle Jess and my deep appreciation and understanding of how they think and work together was learned from Mr. Love, a dear friend and bee mentor in Virginia.

Before I had my own bees, Mr. Love taught me about the division of labor within a hive and how to extract the honey. We would sit outside his hives for hours and he would explain what the bees were doing. Some were collecting pollen, some protecting the hive. And some cleaning and cooling.

S of the bees appeared to be dancing at the hive entrance. "Mr. Love, what in the world are they doing," I asked. "Ah, Mike," he said, "They just deposited their pollen and they're telling the others where the good blooms are." With a troubled look he said, "Oh Mike, if only man could learn to work together like a hive of bees. Look at them. Isn't it a beautiful sight? What a story: All working together for a common cause…the success and survival of the colony."

In time and with his patience, I began to appreciate the complexity of a hive. Then suddenly, that cute little honeybee was flying directly toward my nose and I returned to the present. They're not quite as agile when loaded down with pollen. Funny how certain events trigger memories. And how those memories can make us think about the future. Then, it suddenly dawned on me: The key to a successful anything is to act like a hive of honeybees. Yes, it's true. Their social and cooperative structure is the key to their success and could easily apply to our government (local to federal), businesses, clubs, schools, and "anything. If you think I've been stung one too many times, let's look at the anatomy of a hive, through the large eyes a honeybee and with a little imagination, apply these characteristics to any successful group.

In a hive (business) there is a distinctive division of labor with three specialized groups. At the very top is a Queen Bee who manages the hive. Her main purpose is to create and motivate worker bees. Motivated bees mean more (money) honey! The queen also regulates the behavior and activities within the hive. Remember, use your imagination!

There can only be one queen (leader). If the hive becomes too crowded, the old queen will leave, taking half the hive with her, like a corporate split. With the old queen gone, a new one emerges in a few days.

The second (and largest) division in the hive is Worker Bees" and they earn their title. They gather the pollen and nectar, protect and build the hive, clean, and show the young ones how to be good workers. They are the colony foundation. To be successful, they must be in the right place at the right time. For the record, they are females.

Next is the Drones – males. Their sole function is to keep the queen happy by providing the means to produce more bees, a role critical to the survival and success of the colony. During the winter (lean times), they leave or are expelled from the hive, their version of work-force reduction.

In addition to this structure, honeybees have unique eyesight. Each eye is made of hundreds of smaller eyes, enabling them to see in many directions. It's no wonder they're successful, they have leadership, a well-trained work force, a social structure, an emergency plan, and a vision for the future.

And above all…they work toward a common cause. Key ingredients for success. A flourishing organization (anything) already sees the world through the eyes of a honeybee. For the others, perhaps they need to hire a beekeeper. Just to keep things 'buzzing.'

Every successful business seminar should make time for a beekeeper presentation and a detailed look into hive operations.

Well, it's just...

*"There is no such thing on earth as an uninteresting subject;
only an uninterested person." – Gilbert Keith Chesterton*

There's something strange going around. It is not the flu or a cold. The symptoms are much different. Children usually aren't affected and it rarely affects young adults.

Strangely enough, it seems more prevalent in older adults and it is an equal opportunity affliction because it doesn't discriminate based on gender, education, or income.

It is not a disease because it has no medical symptoms. The cause could be environmental, but I doubt it. One thing for sure, it's real and it's very damaging to those exposed and the person who has it.

It's been around for a long time, yet it has no label...until now. The main symptom is, when someone is excited about a new project or a new anything, then a friend or colleague approaches them and says, "Well, it's just garden club." Or, "Well, it's just a play." Or, "Well, it's just..."

You fill it in, because at one time or another you've probably had the wind taken out of your sails by a thoughtless person suffering from, "It's just." In the early stages, a person may say this out of habit, indifference, or lack of understanding. In the advanced stages, a person may say this out of jealousy, a false sense of superiority, or just plain meanness.

The reason it's uncommon in children is because they can become excited over the simplest of things such as a sand pile, a mud puddle, a pile of rocks, skipping stones, or a bouquet of dandelions for mom. When done, it's off to the next venture with new mountains to conquer.

The affliction is also uncommon in young adults. Because they are too busy with their version of *The Dating Game*. Or, "How to Quickly Climb the Ladder of Success." However, when that young adult enters the older adult world with a secure job, 2.5 children, two cars, and a hefty mortgage, strange things can happen. Not always, but sometimes.

What causes someone to become this negative "I want to rain on your parade" person is hard to understand because there seems to be no common denominator. One thing for certain, it doesn't happen overnight. Personal tragedy can accelerate the process, but it usually isn't the sole reason. It typically creeps up, like multiple vines of poison ivy. Some may be so involved in life nothing seems to satisfy them anymore. They become dissatisfied and lean toward more involvement for answers. Just like a fast spinning merry-go-round, it's fun, but it can make you sick.

Being involved in the community and/or a cause is admirable, if it's for the right reasons. Not for these reasons: "It's expected of me. It helps my image. It's the thing to do. All the important people are members. It'll help me climb the social ladder."

However, over-involvement, personal dissatisfaction, and tragedy are just a few reasons behind this affliction. Because it's not a disease, it can't be cured with a pill or shot. But, it can be dealt with and eventually controlled.

Try this: When someone says, "Well it's just... (fill it in)." Don't take it personal. What they're really saying is they're too busy or just not interested. Or, they don't understand why you're so excited. Some people just resist new ideas, change, and challenges. Comfortable is... comfortable.

Nonetheless, you might try explaining your enthusiasm. They probably won't join up, but at least you gave them something to think about. And, in a round-about-way you told them, "Regardless of how you feel, I'm excited and will stay excited!"

Now the hard one: Dealing with your own affliction. If you have said, "Well it's just..." to someone in the past, you'll probably have the urge to do it again. When the time comes, stop and think, "I may not understand or be interested, but I don't want to discourage." The next step: Try saying, "Tell me more."

Either way, the results may be surprising. Like an old surfer friend of mine once said, "When you learn to ride the waves, the view is magnificent."

Never, ever down play what is important to you –
for any one, under any circumstances.

When the Baton Is Raised

"Finding unity among diversity is one of civilizations greatest challenges, yet working together is essential to the wellbeing of the whole." — Steven Covey

One-by-one they entered the stage. After sitting, some chatted quietly while some began to warm up their violins. Many in the brass section were softly playing scales and a few flutes, clarinets and piccolos in the woodwind section could also be heard. In the percussion section, some musicians would place their ear close to the head of their instrument, tap it lightly and adjust a turn screw or a pedal below. It was like each of the four sections was playing a different piece…the notes constantly clashing.

Then one of the musicians stood up holding an oboe, which to me looked like a large clarinet. The others stopped what they were doing and focused on the notes she was playing. She was the principal oboe, to which all others tune. After a few minutes, the entire symphony orchestra adjusted their seats, positioned their instruments and waited.

From the left side of the stage, greeted with respectful applause, walked a single musician carrying a violin. He is the concertmaster (first violin), subordinate only to the conductor. He plays a single note on his violin; all the other string players check their tuning to his. Then the house lights dim and a spot light brightens stage left.

From behind the curtains, greeted with enthusiastic applause, walks JoAnn Falletta, the conductor (maestro) of the Virginia Symphony Orchestra. She bows to the audience, shakes the hand of the first violin, who then takes his seat in the first chair of the violin section. The maestro then steps to the podium. With all eyes upon her, she raises her baton and another symphony concert begins. Stay with me. This'll all come together in a few minutes.

The conductor, the most important person in the orchestra does not play an instrument. At the most fundamental level, the conductor's job is to indicate the beat of the music, whether slow, fast, aggressive, loud or soft. Few in the audience may realize the years, months, weeks, days, and hours of preparation required of the musicians and the conductor.

As conductor, she is responsible for scheduling rehearsals for individual sections as well as the entire orchestra. No matter how accomplished the conductor, the quality of the performance is based upon the excellence of the musicians, their ability to play as one, and how they react to the conductor.

An outstanding symphony orchestra, like the Virginia Symphony, is no different than any other successful business or organization: Results are based upon leadership, exceptionally well qualified people, creativity, and the ability to work together. Qualities these organizations possess: Microsoft, Stewart-Hass Racing (Tony Stewart Racing) and the Pittsburgh Steelers, just to name a few.

Now, think close to home. Think about your church, club, city government, non-profit organization, or any group you relate to. Then ask yourself, "What would make them more successful?" Then apply the Symphony Test: Is the organization comprised of top quality people? Tony Stewart recently said, "I learned from the master (maestro), Coach Joe Gibbs. Surround yourself with good people and let them do their jobs."

Next, do you have a principal oboe? Someone who others can tune into for direction.

Do you have a concertmaster? Someone who has the respect of the entire group (symphony). Do you have someone who could take over in the absence of the leader (conductor). Finally, is the person in charge (maestro) well qualified and able to communicate their wishes to those working with them (musicians)?

JoAnn Falletta is a graduate of the Mannes School of Music in New York. She received her masters and doctorate from The Julliard School. Joe Gibbs has won three Super Bowls and two NASCAR Championships with Tony Stewart as his driver. Stewart now owns his own race team. All three know something about leadership and communication. They can shape and form ideas, keep everyone focused and on the same page, and give the right cues when changes are necessary.

Now, how does your orchestra measure up? Not as good as you would like? Well, perhaps it's time for some changes.

Next time you attend the symphony, take your business model with you.

CHAPTER II

Family and Friends

Circle of Life

"We all face struggles and conflicts, and we all want to deal with them courageously, with what I call grace under pressure" – Ernest Hemingway

When we are born, we are totally dependent upon our parents. They feed us. Change our diapers. Keep us warm and secure. And comfort us when we're sick. They teach us everything: How to speak. Walk. Know right from wrong. And hopefully how to make the right decisions when they're not looking over our shoulders.

Furthermore, they see to it we're educated. They watch us grow and they grow with us, for we are both young. They do a lot of hoping and praying, for all too soon, that tiny helpless infant they once held tightly will pack their bags and journey down one of life's many roads

Their chosen journeys will keep some near and some will travel far. The years will go by way too fast for both and then then one day, that road taken many years ago, begins to bend. Through the eyes of a mother and father they will always see a child, a 10-year-old walking to school or a teenager getting ready for the prom.

But as the road continues to bend, that child who has now grown into a mature adult, sees a much different picture. They see a mother who can no longer hold a cup of tea or complete a hem stitch. Or a father who has difficulty walking. It seems like only yesterday they were together in the yard playing catch.

As that road continues to bend it may eventually form a circle, reversing their roles completing the "Circle of life." That child, who is now an adult, is faced with caring for aging parents. Difficult decisions. Different circumstances. No one answer is the right answer, or the only answer.

We all want to maintain our independence, but at what price. When do we give up our automobile? When is it no longer safe for us to stay at home or alone? Of course, everyone wants to stay in their home if possible. Do we bring our parents to live with us? Do we encourage our parents to move into an assisted living or nursing facility? What if our parents are not capable of making these decisions on their own...then what?

I'll never forget what Susan (a childhood friend) said to me at one of our high school reunions several years ago, after her grandmother was moved into a nursing facility, "Mike, you know what. Making adult decisions isn't much fun." Her words have stuck with me over the years. Tough decisions are never easy. but they must be made. In an ideal world, families should talk about their options and make their wishes known to one another before it's too late.

This is what happens when they don't: Siblings living far away may stick their heads in the sand and ignore the obvious physical and/or mental challenges of a 90-year-old mother living alone. Out of sight – out of mind! Some siblings may place the responsibility on the closest one and then criticize their decisions or not contribute financially. "Oh, I'm too far away to help. I have my own family."

Some may think being an only child makes the decisions easier. Well, it doesn't because there's only one pair of shoulders, shoulders that must bear the entire responsibility and decision making, unless there was good communication before the road became a circle.

What about the couple without children or who the couple who survived their children? They face some of the toughest decisions, for some day, there will be only one. Wishes should be in writing and placed with someone who'll see they're carried out.

Even if families have communicated well and wishes known, there's no guarantees. The parent before us today may not be the one we see tomorrow. Tough decisions, regardless of the scenario.

But we must never forget, "Once, we were their responsibility. Now, they are ours...it's that simple." No matter what decisions you make, remember to consider everything and everyone and reassure them, "They will never be alone."

She has experienced more in her lifetime than I can ever imagine.
I must always respect her wisdom.

Deviled Eggs and Homemade Applesauce

"There is a communion of more than our bodies when bread is broken and wine is drunk." – M.F.K Fisher

Through the eyes of a teacher, the world appears vastly different. Teachers learn very quickly to never take the little things in life for granted, little things like a quiet lunch in your favorite restaurant.

For the working civilian (non-teachers), the opportunity presents itself almost every day to step away from the hustle and bustle of the workplace for lunch. Teachers seldom have this luxury. Their choice is usually limited to a crowded teacher's lounge or a very noisy student cafeteria, and always under a time crunch. Eat fast because the next interruption is only a knock or an intercom call away.

After spending 32 years in public education, my personal best was consuming a five-course lunch in 12 minutes and 37 seconds. A parent needed to see me and the only time we could meet was during her lunch time.

Keeping this in mind, teachers look forward to in-service days (days when the students are not there) for many reasons. Although leaving for lunch was nice, my personal favorite was when the departments organized potluck lunches. My love of cooking is only surpassed by my devotion to eating. I was fortunate to be in a high school located in a multi-cultural city which provided many exciting culinary opportunities.

Our potluck lunches were like a United Nations celebration. We often enjoyed dishes from around the world, including foreign countries like Maine, Mississippi, and California. One of the simple pleasures was sharing our special recipes. Imagine that…sharing! What a novel idea.

With my wife, Sandra in a middle school and me in a high school, we had the opportunity to accumulate many interesting and delicious recipes. We looked forward to these events because you never knew what would end up on the tables. For me, it was the excitement of the unknown, " I don't know what it is but it sure smells good. Gotta try it. Looks like "Man Food!"

Just the other day, Sandra told me about a potluck event she attended in which the host-members always bring copies of their recipes to share.

Someone had brought a beautiful tray of deviled eggs which always seemed to disappear quickly. One of the charter members brought her special tea. Apparently, her tea has legendary status.

Another lady made homemade applesauce. And there were endless pastries, salads and casseroles. Toward the end someone remarked, "And the beauty of it all is it's not a lot of work for anyone. Just a little work for everyone." That reminded me of what I read in the January edition of A *Taste of the South*, "Potluck dinners are the best kind of entertaining because everyone shares in the cooking responsibilities."

Another joy of these dinners is hearing the history behind some of the old family recipes. And believe me, there's a story behind every recipe: From "Deviled eggs to homemade applesauce." Yes, potluck dinners provide not only good food but also an opportunity to bring people closer together.

But low and behold, "I heard it through the grape vine," that there are some people who do not like potluck lunches. Are they aliens? Anarchists? Or are they just *Grumpy Old Men* or women (in attitude not necessarily age)? To find the answers, I polled some friends and here is what they said: "I think some people think they're too busy to fix something." I can't accept that one. If you chose not to cook, buy a bucket of chicken and a tub of slaw, or stop at the deli or bakery on the way to the event.

Another friend said, "Some might think they're too important. They want to be served and not serve. For them, it's all about image." He might have a point with this one. Perhaps these people need to think less about who they are and more about what they are. To me, it is important to be real!

My third friend said, "Some people just don't know what they don't know. Preparing and sharing...one of life's simple pleasures." I smiled, nodded and thought about "Deviled eggs and homemade applesauce."

I have no time for people so high up the ladder they have forgotten the many steps it takes to reach the top, or how far it is to the bottom.

Friends & Acquaintances

"But friendship is precious, not only in the shade, but in the sunshine of life." – Thomas Jefferson

Before reading further, have a pen and paper handy. Now, write the names of two good friends, and then, two better friends. End the list with your two best friends. Take a few minutes and think about why they are on your list. No, do not go back and rearrange them.

Think: Are they friends or acquaintances? Friends, a title often used but given little thought. We have friends we played with as children and ones who were classmates and some teammates. Some went to war and a few never returned. All were good friends, some were better than others, and a few became best friends.

When I entered junior high, life really started to change for me and around me. By then, my guy friends were mostly teammates. Quickly, I realized girl friends could become girlfriends. Those were the ones who made you say and do stupid and scary stuff! In a blink, it was the end of my senior year of high school. Graduation only weeks away.

At that time of my life, I looked around and saw good friends, better friends, and best friends. Many, I knew since age 4, ready to go in different directions…. college, work, and war. Suddenly, everything was different. We were entering the *Twilight Zone.* The unknown world of growing up not realizing (then) careers, marriages, and oceans would pull us apart. My better and best friends would always remain my friends…but how?

For some reason, girls seem to be better at the friendships than guys. Yes, girls are different, something I learned in junior high. Let's use my wife Sandra and three of her friends as my case study. Using a line from the *Dragnet* television series, "Their names have been changed to protect the innocent, " all except Sandra's.

Sandra met Lynn in seventh grade at Central Junior High School in Clarksburg, West Virginia. That friendship became a threesome - Sandra, Lynn and Lynn's 55 Dodge. Oh, the stories that Dodge could tell – and never will. Years later, Sandra helped Lynn choose her daughter's name, who later was the flower girl in our wedding.

Sandra met, Elaine, who now lives in Raleigh, North Carolina, in nursery school at the First Presbyterian Church in Clarksburg. Together, they went from finger paints to hair color. Sandra met Carol in high school, even sharing an apartment a few years later. That apartment seemed like a century ago, but it was only 21 plus 10 years.

Although years, careers, marriages, and just life kept them apart, these friends remained best friends. On the phone, they sounded like teenagers. No longer talking about boys, hair styles, clothes, who are dating, or who kissed who. Now, it's about china patterns, decorating, illnesses, and parenting dilemmas (what comes around goes around).

There's something special about friendships born in a small town. When I think about them, I wonder, "What do girls know about friendships that most boys never get?"

For most men, a good friend is someone who shares outside interests, possibly from work or community, usually a casual-social thing. A better friend is one he invites to a ball game (having season tickets) and shares a couple of beers. A best friend is one he lets use his season tickets for their son's birthday.

For women, well, they're just different. For her, a good friend is one who is just as honest and truthful when she talks with her as when she talks about her. Her better friend is one she shares her feelings and knows they won't be shared. Her best friend says, "I don't care what time it is, I'm on my way!"

I'm convinced, when men say they have friends, they really mean acquaintances.

When women say, they have friends, they mean somewhere between better and best. In John Gray's book, *Men are from Mars, Women are from Venus*, he attempted to explain the differences between men and women, while offering advice. It made me laugh but it also made me think. It made me think, "I'm not too old to learn about friendships.

In the words of Henry Wadsworth Longfellow "Ah, how good it feels! The hand of an old friend." Excuse me now, I have a flight to catch…to Venus!

The names in this story are fictional, but their characters
are real. Some live so close I can see their lights.
Some so far, I wish we could share the light.

Michael S. Lambiotte

Gimmie back my 48 Hudson

"Nostalgia: A device that removes the ruts and potholes from memory lane." – Doug Larson

"They don't make'em like they used to!" A phrase often used when we're upset at the present and long for the simpler past. Although used to describe many aspects of American culture, no where is this phrase more relevant than when applied to the all-American status symbol - the automobile.

Automobiles, they bring us joy, misery, and frustration. If you have lived long enough, you have earned the right to complain, especially about the cars of today. Here are some of my favorites:

Today's cars rust too fast. They're not like my old Buick.

Too much plastic. I want chrome, metal, and fins. Like my 57 Chevy.

My last car cost three times what my first house cost.

It cost me $60.00 to fill'er up.

They're too small inside. Gimmie back my Olds Custom Cruiser station wagon. It was over 19' long. I could haul my entire bowling team and their wives.

New cars are too low. I can't get in and out. Gimmie back my 1960 Ford Galaxie with plastic seat covers any day.

I enjoyed tuning up 'Old Blue.' Where's the hell is the carburetor in this new car?

198

Nothing fits this nostalgic look more than my parent's 1948 Hudson Club Coupe. "Snow never stopped 'Ole Hud," as my mother often said. Although, weighing in at two tons might partly explain its 'snowbility.'

Let's take a closer look at that 48 Hudson: For its time, it was quite an automobile: Low, sleek, fast, and expensive (for 1948) with a price tag of $2,469.07. It was equipped with a 261-cubic inch engine, producing around 128 horsepower, and got a puny 12 miles per gallon.

Let's do some comparisons between then and now. The average cost of a new house was $7,700. Average wage was $2,950. A gallon of gas was 16 cents! And a loaf of bread cost 14 cents. Sorry, everyone always throws in the cost of bread. Trust me, this is relevant. So, don't forget these figures.

Now, with the image of your favorite nostalgic car firmly planted in your mind, consider some possible advantages of that $45,000 COT (car of today): When's the last time you jacked up a car and put on snow tires for the winter or slopped around trying to put on chains? I remember as a child, seeing windshields shattered from summer heat. I remember hearing dad tell mom, " Don't forget to pump your brakes. They might fail." When's the last time you thought about that one! Talking about rust. With bodies an inch thick, that might explain why they seldom rusted through. Remember the 4,000 pounds.

What about safety of the cars back then: Nothing like a full metal dash board colliding with your head to get your attention or the bigger than a bushel basket steering wheel to challenge your teeth. Today, a broken nose or collarbone from an air bag or seat belt is a small price to pay if it prevents you from becoming a hood ornament.

Going back then: When's the last time you experienced the exhilarating feeling of watching steam poor from your radiator because of a broken fan belt? Ah yes, and who could forget driving down the highway and suddenly, your lights go out! Hasn't happened, lately has it? Oh, but it did.

Still back then: Gas. Yes, Dad could fill up the Hudson for $2.72. But his salary was only $4,564...in 1948. A car cost $2,469 and gas was 16cents a gallon. Compare that today. You do the math! Interesting conclusion, isn't it? Yes, those who profess, "They don't make'em like they used to" are right. They don' and I I'm glad they don't. For I like living and driving the present, although, I wouldn't mind cruising the Satellite

Drive-In, a popular hangout in my home town, in my 60 T-Bird…just for the memories.

For as Hubert Humphrey said, "The good old days were never that good. The good new days are today, and better days are coming tomorrow. Our greatest days are still unsung."

For no doubt, in 2068 someone will write, "Gimmie back my 17 Mustang. They don't make'em like they used to."

Just look at the cars of today…

The Hudson in the picture belonged to my parents, Jean
and Betty Lambiotte. The picture was taken in 1948 while
they were vacationing in Virginia Beach, Virginia
I found the sales slip when I was shuffling
through some of their old papers.
Memories.

Jack & Master

"When asked what is most important to them, most people say family. Yet, oddly enough it is often family that is first to be pushed aside from busy schedules." – Stephen R. Covey

Jack of all trades and Master of none. Or is it, Jack of all trades and Master of all. It doesn't make any difference because we all know a Jack! Let me share the story of my friend who was a pretty good Jack and spent most of his adult life striving to be a Master.

As Sir Francis Bacon said, "Knowledge is power" and my friend did his best to acquire as much knowledge as possible, and turn it into a master career. "Jack and Master." During the years we worked in Virginia, my friend Jack earned a Master's Degree and an Ed. S, while teaching and coaching three sports. He wanted it all and right now! Nothing would stand in his way of becoming a master. But, the question was, "A master of what?"

Jack served on every committee he felt would promote his career. Interest didn't count. Certification points did! The focus was on knowledge and power. The City-Wide Lecture and Art Series he produced carried his name beyond the school district. Spreading his wings further, he got involved in city government, not as an elected official, but a campaign planner and worker. Jack also aligned himself with a very popular School Board member, who later served several terms on City Council. He even worked for the Mayor!

Jack spent most of his time being with the right people, at the right time, and in the right place. Ah yes, Jack had it all. He finally reached the summit of the career mountain! Or had he? He so enjoyed the view, he didn't notice the snow and ice melting below. You see, during this very long and difficult climb, Jack didn't heed the warning signs.

Jack worked *8 Days A Week*. He loves the Beatles. Oh yes, he was a member of all the right committees, councils, and clubs. Never mind the missed meeting here and there. When there were two scheduled at the same time, no problem! There was an easy solution, leave one early and go to the other late. Never mind the frenzied deer in the headlights look!

He was slowly entering the world of "Jack of all trades and Master of None!" The brightest signs were at home, but Jack was blinded by the reality of it all! In the early years, weekends were for family, but as Jack was going up the ladder, weekends were spent attending political meetings and picnics. Sometimes, he had to go to work to catch up! The family dinner became a rarity and replaced with eating out or grab and stuff. It seemed Jack was always needed somewhere else.

Through all this, Jack's wife always supported his ventures. While holding down a demanding full time job of her own, she took over the total responsibility of the home, a responsibility once shared! Fortunately, Jack's wife knew when it was time to come down from the mountain, even if he didn't! She knew he would recoil into 'man-place' if met head-on, so she chose a subtle approach.

One night, while serving dinner, the sign around her neck said, "Hi, I'm Jill- Remember Me?" The note on his pillow said, "Please introduce yourself." she now had Jack's attention! That began the 'Transformation of Jack.'

It was a long and slow journey down the mountain, but he made it before the ice melted! Tragically, some Jack's never make it and the ice melts under their feet. Oh, don't get me wrong, Jack still loves to climb mountains and always will. But the mountains are much smaller...and the view much grander!

Today, he's a "Jack of many trades and master of maybe one." Perhaps you know Jack? The one who wants it all, at the expense of the only thing that really matters - family! He could be your brother, sister, or your neighbor. Trust today's Jack! He now knows! When the family suffers, it creates a ripple effect in the neighborhood, in the community, and in society.

Unfortunately, not every Jack has a wife like Jill… walking beside him and then, knowing when to lead.

> What we really need to do is create a neighborhood full of men
> and women who each are good at something… and then do
> away with jealousy and work toward neighborhood good.

Making the Most of What You Have

"It is not for the benevolence of the butcher, the brewer, or the baker that we expect our dinner, but from their regard to their interests." – Adam Smith

My wife Sandra shared an interesting story the other day and it went something like this:

I was standing by the poultry section of a local grocery store looking for the perfect roasting hen when I noticed the woman beside me. She was an older woman who appeared to be of Asian descent. She had several chickens in her cart. She looked toward me and said, "With these four chickens, I could feed my family for a month." I smiled and said, "And I bet they will eat well."

This story made me think about how some individuals and cultures seem to be more creative than others when it comes to providing necessities for their family. So, out of Sandra's story came this story, "Making the Most of What You Have, " a story I also call, "The 4-Chicken Stretch."

If the woman in Sandra's story could feed her entire family for a month on four chickens, I thought, "What could a real culinary expert (Executive Chef) do with four chickens?" As my plan evolved, I went to the store to make my list: Four-5lb chickens, 10 lbs of potatoes, 6 lbs of onions, 4 lbs of carrots and 4 lbs of fresh green beans. I purchased all the items for under $30.00.

My plan was to contact a local chef and present my challenge as a *Mission Impossible* spin-off: "Your mission, if you accept, is to take these ordinary foods and create some extraordinary gourmet meals using everyday spices and pantry items. You will be feeding two adults and two children for seven days. This e-mail will self-destruct in 10 seconds."

My target was Scott Duarte, a graduate of the Pennsylvania Institute of Culinary Arts who now oversees the development and operations of Charles Pointe's Hospitality Division., in Charles Pointe, Bridgeport, West Virginia. He is their Managing Director, Executive Chef, and the General Manager of the Bridgeport Conference Center (BCC). Before assuming these positions, he was a chef at the Greenbrier Resort in White Sulfur Springs and at the world-renowned Pinehurst Resort and Country Clubs in Pinehurst, North Carolina.

He was the best in the area and I fully expected rejection, "Too busy right now." However, I was pleasantly surprised when he accepted the challenge, "Sure. We'll get to work on it right away." Scott enlisted the assistance of Tim Goots, Executive Chef at the BCC, also a graduate of the Pennsylvania Institute of Culinary Arts. Tim did his internship at Westin William Penn Hotel in Pittsburgh. Locally, he headed food production at Jim Reid's in Nutter Fort, West Virginia and owned Johnnie B's, in Clarksburg, West Virginia before joining the BCC.

Both are excellent chefs but could they do "The 4-Chicken Stretch" - take a limited amount of everyday food and create seven gourmet meals for a family of four? In just a few weeks I had my answer when Tim responded with these recipes: A "Chicken Stock" and a "Brown (or roasted) Chicken Stock" using chicken bones (or parts) including carrots and onions. There was an "Herb Marinated Slow Roasted Chicken" which incorporated six different herbs, served with roasted potatoes and vegetables. A "Garlic and Rosemary Chicken" with green beans, sautéed onions and buttered egg noodles. "Grilled Chicken Breasts with Dried Cherry Barbecue Sauce" (4 breasts). The marinade and sauce are made from scratch.

They also included recipes for "Braised Chicken with Soft Polenta and Tomatoes" and "Cajun Chicken." One chicken was transformed into "Honey and Tarragon Chicken Salad," reserving the bones for stock. And your standard "Chicken and Dumplings" was anything but standard. It included buttermilk mashed potatoes and herbed green beans and carrots.

The piece de resistance was a chicken pot pie to die for…all from leftovers.

Together, these chefs not only met the challenge, they exceeded my expectations. Proving it is possible to create excitement from the ordinary, "Making the most of what you have."

To Scott, Tim and the BCC culinary staff…Bon Appetit! And thank you.

If you are interested in any of these recipes, contact me at michaelslambiotte@gmail.com or on my website michaelslambiotte.com

The Asian woman in this story probably didn't create
gourmet recipes from her chickens. But, her children
weren't hungry when they went to bed.

Mom, Please Not Those!

"We do not remember days, we remember moments" – Cesare
Pavese

Every parent has them. It's their right because it says so in the manual,
Parenting 101, Chapter 4, page 29, "It's the right of every parent to take
embarrassing pictures of their children." To parents, these pictures are
wonderful innocent memories. But to their children, they want to stick
their head in the sand and die. Let's look at one of my favorites. At the age
of 2, I was in my grandparent's back yard and was standing in a washtub
wearing my cowboy hat and a Roy Rogers Colt 45. That's all! Fortunately,
my manhood was covered by the Colt 45.

My relatives would look at these pictures and smile and nod their
heads, while I was dying. A Friend in Virginia even staged his pictures and
picked the moment of truth for his daughter. When she was 3, he took her
picture on his friend's custom Harley-Davidson. She wore a Confederate
flag bandana, sunglasses, leather vest and shorts, with stick-on tattoos on
her arms. He said, "I can't wait until her 13th birthday party."

For her sake, I hope his wife has it under lock and key. Every child
vows never to do this to their children. However, guess what, they end up
doing it. Maybe it's twisted revenge. Who knows?

But parents, beware! Some where, deep in those closets or in the
attic is "The Box," pictures of you as a teen or college student. Funny or
cute at the time, until your teenager finds them. For me, it would be me
wearing Navy bellbottoms, tie-dyed T-shirt, Bob Dylan hair style, and Joe
Namath-type Fu Manchu mustache. Really cool in 1970, but today, let's
just say, "I would stand out."

I remember the picture a student brought to my Political Science class
in 1986 when I was teaching a course on the Vietnam War. It was his
father in Vietnam, shirtless, sitting on the barrel of a tank with a long red
bandana tied around his head and a peace sign on his chest. Painted on
the barrel was, "The Good, The Bad, The High." The boy knew what it
meant but asked his father anyway, just to watch him squirm. His dad said,
"Uh, well, we were in the mountains. Where did you find that picture?"

Don't forget the college pictures. I recently heard about the infamous

"Green House 7," a group of college girls who shared a house in the Sunnyside section of Morgantown, West Virginia, near the Superette. This house hosted many "celebrations" with pictures as proof. Thelma and Louise (not their real names) were residents of the Green House. The house is now under the federal witness protection plan.

It was recently painted to conceal its shadowy past. Here are some of Thelma's (securely hidden) pictures: Thelma in a pink bandana, matching pink sweatshirt and fringed Daisy Duke shorts. One housemate is wearing a rainbow striped matching ski jacket and sweater - disco material. There is a picture of Louise having breakfast using a cool whip bowl and ladle. Certainly, these types of pictures are ones your teenagers would love to get their hands on. Warning! Guard them well.

When you least expect it, your child will hand you a taped box and say, "Mom/Dad what's in this?" Then, your heart sinks; it's now time for "Truth or Lie." Sorry, can't help. You're on your own with this one.

Why do we keep these incriminating or embarrassing pictures? For the same reasons our parents (and you) kept those baby pictures. As Ralph Edwards said in 1952, "This Is Your Life." That 6lb. 7oz. baby became a 235lb. adult - overnight. One day you are holding your twins. The next, you're holding your grandchildren.

Those college or military pictures...they make you laugh and cry, but nevertheless, "This is Your Life." As you look through those pictures, think how fortunate you are to have the memories. Yes, some may be embarrassing at the time, but, try to imagine what it would be like growing up not having, or not being able to "remember the days or the moments."

In the words of Victor Hugo, "The supreme happiness of life is the conviction that we are loved."

Not being a parent, I will never understand why a mother or father feels the need to tell an embarrassing childhood story about their 65-year-old son in public.

Next Stop...Georgia!

"As you walk and eat and travel, be where you are. Otherwise you will miss most of your life." – Buddha

It was 1958 and school was over for the year. Like most boys my age, it meant swimming, baseball, waiting for the ice cream truck, and our annual family vacation. I was only nine, so I it really didn't matter to me where we went as long as it included sand and salt water.

Last year we went to St. Petersburg, Florida and this year we were we were headed for Miami. Mom's job was to pack the suitcases, fix the snacks, lunches, stock the cooler, get the traveler's checks, and anything else moms did in 1958. Dad's job was to pack the car. My job was simple, get in the car.

Mom's final words, before climbing into our 1956 black and yellow Buick Special were, "Don't forget to go to the bathroom. You know your Dad. The next stop will probably be Georgia!"

Yes, Dad was one of those men who focused on the destination. With a full tank of gas, plenty of food and water, and a map on the seat, it was "Miami or bust!" If not for a few well received gas stations, bust it would have been. If he could have refueled while driving, like a fighter jet refuels in the air, we would have never stopped, until we reached the Miami Fontainebleau Hotel. At that time, the Fontainebleau, which opened in 1954, was affordable for us blue collar folks. Now, it's a 'haughty tot tot' 5-star resort.

But, back to my story. As our trip progressed, Mom slept or had her eyes closed from terror, and I watched the telephone poles take on the look of a picket fence. Through Dad's eyes, there was no time for sightseeing, he could see Miami from the West Virginia – Virginia border. All I could remember was the ground getting flatter. And suddenly, there it was... Miami Beach.

As the years flew by, those Florida trips became a distant memory. However, I realized I had inherited dad's destination desire. When planning a trip (any trip), I would always look for the quickest way, with no time for scenery. No, can't stop. Gotta get there.

When my wife Sandra wanted to stop at a scenic overlook or some useless antique shop or garden center, I would say, "We'll stop on the way back. Besides (as I accelerated), there isn't any place to turn around."

Even when we went on a Mediterranean cruise for our 25th anniversary, I spent as much time planning the shore excursions as relaxing on the ship. However, she never gave up on trying to alter my genetic disposition for 'destination desire.'

But change I did. I'm sure most of it was because of her. I think it started when she took me to Bald Head Island, North Carolina for my 50th birthday. She packed the car, planned the trip, made the reservations, and never told me where we were going. She just said, "Drive!"

And you know what, the whole experience was incredible. As we were driving, I not only saw the tobacco and cotton fields, I smelled them. When we entered the small village of Southport, North Carolina, I could see the fishing and shrimp boats tied to the docks, as seagulls circled overhead. I was secretly hoping this was not our destination. For once, I was enjoying the trip. She then pointed and said, "That ferry will take us to our destination."

Three days of quiet nothing opened my eyes to the joys of the journey. Since that experience, I now know why my grandparents so enjoyed packing their cooler and just taking a country road to see where it goes. I understand why someone would take a 3-day cruise to nowhere and why the back roads are now so alluring.

Oh my, how much of life I did miss. Always in a hurry. I can't change the past. Nor can I foresee the future. But, I can now take pleasure in the present.

Because, I finally realized the journey is part of the destination.

Age closes so many doors, but it also opens
so many eyes – at least these eyes.

SPLAT!

"Open your eyes." Alexandra Stoddard

"Don't worry, I'll be careful." A familiar phrase used by young and old in every day conversation. It just rolls out with little thought regarding being careful or about consequences. Granted, no one sets out to be careless, but accidents do happen and that is why they call them accidents.

In my opinion, most home accidents happen because of carelessness and/or overestimating one's physical ability. In other words, carelessness is a result of mind and body not being on the same page, especially when it comes to daily routines.

For instance: I was recently taking garbage from our large outdoor wooden container. The wooden lid, which was secured by a chain, came crashing down on my ring finger nearly severing it. My mind was looking forward to a nice bottle of wine and a wonderful meal, while my body was working independently from routine.

Later that evening Sandra, who is a firm believer in predestination, said "Everything happens for a purpose. If you don't slow down, God will slow you down." Not exactly what I wanted to hear, but it has slowed me a bit.

That being said, because of my recent experience with accidents and a personal interest in falling, let's talk about some preventative measures. When I was 10 years old, I got up in the middle of the night to go to the bathroom. I made a wrong turn and fell all the way down the stairs. Dad heard the commotion and almost beat me to the bottom of the stairs. Fortunately, 10-year-olds bounce well and there was no injury, just a dazed look, "Where am I?" That experience taught me to wake up and open my eyes before walking, which isn't always easy for a 10-year-old.

Now if I fall, all I can think about (after the initial embarrassment) is, "I hope all the body parts work and are still attached." As we get older, one of the many difficult things to accept is the physical changes age brings, especially when our mind says, "We can still do it" but the body says, "Are you nuts! Look at our driver's license. We're not 20 anymore."

So, for those of us slightly beyond our physical prime, here are some additional points to ponder: Remember when you were 10 years old? You could jump up and twirl 360 degrees and land perfectly straight. Now, you can lose your balance when you turn your head too fast. Just a thought, maybe you should let someone else fix those loose shingles.

Additionally, perhaps it's time to give up the hedge clippers when the extension cord has more splices than a 6-foot sausage link. Think: Before you get that step ladder to change a light bulb remember, "Last week I lost my balance stepping up on the curb."

Don't let overestimating your physical ability result in a careless accident. Keep your ego in check! Of course, some accidents happen because we overlook obvious hazards, especially in 'Accident Central' - our homes. A few weeks ago, an acquaintance was serving dinner wearing slippers with no heel. He fell resulting in a compound fracture of his ankle. Those slippers are for people who still bounce.

Looking around your house you'll probably see a few throw rugs or what I like to call fall rugs. They are nice to look at, but not while you're face down, up close and personal. Do with them what their name indicates… throw them away. Remember, children bounce. Old children go splat! Finally, look carefully at your electrical outlets. Do they resemble a 1940's telephone switchboard with multiple plugs and wires? Save time, just throw a match on your sofa.

In the end, accidents do happen for many reasons. That's why they call them accidents. No one walks outside and says, "Gee, I haven't fallen for a long time. I'll try it and see how it feels." If we open our eyes and think, many can be prevented. Don't go through life saying, "Don't worry, I'll be careful" and brush it off. If nothing else, think about how your carelessness or overestimating your physical ability will affect the people who love you.

Yes, I'm talking about you! And, I hope you're listening.

It's is truly tough raising parents.
They won't listen to reason and they think
they can do anything they want.

The Other Side of the Moon

"To finish the moment, to find the journey's end in every step of the road, to live the greatest number of good hours, is wisdom." - Emerson

Over the years my mother-in-law's strengths have become a curse became a curse in her final years. That being said, this story is dedicated to those blessed with remarkable health well into their 80's and 90's. Those whose mind says, "Let's give it a try!" And the heart responds, "Why not. Together we can still mow that lawn, trim that hedge and climb that ladder."

WE are forever confident in our physical abilities, even if their driver's license says, "Excuse me! Look at this picture. You're past 80." Meanwhile, the children or spouse worries, "What if they fall? Slip under the mower. Miss a stop sign. Cut themselves with the hedge trimmer." Sometimes, we have to stop and look at "The Other side of the Moon" and notice very mature person who can still do and still does.

This leads me to the true story of June and her son Stephen and the lessons they both learned. The names have been changed to protect the guilty. Stephen's mother is 78, still did her yard and inside work, continues to drive where she wants and shops till the stores close. However, with each passing year the lawn became steeper, the hedges taller and the vacuum and groceries heavier. Yet she manages, something that always amazed Stephen.

Being fair, he lived out of state and only came home a couple times a year and really did not see what was happening, that is until he retired and returned home. As he began to help around her home, his concerns rose, "Mom" he said, "Do you think its time to give up the hedge clippers? Your extension cord is spliced so many times it looks like linked sausage." Fearing she would fall while mowing, he replaced her industrial sized electric start self-propelled mower with a light-weight pull start, one he could use and one she couldn't start.

When she turned 82, Stephen's worry list grew: She still drove, but not at night, that is until her cataract surgery. She enjoyed working on the river bank and promised she wouldn't roll over the ban. Her best friend was her stepladder. Her electric string trimmer became a multipurpose tool for grass, weeds and poison ivy. You name it, she trimmed it.

There was nothing she couldn't accomplish with a snow shovel and a long stick. Adding to Stephen's fears: She worked outside late into the evening because she couldn't take the heat. When June turned 83, Stephen finally realized life had come full circle. It was his time to worry and protect her, as best he could.

One day he said, "Mom, we need to talk." Half way through their conversation she looked at him and said, "I just can't sit around the house all day. I can still do things and I need to be outside. I want to drive if I can." Stephen paused, remembering the words of Jonathan Swift, "May you truly live all the days of your life."

At that moment, he realized his mother needed to live her life, with a few concessions. For them, this is what "The Other Side of the Moon" looks like today: Stephen does the mowing and hedge trimming. "June does her own weeding, clipping and snipping and promises to be careful. The snow shovel and ladders are off limits – she promised! However, just in case she weakens, they mysteriously disappeared. They talk every night after all the doors are locked. Three telephone rings in the morning tells Stephen, Mom's up and the coffee's hot. When she goes on a road trip, she calls before she leaves and when she gets back.

Through it all, she learned a valuable lesson: When the mind and heart tricks the body, listen to the body. And occasionally your son. As for Stephen, "Sometimes, it's really tough raising mothers. God needs to look over them also" – right Mom!

If you ever see "The Other Side of the Moon," love them for who they are. For one day, we hope we will be them.

Still, people who know my mother and me often ask, "How's she doing?" "Wonderful," I reply, and that presents it own problems.

When I Grow Up

"The future belongs to those who believe in the beauty of the dream." — Eleanor Roosevelt

I wanna be a cowboy when I grow up!
I wanna be police officer when I grow up!
I wanna be a fireman when I grow up!
I wanna be an astronaut when I grow up!

At one time or another, I wanted to be all of them. As a child, every Saturday I watched Roy Rogers and Gene Autry riding, roping, and shooting (to wound). To satisfy my cop dreams there was Broderick Crawford in *Highway Patrol*. Unfortunately, I cannot remember any special fireman movies or characters. I was just attracted to the big red trucks, sirens, flashing lights, water hoses, and chopping down doors. My astronaut dream was the result of watching Allen Shepherd fly into space in 1961.

All this was serious stuff when you're 12 years old or younger. I wonder, do you know anyone who fulfilled their childhood dreams? I mean the 10-year-old who dreamed of becoming a fireman and became a fireman - because he/she wanted to. Or the 12-year-old who drove everyone in the neighborhood crazy by putting a siren on his bike and putting fake tickets on windshields and became a state trooper. Or, the little girl who rejected Barbie dolls in favor of model airplanes who is now an Air Force fighter pilot.

The likelihood of personally knowing someone like this is very slim, In my opinion.. As children, we all dream, and that is beauty of being a child. However, very few carry those dreams from childhood, through the teen years, and into adulthood. If you disagree, ask yourself, "What did you dream of becoming when you grew up? And what have you become now?"

Chances are, that young astronaut is now an accountant. And the teenager who dreamed of rodeos and bull riding is now a postal worker. What about the young girl who wanted to be a policewoman and was never encouraged and probably discouraged, she's now a librarian. What about the high school graduate, who dreamed of becoming a fireman, but felt obligated to join the family plumbing business.

I'm not saying these people aren't happy with their accomplishments. Quite the contrary. More than likely, they are happy and successful, but I suspect there is always that little voice that keeps saying, "What if."

Of course, life's circumstances lead us down many different paths. Although, the main difference between the 'What ifs' and the 'Dream come truers,' is for the come 'truers,' someone was there to listen, to ask questions, encourage and help create opportunities. Some parents truly listen, "Mom, when I grow up I want to be an interior designer. Oh really. Do you know what an interior designer does? Let's go to the library and check out some books. Maybe talk with your school counselor. It's never too early to plan. In the future, maybe we could contact your school and see if they have a Shadow Day. Perhaps you could spend a day with a local design company. Or volunteer to help out during school breaks."

Unfortunately, this is what many children hear, "Interior design... are you crazy! You'll never make any money doing that. If I'm paying for college you're going to be a nurse. That way, no matter where you go, you'll be able to get a job. End of discussion!"

Extreme examples? Maybe. Maybe not. In the first instance, the child may realize he (or she) has a real passion for design. That's the beauty of the dream. On the other hand, they may find there is more to interior design than pretty colors and lace toile.

Either way, it's their choice because it is their future.

In the second case, the dream went up in a cloud of smoke because the child was discouraged from the very beginning. One of the hardest, and one of the most important, things an adult can do for a child is to support a dream they don't understand. When you hear these words, I encourage you to listen, . "When I grow up I wanna be..."

These childhood dreams could be more than starring out a window. They could be a looking at their door to the future.

I had the opportunity to grow up to be what I
wanted to be. I wasted the opportunity. Sad.

When Teenagers Grow Up

"The more we accept responsibility for who we are and who we can become, the greater will be our progress and contribution." – Stephen Covey

"But Dad, all my friends are going! I'll be the only one not there." "Mom, it's my nose and if I want to get it pierced it's my business! After all, I'm 15." "No, you can't buy that 'micro' bikini. Case closed!" "Son, no tattoos…at least as long as you're living in this house." "No, you can't go on that Senior Graduation Cruise. I don't care if the whole world is going. You're staying right here and that's final…no ifs, ands, buts or maybes!"

The last years of my educational career were spent in high school administration. Much of that time was spent listening to teenagers complaining about their parents.

Generally, we'd just sit in my office and I'd let them vent about how they had the world's worst parents. I always shied away from these common clichés, "It's for your own good. They are your parents you know. Someday, you'll understand."

At some point during the venting process, they would always stop and say, "It's just not fair!" Side Bar: The average teenager uses "It's not fair" 8.6 times a day and it is their favorite way to end a sentence. At some point, I would always interrupt and say, "You're probably right, it's not fair." That always caught them off guard.

Continuing, I would say "Raising parents isn't easy, is it? For the past several years you've tried and tried but they don't seem to understand how difficult it is to be a teenager…the peer pressure and stuff. Your parents were born old, weren't they?" After a couple minutes of this approach, I received looks somewhere from bewildered to slightly contemptuous.

After a planned pause, I would look them straight in the eyes I say, "You know why dad or mom won't let you buy or do some of the things you want to buy or go some of the places you want to go?" Their standard response was, "Yea, because their stupid and they don't understand." "On the contrary," they understand perfectly. Because they were once 17 and they vividly remember how a 15, 16, 17-year-old brain works. They also suffered from peer pressure and stuff. They love you and want to protect you from bad things and from yourself. So, give 'm some slack. Raising a teenager isn't easy either. Remember, someday you'll walk in their shoes and you will become your parents."

Of course, most adamantly disagreed, yet as they were leaving my office, many would turn around and say, "Thanks for listening, but it's still not fair." I would nod and say, "I know."

Fortunately, as the years pass most young people learn that being a teenager wasn't nearly as stressful as being an adult. And the phrase "It's not fair" falls by the wayside.

Unfortunately, "When teenagers grow up" their adult anthem (favorite phrase) becomes "I'm too busy" or "I don't have the time." I'm too busy to help with that club project. I don't have the time to volunteer to bake cupcakes. I'm too busy to take the kids fishing. I don't have the time to... (add your personal favorite).

In my opinion, "too busy" or "not enough time" is purely an excuse for what many parents are really thinking, "Just not interested" or "Got something better to do." Unfortunately, these excuses are acceptable for most people nowadays. I wonder where we would be if Michelangelo, Mother Teresa, Thomas Jefferson, Shakespeare or Albert Einstein had said, "I'm too busy to....?"

Luckily, most teenagers move beyond "It's not fair" rather quickly. However, I ask you, "How old do adults have to be before they stop saying 'I'm too busy' or 'I don't have the time?" Regrettably, these excuses often prevent us from exploring new opportunities and possibilities. I for one admit I am a frequent practitioner of these two common phrases, "I'm too busy" or "I don't have the time."

Nonetheless, I am pledging to stop and reflect for a few seconds what really lies behind these excuses and then attempt to turn them around and see where they take me. Won't you consider the same?

As Shakespeare said, "The fault is not in our stars, but in ourselves."

My neighbors wonder why their sons seldom visit.
They must look within themselves for the answers.

216

CHAPTER 12

Oh, Those Beautiful Brown Eyes

Merry Taught Me the Meaning of Real Love

"Until one has loved an animal, a part of one's soul
remains awakened." — Anatole France

This chapter contains stories about many of our memorable pets – our cats Jessie, Sydney, and Mr Gray. There are also stories about Merry, a very special Larbrador retriever. Merry – the name suited her so wellfor she so Merry, Merry to the very end.

This story is dedicated to Merry and to her memory., for she taught me the meaning of real love. She taught my how to live a better lifeand how to become a better person.

So, this is for you "Merry Wiggles."

Love comes in a wiggle: Even as a puppy, she knew how to touch my heart. When I would pick her up, from the tip of her tail to the end of her nose, everything was wiggling. That is how she got the nickname, Merry Wiggles. which was just one of her many deserved nicknames. Her eyes were so black they looked like shiny lumps of coal. It was only as she grew older that they changed to a deep brown. Her eyes said, "Thank you Dad, for holding me so close."

Master of non-verbal communication: Unlike most, if not all dogs, Merry knew how to get what she wanted (or needed) with a look – never a bark or a growl. When I was reading the newspaper, she would stand in front of me and just stare. If it was 7:00 a.m.,12:00 p.m., or 5:00 p.m., her look said, "Dad, I'm hungry. Time to feed me!" If I did not respond in a 'Merry Moment,' she would take her nose, flip up the paper and place her muzzle on my knee and cut those beautiful eyes. Then, she got what she wanted or needed. When the last crumb of food had disappeared, she would look up at, head slightly tilted, ears up high, lick her lips, and her eyes would say "Thank you. Any chance for more?"

If my wife Sandra and I were in the kitchen and we had been negligent in filling her water bowl. She would stare at the empty bowl, look directly at us, bowl, us, bowl, us – until we got the message. When Merry needed to go outside, she would walk to the door, stare at it, then turn her head and stare at us – repeatedly, back and forth. She never barked. Her way of saying, "Dad, Mom, one of you needs to let me out. You know I would die before I had an accident in the house." If I was somewhere else in the house, she would stand in front of me and just stare. The time of day or night determined back door, food, or water bowl.

Always a happy greeter: When she was a puppy and saw me enter the driveway, which was 400' long, she would wait until I got out of the truck and then would run full bore, leaping into my arms, "Dad's home. Dad's Home. Can we play now!" She knew I would catch her. I always did. That is, until she began to gain weight and length. Catching a full speed Labrador that weighs 50 pounds and is still growing becomes a challenge. Eventually, we had to stop the 'Leap & Catch.' Stopping puzzled and may have even hurt her feelings, but my kneeling down and vigorously scratching her back, combined with a good belly rub was a good substitute – she said so.

From the day she arrived in my life to the day she died, she always greeted me with happiness and kindness.

I forgive you Dad: Merry was not perfect, but near perfect. I was the one who had the personality issues. At times, I was verbally a bit rough during her training or when something in my life went wrong, I would occasionally take it out on her. She never deserved either.

When I would raise my voice, she would drop her head and retreat. Regardless of how I acted, she would always return to me, tail wagging. Her eyes said, "Dad, I'm so sorry for whatever I did. I try so hard to be good but sometimes it is so hard. Please hold me." She taught me that all she needed was a firm voice. And lots of love. She taught me about forgiveness.

Oh, how I love the simple things: It didn't take much to make Merry happy. True, she had more stuffies than one could count and a bed on every floor – even an orthopedic bed for long night sleeps. She always had fresh water and the right kind of food. We exercised together and we played together and she had the best medical care possible.

Nevertheless, it was the simplest of things that gave her great joy. Going for any walk became an event. She would jump up and down at the door making yodeling, moaning sounds of excitement. Getting her choker and bandana on her was a chore because she would not stand still. Side note: One day, even with all the excitement, I forgot to put her bandana around her neck. I opened the door and she stopped dead, turned her head, and looked at me with eyes that said, "Dad, you forgot something. I can't go out half dressed." With bandana around her neck, I would open the door and she would leap from the porch and sprint to the back door of the garage. A simple walk – one of life's simpler pleasures.

Somehow, she could read our body language and knew when she was going for a car ride. No, I didn't reach for the keys until the last minute. It was the walk routine all over again. However, when we got to the truck, she could barely contain herself while I opened the door. With one massive leap, she was in the back seat, bouncing from side window to side window. The only way to calm her was to begin moving and crack the window a few inches She didn't care where we were going. She just loved to see new things and smell new smells. Another simple pleasure. As the years went by, she never lost this joy, even when she needed a ramp to enter the back seat. It folded up like an accordion and stayed in the back of the truck.

Merry taught me how to love the simplest of things and activities:

Sitting in the back yard watching a butterfly. Hearing children playing up the street. Watching hummingbirds compete for feeder space. It has been a year since she died. But, she still walks with me. And, I still find her black hairs in the truck. Occasionally, one will float around the cab as a reminder, "Dad, I love car rides."

I am so tired. I just can't do it anymore: Merry taught me about limitations. She taught me that growing old(er) is a gift from God. As the years went by, the simplest of activities became more difficult and eventually impossible – for her and me. The difference between us: was she was smart enough to accept, "I just can't do it anymore." She would always go up the stairs with us for a good night's sleep. One evening she stopped at the bottom of the stairs, moving from side-to-side, picking up the right foot then the left. She wanted to try the stairs so bad, but eventually sat down and just looked at us. Her eyes and body language said, "I want to so much, but I just can't. It's hurts too much."

We brought her upstairs bed down to the main floor, along with her stuffies, and just sat with her for a while. She was content and knew we loved her. In my younger days, I would have gone down the stairs and encouraged her to again, try the stairs. She taught me: We all have limits and pushing those limits not only hurts us, but it can hurt those around us. Merry taught me compassion and understanding.

True love means making the most difficult of decisions: As Merry reached the age of 10, her health was beginning to fail. At 11, she was visibly tired. I could see it in her eyes. She was losing a little weight, arthritis was slowing her down, and she had already been treated for a small malignant growth. However, she still had the heart of a lion and the will of an Olympic champion. The desire to rip and tear was still in her eyes, but she accepted the realities, "Dad, let's go for a short walk in the back yard and lay in the sun for a while" She still had her dignity. And we vowed we would never allow her to lose that dignity.

The next story, "Merry's Last Car Ride" is about dignity and the most difficult decision we ever made.

Merry, we love you! Thank you for showing us how to love life.

Merry's Last Car Ride

"God's finger touched her, and she slept."
-Alfred, Lord Tennyson

It was August 2015. Merry, our so precious Labrador retriever was 11. Converting to human years, she was 77. She always looked forward to going with my wife Sandra to the gardens. Merry would smell the flowers, attempt to chase a bee or two, watch a butterfly erratically flying from plant to plant and lay in the sun a few minutes. Funny though, no matter where Merry was, she always kept Sandra in her sight.

No matter where Sandra was, Merry was always close. Merry had to see her always. However, when the sun began to heat things up, Merry had enough and would walk to Sandra and just stare at her. The eyes and head tilt said, "Mom, I'm too hot and I need to go inside." For years, this was their routine and part of their special times together. Everyone needs a special time and a special place. Sandra and Merry found their 'Special' in the garden.

Through May of this year, this was their routine. Sandra would take her coffee and garden snips and head to the garden with Merry by her side. However, as we entered the heat of June, Merry changed. I didn't notice it but Sandra sure did. One morning, when she opened the door to go to the garden, Merry just sat there. Then, she laid down on the cool kitchen floor, dropping her eyes. The eyes spoke, "Mom, it just hurts too much. I'm sorry. I just can't do it today. Maybe tomorrow."

This was a sign, one I never recognized or refused to recognize. When July came, Merry's conditioned continued to slip. Some days, she would go to the garden and some days it was just too difficult. Sandra attempted to talk with me about Merry's decline but I refused to accept the inevitable. I always did.

On Merry's good days, I would take her for a walk around the back yard. Being my selfish self, I would encourage her to run to me. Merry did her best – with a limping gate and hind legs that could not keep up. Taking her to the front yard was off limits. She became too excited and we were afraid she would fall.

Visibly, she continued to lose weight. A small growth on top of her foot was beginning to enlarge. The small hard masse in her abdomen was still there. However, her appetite had never changed. We fed her three times a day, limited amounts, and she polished off every single drop. She drank three or four bowls of water daily. Although arthritis limited her physical activity, she still had the heart of a lion and her mind remained sharp. However, she was tired. You could see it in her eyes. The sparkle was gone.

Sandra wanted to talk. Me, being me...I shut out the thoughts. In the meantime, we agreed that Merry needed to visit her doctor for an evaluation. Deep down, we both knew what was coming, but I fought the inevitability. Sandra, being the strong one said, "We must never let her suffer or lose her dignity."

It was August 4. I went to the truck to prepare her ramp. When I returned to the house and opened the kitchen door, Merry was standing there, staring at me, then at Sandra...back and forth. Somehow, she knew it was Car ride time.' Getting her choker and bandana around her neck was always a chore, and this time was no different. So, she would not attempt to leap off the porch, I had to attach her lead and walk her, slowly, down the steps and then to the truck.

As we stood by the open back door of the truck, she tried he best to walk up the ramp, but could not. The strength just wasn't there. With my arms around her midsection, I helped her into the back seat. As usual, I turned on the air conditioner for Sandra and partially opened the back windows for Merry.

Merry, unlike most dogs, enjoyed her visits to the doctor. She greeted everyone with a wiggle – even this time. During her examine, our worst fears were confirmed: Removing the growth on her toe would require removing part of her foot. Her lymph nodes were enlarged. The weight loss, despite a ravenous appetite, signaled serious internal problems, although she experienced no digestive issues.

What I wrestled with most: I looked at her with eyes that refused to see the obvious. She was old(er). Gray around her muzzle and eyebrows. A little stiff in the joints. But, she still loved to eat and get out and play a little. A little like me. Fortunately, there was this little voice inside me, "Mike, quit being selfish. This beautiful little girl deserves the best. Don't wait until you know she is in pain."

Merry's doctor was so kind. She explained our options and percentages. Sandra and I just looked at one another. Merry's doctor asked if we wanted a few minutes by ourselves - all three of us. We said yes. I looked at Merry and wanted to see that two-year old that once knocked me down. All I saw was tired eyes that were trying their best. Sandra looked at me, "We must never allow her to suffer or lose her dignity." I agreed. Then, I knelt beside Merry, with my arms around her, "I love you precious and I will never forget everything you taught me." She licked my nose and I knew everything would be all right.

A few minutes later, with me lying on the floor beside her, and Sandra holding my hand, Merry passed away – and Merry never suffered or lost her dignity. The sadness we shared on the ride home was beyond words. Tears freely flowing from both of us. The reality of it all was overwhelming. This was *Merry's Last Car Ride.* The first time in 11 years Merry was not with us.

It has now been slightly over a year since Merry passed away. Her choker and bandana still hang beside the back door. Her lead is the garage. Her collar on our book shelf. Not a day goes that I do not look around the yard and see her having an experience as we referred to her running wildly around the yard. I still see her on her back, legs straight up, wiggling from side to side. Her black hairs still show up – everywhere.

When Sandra and I sit together in the library, across from our chairs is Merry's picture on my great grandmother's writing desk. She is laying in the green grass of our back yard wearing her signature red collar. Her forehead wrinkled with ears perked. Hanging over the edge of the frame are the two tiny bells Sandra had around Merry's neck when she entered our life.

I do not need a picture to remind me of the companionship and love she provided us over the years. But, it does provide comfort. And, at times, I look at her picture asking myself, "What! Now what do you want?" And I smile.

Today is September 25, 2016 – Merry's birthday. She would have been 14. There has never been a day that I question the decision Sandra and I made. For we made the decision for Merry. Not ourselves.

"Merry Wiggles, you never suffered or lost your dignity"

Isn't is a shame our society does not allow us to make these same difficult decisions for family members we have loved and have taught us so much.

They should not lose their dignity.

Cat Tales...Through Our Eyes!

"The world is full of magical things patiently waiting for our wits to grow sharper." – Eden Phillpotts

Good Morning. I'm Jessie and I'm Sydney, Mike and Sandra's cats. This story is about two well-bred, noble, confident, and independent American short-hair felines. It is about us! If I may, Dogs are from Saturn. Cats are from Jupiter.

We concede: Dogs have certain endearing qualities. However, their willingness to please, often sacrificing their dignity, is totally unacceptable in the regal and sophisticated world of cats. Tail wagging, guttural sounds, running and jumping to please, drooling, and sitting on command are absolutely disgusting, at least through our eyes.

On the other hand, we'll give Merry, our black Lab sister some credit. Dogs do an acceptable job of teaching basic human behavior - the foundation. However, it's the job of felines to take this foundation and upon it, create a sophisticated society...ie: a well-rounded human being!

Therefore, we're proud to present, "Cat Tales...Through Our Eyes." Jessie, because you're the oldest, you go first. One of the many lessons taught by felines is the importance of being independent. We would never lower ourselves to come running with ears flopping, tongues hanging out, and tails wagging.

We're way too free-spirited. Granted, at times we may come when called, but to please us...not you. On the other hand, we may stare at you with keen vertical slit eyes and a look that says, "Not today, I'm too busy" and walk the other way. If we really want to be independent, we will ignore you and hide, even though we're only a few feet away. Sometimes, we just want to be alone. Rejection is part of life, accept it.

Sidney, you do the lesson on personal and environmental hygiene. Notice we're always grooming ourselves. We take pride in looking neat and clean. Remember the time our older brother Punkie, who passed away a few years ago, was playing in the coal bin at Grandma's? It took him a couple of days, but three fur balls later, his coal-gray fur was once again bright white. Learn from us!

On the topic of environmental cleanliness (aka... keep our house clean): When we miss the litter box, I assure you it's on purpose! Just our way or reminding you how important it is to keep a neat and clean house.

We also teach how unpredictable life can be. Like when you curl up in your favorite chair and suddenly, we leap onto your lap. A subtle purr is all you'll get. A gentle nose nudge indicates a light head stroking is desired. And, with no warning, it's claws to the leg and chest or fangs to the fingers and we're gone. Learn to deal with the unpredictable.

Jessie, you do the part about sharing. I need a snack and a nap. When some of our country/outdoor relatives deposit a snake, mouse, or something you can't identify on the back porch, don't scream and slam the door. We're just teaching the importance of sharing.

Hey Sidney, wake up! Remember hearing about Punkie climbing the Christmas tree to capture the mouse and then bringing it to the Christmas table as his contribution for dinner. Everyone appreciated the thoughtfulness, but graciously declined his offering. It was the thought that counted. Punk got a small piece of turkey. Sharing is important. Learn from us.

Sydney, get up! We both need to do the lesson on observation and patience...cat style patience. You humans really need to take a lesson on this topic. Why do we lay flat as a pancake or sit motionless for what seems like hours ? Staring. Listening. The answer is simple. We have our eyes on the prize. We are willing to sacrifice whatever it takes to accomplish our goals. Through our eyes, many of you quit too easily and too soon. Learn from us.

Lastly, as cats, we teach the importance of a good nap. Nothing beats a well-timed nap. Unless we are hungry.

From Merry, Jessie, and Sydney, this has been a few of life's lessons.

Cats are "snooty" by nature but they love us
the same as dogs, but by their terms.
Don't forget to love them back.

Every Precious Moment

"Life's short and we never have enough time for the hearts of those who travel the way with us."- Henri-Frederic Amiel

This story is dedicated to Dr. J and Dr. G, veterinarians at APAC and veterinarians everywhere, for they have dedicated their lives to treating patients who cannot speak.

In late July, Merry, our 8-year- old Labrador retriever almost died after developing pancreatitis. Without sounding too clinical (which is a struggle for me anyway), the pancreas plays an essential role in digesting food. When it becomes inflamed its enzymes can leak into the abdominal cavity and damage other internal organs, often leading to death.

The causes are varied: certain medications, infections, obesity, metabolic disorders, trauma, shock and high-fat diets are all possible causes. However, none of these applied to Merry other than my carelessness when she was a year old. Taking 'stupid' to new heights, one evening I placed our french fryer on the back porch to cool (uncovered) and forgot about it! The next morning, I let Merry out to survey the yard for night-time trespassers. When she returned, her muzzle was covered with oil. Saving all the details, we rushed her to our veterinarian, with my wife Sandra lecturing me (deservedly so) the entire way.

Warning! Never give your dog table scraps, fatty-stuff, bacon, pork, etc., which we do not, at least not anymore. In addition, never, never leave the fryer unattended! The only symptoms Merry had in this July episode were vomiting and a little discomfort getting up and down. No fever, no loss of appetite, no diarrhea, no depression.

When she vomited (for the second time) undigested food from the day before, we were on the way to see Dr. J & Dr. G. After drawing blood, we took her home and waited for the results. Later in the afternoon our worst fears were confirmed: Merry tested positive for pancreatitis.

For the next two days, she was hospitalized, given fluids intravenously and antibiotics. These were the longest two days of our lives. Not knowing whether she was going to live or die. When I saw one of her stuffies (a pheasant) on the dining room floor I said to Sandra, "Just don't touch it. Leave it for her when she returns."

We were fully aware she might not return. Every room had reminders: Her bowls in the kitchen. Her bed in the library. Another bed in our bedroom. Every room had a stuffy lying around. She never puts her toys away. When I walked out the back door I would see her signature red bandana hanging on the hook. Every morning she got us up, but not now. Every time we came home she was always there to greet us, but not now.

Every two hours we would call to check her progress. "She's stable, not vomiting and doesn't have a fever," they said." "The key is if she can keep her food down." During the second day Sandra looked at me and said, "I knew we would lose her someday, But not now. Not like this. If she makes it through this, we must savor every day with her and never forget the joy she brings."

And then, at the end of the second day we got a call from Dr. J, "I think Merry's ready to come home." Tears of joy were shed all the way to their office and all the way home. When Merry saw us she did her best-ever wiggle dance saying, "Boy, it's good to be going home. What's for lunch?" She never lost her appetite. We were told with antibiotics and a temporary special diet, Merry should make a full recovery. We might not, but she probably will.

I'm better now than before Merry's illness. Almost losing a beautiful 90-pound friend has taught me what it means to truly savor "Every Precious Moment."

Finally, I raise my glass to you Dr. J and Dr. G! And the technicians at APAC. How do you do what you do…treat patients who can't talk? Can't answer your questions. Can't tell you what hurts.

In comparison, human doctors have it easy.

Don't let "careless" haunt you for the rest of your life.

Merry & Me

"Until one has loved an animal, a part of one's soul remains unawakened." – Anatole France

In 2005, John Grogan wrote "Marley & Me." "Life and Love with the World's Worst Dog." I would like to present the story of "Merry & Me." "The World's Best Dog," at least through these eyes!

Merry, is a Labrador retriever who came to me as a Christmas present form my wife Sandra in 2003. Apparently, I had developed some bad habits only a furiously rambunctious and fearless 8-week-old Labrador puppy could cure. Merry knew I couldn't resist sweet-smelling puppy breath, a non-stop tiny tongue and the unconditional love coming through her brown eyes.

I'm sure many blessed dog owners feel their companion is the 'World's Best,' but I feel Merry is the benchmark. Here is why: After leaving her mom and litter mates, she only cried for two nights. On her third day, her eyes said, "Enough! Time to explore and have fun (the Labrador anthem). Let me outside. I need to find a stick."

She was totally house trained at 10 weeks, with the full run of the house at four months. No, she never did and still doesn't get on furniture. Trust me, 90 pounds of black fur is easy to detect. Her only destructive behavior was puppy-bed shredding. Our Virginia veterinarian said, "Labs are very high energy dogs and usually destructive only when they're scared or bored. They love their family and need to be with their people." He should know. He had five Lab boys, three human boys and a saint for a wife.

By six months, Merry was no longer scared or bored and her bed became her safe place. It didn't take long for her to 'Stare' train us. No barking, whimpering, whining or scratching doors. Merry just stares. To go outside, she stares at the door. If we don't react in a reasonable time, she turns her head and cuts her eyes. Eyes that say, "Excuse me! I need a restroom break." Or, "Let me out. I gotta find a stick and make mulch."

To get back in she paws once and a little more forcefully the second time if I'm too slow. If we're in another room, she'll sit and just stare. It's our responsibility to determine if its yard-break or dinner time. Yes, Merry joins us at the table, but with Lab-class, meaning no drooling or other obnoxious behavior. She stares! Only rarely putting her paw on my thigh or possibly her chin (major pity ploy).

However, Sandra's my strength while at the table, "Don't you dare give in! You want to give her pancreatitis." Merry also teaches the value of routines. Every morning, "immediately" after I open the paper, sit down and reach for my coffee, she stares and/or chin on the knee with eyes that say, "Dad, gotta survey the front and back yard for nighttime trespassers."

Somehow, she knows if its walk or car ride time as soon as I get up. Labs can read minds! She'll run to the back door, bounce and stare at her traveling clothes - her necklace and her signature red bandana. One day I opened the door without having her leash in my hand and she just sat there, staring at her leash.

Periodically we gather her (many) stuffies, placing them in one large basket. She won't take them out. She simply stares at the basket until we empty it. She doesn't want to make a mess.

There're only two slight cracks in her perfection armor. She has experiences, as we call them - adrenalin explosions resulting in wild-eyed, paws spread wide, back humping, hair up (fins up) uncontrolled running fits. What causes tis experiences varies: a leaf, a falling nut, a bird with a death wish, Dad's teasing, our neighbor and her bulldog, who knows what sets her off. The other crack: Merry, like most Labs, is a lousy watch dog. She barks at strangers, but it's an expression of pure joy at the chance to meet and wiggle at somebody new, not a warning.

These are just a few reasons Merry wears the crown as "The World's Best Dog." Of course, I'm biased!

I leave you with this thought, "Dogs never lie about love." – Jeffrey Masson

I know you think your dog is the "best" ever.
But, have you ever been loved by a Labrador?

They are the best.

World's Luckiest Labrador Retriever

"Treat me kindly, my beloved master, for no heart in all the world is more grateful for kindness than the loving heart of me." - Beth Norman Harris

If this was a featured front-page story, the subtitle would be, *"She survives despite Dad's weaknesses, carelessness, and lack of knowledge."* This story is about Merry our black Lab and how she survived "Dad." The dad who was weak, careless, and just didn't know about the "bad" things dogs shouldn't do or eat. I hope by sharing her story it may prevent others from making the same mistakes I made.

Now, the "World's luckiest Labrador retriever:" From a puppy and until the age of two, Merry had free range of our farm and orchard in southern Virginia. This included blueberry and blackberry bushes, grape vines, fig, apple, peach, pear and chestnut trees.

She would help herself to anything that would fit in her mouth She was a canine vacuum cleaner. She even ate the green spiny capsules around a chestnut. Ouch! My wife Sandra kept yelling, "Don't let her eat that stuff." My response was, "Ok." And then I went about my business and Merry went about her business - browsing for tasty morsels.

She would frequently top off her fruit meal with a hearty helping of grass, followed shortly thereafter with a nice case of vomiting and occasional diarrhea. All this came to a screeching halt when my resident "vet" (Sandra) observed the unfortunate results of Merry's menu choices and my negligence. To me it was just fruit and salad. Fortunately for Merry, more responsible heads prevailed. Lesson: Dogs should eat only dog food!

I also learned carelessness can lead to tragedy. After fixing a batch of french fries, I set the fryer on the back porch to cool. The next morning, I forgot about the fryer when I let Merry out. When I let her back in I saw oil all over her mouth. I looked down and saw half of the fryer oil was gone. Sandra didn't even wait for an explanation. She yelled, "I'll call the vet. Get her in the truck." She yelled a few other things and many unprintable. While in the vet's office Merry made quite a mess on the floor, which turned out to be a good thing. Not digesting the oil was a blessing.

Our greatest fear was pancreatitis, which can cause organ damage and possibly death. We followed the doctor's orders and fortunately she made a full recovery. Our vet nicknamed her 'Grease Ball.' I've never forgotten how my carelessness could have ended. Lesson: Carelessness can kill. Fatoily stuff can kill. Keep the chemicals and poisons secure.

A few years later we moved back to West Virginia. I'm still learning how to be strong-willed: No table treats. But it's so hard. Those big beautiful brown eyes and a paw on my thigh makes me so weak. However, in my moments of weakness I can rely on, "Are you nuts. You want to give her pancreatitis!" Thanks Sandra. I needed that.

I also found sharing grapes: one for Merry, one for me is very unwise. Grapes (may) can cause diarrhea, as Merry found out. Sandra made the mistake of leaving us alone one evening without adult supervision. I also found out Merry had not lost her country ability to scavenge for food.

The saga continues: Last spring, she helped herself to the red dogwood berries which had fallen from the tree in our front yard. The results were predictable: Dog + Berries = Vet Trip. And another lecture from my personal vet, "You idiot, you need to watch her all the time!"

Now you know why I call Merry, the "World's luckiest Labrador retriever." She survived me. We now have two superb veterinarians who have a very informative website. See if yours has one. One section is called "Common Sense." I think it was written because of me. I'm trying to follow their philosophy: "Dog food is for Dogs. People food is for People."

Finally, I encourage all pet owners to read the entire poem titled *"A Dog's Prayer"* by Beth Norman Harris, also on their website.

I wish I had room to print it. My opening quote is from her poem.

Our pets trust us beyond human capabilities. Do not betray that trust.

CHAPTER 13

When You Stop Learning – You Stop!

Caught Being Good

"(The word) takes hold of one today and falls into his heart; tomorrow it touches another, and so on. Thus, quietly it will do its work, and no one will know how it all began." – *Martin Luther*

John Sutherland was born in Brandon, Mississippi. He received his undergraduate degree from Old Dominion University in Norfolk, Virginia. His Master's Degree and Doctorate (PhD) were from the University of Virginia. Very impressive credentials, especially since he was a high school dropout, joining the Marines at 17. He earned his GED in the Corps.

When we first met, he was an elementary principal, soon to become a middle school principal. He was a leader, a visionary, our mentor, and what we coveted most...our friend. With his short white beard, he roamed the school in jeans and a school sweatshirt, looking more like Santa Claus on vacation than a principal.

However, his vision and goodness were unmatched. His programs were as unique as his appearance. In a school, considered the poster child for toughness, he saw only good and the potential for better. To encourage the positive, he created a program called, 'Caught Being Good.' Everyone was included: Teachers, students, and custodians - everyone! When a

233

student was caught carrying out an unusual act of kindness or courtesy, their name(s) would be submitted, a description of the act, along with an explanation as to why they deserved recognition.

Each week, Dr. Sutherland selected one name from those submitted, identify them over the school intercom, and personally going to their room for recognition. They received a token gift: A voucher for a bag of popcorn and play money, which could be used in the school store. To you and me, not much of a reward but through the eyes of a 12-year-old, the reward was priceless, reaching way beyond money and popcorn. For in this tough school, he saw what could be…not what was. Because of his (their) success, different versions of Caught Being Good were adopted by other schools, school administration, and even by some local businesses. It became an epidemic of goodness and courtesy.

I wonder: What it would be like if people in your city or town adopted a version of Caught Being Good? It might go something like this: You see the dreaded flashing lights in your rearview mirror and hear the shrill siren. You think, "What did I do! I wasn't speeding! The light wasn't red…maybe yellow!" And the police officer hands you not a ticket, but a Caught Being Goo' card. It seems she saw you pull over to help someone whose tailgate had fallen and part of their load was in the road…while others drove on. Or: You open your mail and find a Caught Being Good card from a garden club saying, "For efforts above and beyond. You are being recognized for extraordinary efforts in improving your home, thus our community."

Another possibility: Outside stands a sheriff's deputy with a letter in his hand. You nervously answer the door, but you notice he's smiling. "Does (your son's name) live here? Don't worry, everything's fine. I'm just here to give him a Caught Being Good card from a local grocery store. Last week the store manager saw your son catch an elderly lady's run-away cart in the parking lot. He made sure she was all right and put her groceries in her car. The manager got his license number. He just wanted to say thanks."

This is a novel idea: Names and situations could be sent by individuals to the media each week, with one or two selected for recognition and local businesses could sponsor a reception for those who were 'caught.'

I know. I see the smirks on some of your faces but I can also hear the 'yea, why not's.' I will always remember it was Doctor Sutherland's 'yea why not's' that helped make his program a success. Just think, if it helped turn around a tough inner-city school, imagine what it could do your city

All it takes is one…one with a vision. Why not give it a try?

Who knows…before long, the person who is "touched today, may touch someone tomorrow, and so on."

"Caught Being Good" may not work in all situations,
but isn't it better than watching failure grow?

Escaping from Reality

"We become in part what our senses take in."
— Eknath Easwaran

From the onset of this story, I make no apologies for my position regarding reality television, It needs to go away. Although reality television (people in unscripted situations) began in the 1940's, it has exploded to never-seen-before proportions since 2000. The first one I remember was Allen Funt's *Candid Camera*, which debuted in 1948.,There were others throughout the 1960's and 70's like *An American Family* in 1973 which featured a family going through a divorce. Then in the late 80's, we were introduced to *COPS*, police officers on duty apprehending criminals.

The complete saturation of network and cable television with reality began in the early 2000's with *Survivor* and *American Idol*, both becoming top-rated shows. However, I must admit I did enjoy the original *Survivor*, do in part to Rudy Boesch, the retired Navy SEAL. He and I lived in the same city and I knew a retired SEAL who served with him.

However, since that first episode, *Survivor* has visited almost every bizarre place in the world. Even for me, it has gotten way too weird. *American Idol*, let's just say its star isn't as shiny as it once was, at least not for me.

However, the network executives discovered an easy way to capitalize on their popularity of the original hits. – create spin offs. Let the saturation begin. During the next few years we had *The Amazing Race, America's Next Top Model, Dancing With The Stars, The Apprentice, America's Got Talent, Fear Factor* and dozens more.

Then it became even more bizarre when the spin offs had spin offs: From *American Idol* we had *American Juniors, An American Idol Christmas, American Idol Extra* and even *Canadian Idol*. From *Big Brother* we saw *Big Brother's Little Brother* and *Celebrity Big Brother*.

Sorry, I don't want to see purportedly unscripted dramatic or humorous situations which feature supposedly ordinary people instead of professional actors. I don't want to sit down with a nice cold beer and watch *The Osbourne's*, which is about the dysfunctional life and family of Ozzy Osbourne, the English rock star. I don't want to watch the moderately talented Paris Hilton in *Paris Hilton's My New BBF,* a reality series about her looking for a new best friend.

About now you're probably thinking, "Well, if you don't like them, don't watch them." You're right. That's why I do not, anymore. When I relax of an evening, I want to escape reality, not relive it! Every-day life is already full of dysfunctional families, pain and suffering, men and women in crisis, and people who think they are prima donnas. Do not give me reality television. Give me a well-written dramatic series or one which makes me laugh along with a tasteful comedy. Give me a documentary about an ancient lost civilization or other programming which will make me think. Remember, it's all right to educate me.

Provide me with entertainment but not at the expense of someone's dignity or the misfortune of others. Let me become someone I'm not, if only for a brief time. Allow me to become Allen Shore on *Boston Legal,* defending the rights of a homeless veteran. Actually, I'm more like Denny Crain, slipping in and out of reality. Let me be a millionaire playboy who races fast cars or a secret agent, "Hello, my name is Bond, James Bond." Give me the opportunity, if for only one night, to be a swashbuckling pirate, sailing from exotic island to island who finally rescues the Governor's beautiful daughter.

Allow me to become the teacher who inspires his students to rise above the squalor, drugs and crime of their neighborhood. I remember reading what Franklin Roosevelt said during the Depression, "It is a splendid thing that for just 15 cents an American can go to a movie and look at the smiling face of a baby and forget about his troubles."

I agree, sometimes, even today…perhaps especially today, we just need to escape from reality. For if we do not, "We just might become what our daily senses take in."

Here's to you Denny Crain!

Reality television is a poor excuse and a lesser product,
the result of opportunity and failed creativity.

Cuantos idioms sabe usted habler?

*"Every experience we expose ourselves to improves our lives in
every way because we are broadened by our understanding of
what a rich, diverse world we inhabit." - Alexandra Stoddard*

It's probably safe to say most of you could not understand the title
of this story. I couldn't either, that is why I had someone translate my
thoughts from English to Spanish. The title says, "How many languages
can you speak?"

If you are like me, you are reasonably proficient in English and
remember a word or two from a high school foreign language class.
Unfortunately, many Americans do not care one way or another about
speaking a second language. However, if you look (and listen) far enough
through the branches of your family tree, you'll probably hear your
ancestors speaking Spanish, Italian, French, German, Hebrew, Greek, or
some language other than English.

Chances are you never learned your ancestral language and that is
where we, as (most) Americans, have missed the boat. No pun intended.
By speaking only one language, we reduce our ability to effectively
communicate with many people around the world. Just the other day I
was listening to an interview with Roger Federer, currently the No. 2 male
tennis player in the world. As the international press was questioning him,
he responded in English, French, and German. He speaks all three fluently.

This made me think about the foreign exchange students I taught
through the years and other teenagers who came to permanently live in
the United States. They came from Columbia, Peru, Guatemala, Norway,
Sweden, France, Germany, Spain, Iran, Vietnam, and Cambodia, just to
name a few. In addition to their language, they spoke decent English and
sometimes a third language.

Then I thought, "What is it about their backgrounds and experiences
which makes them so different from me and you when it comes to
languages?" Of course, some of it is explained by geography when small
countries close together present greater opportunities for travel and
exposure to cultural differences. Commonly, Europeans travel much more

than Americans, which can lead to language-blended families like Roger Federer's. His mother is from South Africa and his father is Swiss.

Their schools and vision also play a major role in being bilingual. Many countries (Holland, Germany, France, and Spain for example) either require or encourage learning a second language. not for a year or two, but for several years. However, for some reason, many Americans are indifferent when it comes to a second language. On the other hand, some of this may be explained by our geography, being a large country with few neighbors. But I suspect our American attitude also contributes.

On several occasions, I've heard, "Why should I learn their language. They should learn ours." I totally agree, if they are moving to, or planning to live here for an extended period. In my opinion, there are many reasons for learning 'their' language. For example. it can make travel more comfortable and safe. Consider: Trying to impress a companion by ordering escamole in Mexico because you thought you remembered it from your hometown Taco Bell isn't recommended. It is ant eggs.

This is certainly something to consider: Your becoming increasingly nervous and fidgety in a Paris airport while looking for a public restroom might be misinterpreted by their security forces. If only I could say, "Ou se trouve une toilette publique"

Closer to home: Speaking Spanish to a Spanish-speaking waiter at a local restaurant does so much more than impress your friends. It builds bridges, friendships, and acceptance – yours and theirs. Plus, it will impress your friends! Also, in this ever-growing global job market, being bilingual will certainly move you to the head of the class. Companies and government agencies are clamoring for employees fluent in languages other than English. When multi-lingual, you never know when opportunity will present itself.

Yes, in my opinion, learning a second or third language can broaden and improve our lives in so many ways.

Many Americans may have come to this land by boat, but most Americans have missed the language boat.

"I Yam What I Yam"

"Every day look at a beautiful picture, read a beautiful poem, listen to some beautiful music, and if possible, say some reasonable thing." - Goethe

Raise your hand if you remember Popeye saying, "I yam what I yam." If you don't know who I'm talking about, you're probably under 40, so forget it and just keep reading!

When I was a child, Popeye was a cartoon character who constantly butchered the English language, much like me at the time. Even so, Popeye made me think, "We yam what we yam" because of what we watch, read, do, and listen to. And that can be a little scary.

What do you watch? A few years ago, I overheard a friend saying, "Did you know John and Alice are divorcing? Alice found out about John's affair with Sue (her best friend) and confronted them (drunk) at Sue's apartment." How sad, I thought, until found out she was talking about characters on her favorite soap opera.

Oh yea, soap operas. They are a great resource for building relationships. I really like watching professional wresting but I realize it is scripted entertainment. It's not real life! Also, for those glued to the television advice shows, remember they compete for ratings because they are in the entertainment business.

Some say, "There's nothing but sex, violence, and drugs on TV!" Uh, excuse me. You don't have to watch the bad stuff. You might try one of the other 300 or more channels available. When your focus is one-sided, it's so easy to become negative. Remember, "You yam what you watch."

Now, please take a few minutes and ask yourself the following, "What do I read?" Western romance novels are great, but not 24/7. *Sports Illustrated* and *Muscle and Fitness* are two of my favorite magazines, but I am also exposed to *Fine Gardening, Country Gardens,* and author Alexandra Stoddard, to name a few. Oh my, what beauty and knowledge one misses, by only reading one book or one topic over and over. Remember, "You yam what you read."

Next, what do you do for fun? I'm retired. I do what I want to do, if my wife Sandra approves. I go to the gym 4 days a week and would go 7 but, I'm reminded, "There's more to life than a gym." I need those little reminders. What about you? Is it golf, the fraternal club, video games, the computer, shopping, the local watering hole, or...? They all have their place...but what happens when they become the only place?

Finally, what type of music do you listen to? I'm old enough to remember and appreciate 'doo wop,' Motown, the psychedelic 60's (most of them), *Saturday Night Fever*, country, and today's popular music, if you can call it music. My God...did I just sound like Dad?

I wonder though, if all you heard (for years) were lyrics glamorizing violence and drugs, degrading women, and contempt for the police, how would you evolve?

Maybe an occasional trip to your local symphony orchestra, or a night under the stars at an outdoor concert in a local park might create a little balance. Without good balance, it's easy to fall. Remember, "You yam what you listen to."

The other day, I was listening to Jimmy Buffett's *Cheeseburger In Paradise* and remembered these lines, "Heard about the old time sailor men, They eat the same thing again and again." If I'm not wrong, I think their teeth fell out due in part to scurvy!

However, being creatures of habit is part of being human and experiencing the same thing repeatedly is not a bad thing – unless we become blind to people, beauty, and all there is to learn around us. I cannot imagine going to Radio City Music Hall to see the Rockettes, and only notice the dancer in the center. Or, visiting the Meilland Rose Gardens in France and staring at a single 'Peace' rose, with the beauty of thousands nearby. You miss so much.

As Emerson said, "The good mind chooses what is positive, what is advancing, - embraces the affirmative."

What are you embracing?

There is a huge difference between being entertained and being allowed to think. I soon forget entertained. Thinking is forever.

It's Time to Go

"We should not let our fears hold us back from pursuing our hopes." — John F. Kennedy

"Mom, Dad, I think it is time— my time." Words every parent hates to hear. "Honey, are you sure you want to do this. Maybe you should stay home." Words every teenager hates to hear. As summer winds down, these words are heard across the country. In many cases, college awaits and mom thinks, "My baby is leaving home." Parents are watching images of their child's first birthday flash before their eyes and at the same time, remembering the wild parties portrayed in John Belushi's 1978 movie *Animal House.* Some parents hear "Dad, don't worry. I'm an adult," and then the parent trembles uncontrollably.

That was then, and this is now. Oh, what a different world we have today. The images and emotions are still there: excitement, nervousness, sadness, and fear. But, for many, they are overshadowed by images of the senseless murders at Virginia Tech in April 2007. Or terrified students running from Columbine High School in 1999. Yes, the world is different today. And our schools are becoming safer. They are safer because of the senseless violence taking place in society.

Parents, as your hopes and dreams leave for college, public, and private school soon, make sure you ask those schools these questions. What are you doing to keep my child safe? Look at your area high schools. Do you have security personnel on duty with cameras linked to the local police? Do you have uniformed police officers in the school? Are metal detectors available? Do you allow students to carry backpacks or wear coats once classes begin? Are exterior doors locked once classes start? May I see your emergency management plan and can I observe practice drills. If these seem like extreme questions, think about this:

Last spring, my wife walked through the main entrance (doors unlocked) of a local high school and up the stairs to the principal's office. With no security present, no cameras visible and no one ever questioned her presence. Granted, she didn't look like a threat, but neither did Cho Seung-Hi at Virginia Tech., did Eric Harris or Dylan Klebold at Columbine.

When I was a high school administrator a parent asked, "Can you guarantee my child's safety?" My answer was simply "NO! But you and I working together can make it safer than it ever was before." He just nodded and said, "Fair enough. But, I'll be watching." I said, "Fair enough. I want you to watch."

For the parents helping to pack those cars for college, your fears are real but your children must find their own way. Nonetheless, I urge you to ask the same questions, "What are you doing to keep my child safe?" Does the school provide an orientation for students as well as parents on campus security? Does the Director of Campus Safety review policies and offer safety tips for students? One very impressive security program is the E911. This allows campus security to identify a building and room number when a call arrives. Emergency phones are also located around campus. They also can send text messages to cell phones and e-mail messages to students if there is an emergency. Impressive stuff…too bad it's necessary.

WVU (West Virginia University) has an impressive orientation and video presentation on campus safety. It's all covered: emergency phones, personal safety, dorm, and apartment security. If your child (sorry, young adult) goes to WVU ask them to show you their "Eyes <u>and 'Eers" resource guide</u>. Especially Part 13, "Playing it Safe." You should have them memorize it. You should memorize it.

I have an idea! Maybe the campuses and local police could put on safety and security orientations for the public. In the meantime, we should ask every school, "What are you doing to keep our children safe?" Demand to know! Constantly challenge the system to improve. Question procedures.

Remember, this is your hopes and dreams going off to college or getting on that school bus.

There is one other thing you might do – Go to that school and say, "What can 'I' do to help 'you' keep my child safe."

The safety of a child knows no boundaries.

Michael S. Lambiotte

Learning "Good Speak" Isn't Easy

"My conviction is that we can say marvelous things without using a barbarous vocabulary." - Jean-Henri Fabre

Learning a language as a child is very easy. When we are born we just lie around and our parents take care of all our needs and they talk to us. What they (our parents) don't realize is we are like a sponge, absorbing everything around us, what we see and what we hear.

First, let us focus on what we hear. Many parents and relatives cannot resist looking at our cute little wrinkly faces and use what they call baby talk: "Cuitsie cutsie Q." "Say Da Da." "Does little Jon Jon want his milkie bottle now?" Stop it! Talk to us like we're human. We are, aren't we? How do you expect us to talk well if you don't use complete sentences? We don't expect you to sit by our crib and quote Shakespeare or read excerpts from the Roman philosopher Cicero. Don't you want us to be reasonably intelligent? Or at least sound intelligent? Of course, you do. However, despite the baby talk, we eventually learn to speak your language.

On the other hand, "Learning Good Speak" isn't that easy." Sure, we can speak the language, but can we communicate well? Something I have noticed is that many people (me included, especially me) often use words or phrases that can be annoying or distracting. Such as: You know, uh, um, well, like, man and now.

It's so distracting to listen to someone being interviewed or speaking in public that constantly ends every sentence with 'uh or um.' Or, when asked a question or just making a statement, they begin or end (sometimes both) every sentence with 'you know.'

If you really want to lose my attention, punctuate your speech with, "Man, that was like you know…" For the record, I've been guilty of these annoyances but I am trying to eliminate them one-by-one.

My first major attempt at eliminating the uh's and um's when ending a sentence happened while I was still teaching political science. For one week, I made a conscious effort to eliminate uh's. After a Friday lecture, I was convinced I had been successful.

Especially when two young ladies approached my desk after class and said, "Mr. Lambiotte, that was an awesome class." As my ego was inflating they said, "You broke your previous record by saying 'now' 27 times." Pop goes the ego!

It seemed I had replaced uh's and um's with 'now.' Now, I had something else to work on. However, eliminating these annoying phrases isn't easy, especially if you not aware you're using them. These young ladies provided valuable feedback, unsolicited, but valuable. Without realizing, these annoyances break the attention of listeners and prevent them from grasping what you're saying.

Let me share what I have learned (the hard and embarrassing way) about effective communication. In other words, "Good Speak." Ask for honest feedback from friends and spouse if one dares, but be prepared! Pop goes the ego. Slow down when you speak. I have a habit of speaking very fast and way too often, as some say - a classic case of tongue and brain operating at different speeds.

Furthermore, pause at the end of each sentence and take a breath and think. You will eliminate the uh's and um's and give your listener(s) time to absorb what you said. I was once told that uh's and um's were an attempt to keep others from speaking. Also, pause after asking a question or making a profound statement. This gives everyone time to reflect. When speaking to a group, don't be afraid to record your presentation. If you've never heard your recorded voice, it is an ear-opening experience. We all can't sound like Morgan Freeman (actor), James Earl Jones (actor) or Dennis Haysbert from the Allstate commercials and star of *The Unit*.

Finally, the best advice I was ever given regarding "Good Speak" was, "Everyone is a public speaker. It makes no difference whether it is one-on-one or in front of hundreds. Conquer one annoying phrase at a time."

And that's how I view "Good Speak" ...

It's most annoying when an educated newspaper or magazine editor steps down to "street speak" in their daily reporting. We expect more.

Mirror Mirror: Tell me the truth

"The very purpose of existence is to reconcile the glowing opinion we have of ourselves with the appalling things that other people think about us." – Quentin Crisp

It began like every other day. Stephen got up, dressed, ate breakfast and went to work. That evening, after dinner while in the back yard, he watched the evening turn into night. Later, he watched Humphrey Bogart and Katherine Hepburn verbally spar in the romantic movie *The African Queen*. At its conclusion, he thought, "I wish I was more like Bogart." As he settled into bed, he kept thinking about the movie and Bogie.

At 3:30 am he awoke and made his nightly trip to the bathroom. Looking in the mirror he thought, "Mirror mirror, tell me the truth. I'm no Bogie but, who am I? What am I really like through the eyes of others?" As he turned around he heard a soft voice say, "Stephen, do you really want to know?"

He turned and saw a fuzzy image in the mirror. Not believing what he heard and saw, he still responded, "Yes." The image said, "Are you prepared for the truth, no matter what?" "Yes," his voice now quivering. "OK, Let's begin. First, you talk way too much and too fast. Your attempt to dominate conversations is annoying and slow down when you speak. It's hard for people to process 'warp speed' speech."

Stephen rubbed his eyes, looked at the mirror and the image was gone. He thought, "Maybe that four hotdogs at 9:00 p.m. was too much" and returned to bed. At 6:00 a.m. he opened his eyes and laid there a minute thinking, "Wow, that was really a creepy dream...a talking mirror."

Blaming it on the hotdogs, he once again began his morning routine. However, throughout the day he couldn't stop thinking about that fuzzy image and what it said.

That night, he made his usual trip to the bathroom precisely at 3:30 a.m. He had a 3:30 a.m. bladder. As he washed his hands he looked up and saw that same fuzzy image in the mirror and the voice said, "Stephen, yes it's me again. This time I want to talk with you about one upping people." "What do you mean one upping," Stephen said. "Stephen, whenever you're around people and someone tells a story you seem to have the need to tell a better or a funnier one –'one upping them' Stop it! It's irritating. Let the original storyteller have the stage. You're not the only star in the sky."

Again, Stephen rubbed his eyes, shook his head and the image was gone. This was a new experience for him - reoccurring dreams. He thought long and hard, "Am I really like that?" However, the dreams didn't stop. For the next several nights he was visited by that fuzzy mirror image and a soft voice saying: "Stephen, you don't remember names when you're introduced to someone. Quit thinking of something clever to say and pay attention to their name and what they say. Stephen, when you become involved in a project or an activity, your enthusiasm is often mistaken for trying to jump in and take over. Be more like a plant creep, crawl and run."

The voice continued: "Stephen, you need to do a better job remembering what people say or ask you to do. When you forget, it makes people think what they say isn't important."

Last night Stephen looked in the mirror and asked, "Am I really that bad of a person?" The image responded, "No Stephen, basically you're a good person but many people have this perception of you. Is this what you want?" "Of course not," Stephen said. "Then my friend, perhaps it's time to do some soul searching. And by the way, cut back on the body spray, you smell like a cheap backstreet pimp."

When he awoke the next morning, he thought, "Imagine what it would be like if everyone had a truthful mirror, but it's only a dream."

After tying his tie and combing his hair he turned to leave the bathroom and heard, "Stephen, I'll see you tonight."

Truthful mirrors do not exist. However, truthful friends are priceless.

The Downtown Gallery

"Put your hand in mine and let us help one another to see things better." – Claude Monet

His interest in art began in 1968, shortly after he enrolled in college. During a walking tour of the campus he asked, "What are those buildings at the bottom of the hill?" "That's the art department. The far-right building is the art gallery," one of the football players said. "Forget about those. Only hippies and freaks hang out there."

However, one evening he decided to visit the gallery, just to look around. Above the entrance to one room was painted, "An artist creates a feeling or mood, not just a picture." The statement was just as puzzling as some of the art. Right in front of him was a painting by Andy Warhol, "32 Campbell's Soup Cans." It was 32 –canvasses put together to make one painting. Standing across the room, they seemed to run together like herringbone. At first, they looked alike, but the longer he looked, he realized each can was different.

His first art lesson, "The longer you look, the more you see." On the opposite wall was Warhol's Gold Marilyn., a 7 foot x 5-foot gold canvas painting with a small silkscreened picture of Marilyn Monroe in the center. It was hauntingly beautiful, real but not real. The Warhol paintings were part of a traveling exhibition of a few of the controversial pop artist's finest works.

He found the paintings interesting but confusing, "What was Warhol trying to say? What did the paintings mean?" The answers would come… in time. That was his first step into the art world, but certainly not his last. Over the years, he and his wife visited many galleries and even collected a few highly sought-after prints and a small number of original oils by local artists. When they retired, and returned to their hometown, they became reacquainted with the 'town that is,' not the town they remembered.

They both agreed, "What downtown really needs is an art gallery. One of the vacant store would be perfect." First, they need to gather some like-minded investors and then recruit local high school art teachers to help design the inside and the art students could help. He knew enough about art to realize he knew very little. His vision: Start small but have a dramatic impact.

The grand opening would be a black tie (invitation only) with champagne, caviar and chocolate covered strawberries. The featured collections would be three popular local artists. Future collections would include photography, textiles, watercolors, oils, china and hand-blown glass - all forms of art. A friend even suggested a special exhibit of tattoo art.

"What a great venue for student art show," his wife added. He remembered that Claude Monet, the famous French painter, began selling his caricatures at 15. He saw the gallery growing where they would have juried shows, shows where artists apply and submit their work to a panel of judges, hoping to be selected for exhibition. In the back would be a small coffee shop, reminiscent of one he visited long ago in Greenwich Village. She made this suggestion for the layout of the gallery: As you entered the gallery, you could walk left and enter an intimate replica of a London tea room. Ah, the aroma of a Darjeeling tea, only surpassed by its taste.

To him, it was much more than an art gallery. It could become a community center, a place for teaching and learning, a place of quiet refuge where people could come and reflect. For some, it could become a temporary escape from the chaos of the day, or have coffee or a fine tea and browse the gallery rooms. His vision was to have many overstuffed chairs and benches throughout the gallery.

The boys at the barbershop laughed, some behind his back, "He's an idiot. He needs to go back to the big city. Champagne and caviar, yea right. We're a beer and peanuts town." When he heard what they were saying he thought, "Have you ever tried champagne and caviar? Felt the bubbles of champagne as they chase a chocolate strawberry?" Yes, we're a small town," he said. "But, we don't have to think small."

"The Downtown Gallery." Offering a new way to grow.

The "he" in this story is me. It was the beginning of appreciation far removed from my roots...and I am thankful for the experience.

The Shadow Day

"The future is purchased by the present." – Samuel Johnson

"The youth of today loves only luxury; they have bad manners, reject authority, and lack respect for their elders. They contradict their parents and tyrannize their teachers." Perhaps you have heard these words before, or even said them. By the way, this quote is attributed to Socrates. He was born 469 years before Christ. Even in Socrates' day, some teenagers were rude and rebellious, just like today. However, I am certain Socrates never met a group of teenagers like the group I recently heard about. about.

While playing golf, Steve (who is also a retired educator like me) shared this story. He is a member of a Harrison County, West Virginia volunteer service organization and was asked to organize their annual Shadow Day. A Shadow Day is when local businesses invite teens to join them for the day.

I thought, "What a wonderful opportunity for a first-hand look at how businesses operate, career opportunities, and the skills required for the job." Steve told me two local high schools were selected to participate. "I hope the other schools didn't get their fins up," he said. "We do plan to rotate the schools."

The service club provided breakfast for the students at a local restaurant, where they were introduced to their sponsors. Then, off they went, 50 students, visiting the real world. At noon, everyone met for lunch downtown .The luncheon speaker was the president of a local small university.

As we were carrying our golf clubs, Steve said, "Mike, for a few hours, I was back in my element as a teacher. Seeing them arrive for breakfast at 7:30 a.m. was déjà vu. - back in the café again. Some were wide awake. Some...well, just awake. The young ladies kicked it up a notch when it came to attire. Girls do that sort of thing!

The young men, not wanting to look too cool, were neat but not too neat. Socrates never met this group, I thought. They were on time (at least most were), polite, well mannered, and attentive. However, right before lunch, I must admit to nearly having a small anxiety attack. Imagine, 50 hungry teenagers in a small room with the aroma of 25 pizzas filtering about. Mass release for the pizza line would have been chaos, so I swallowed hard and announced, "Ok, I'm old school. We'll dismiss ladies first, two rows at a time."

As we were putting our clubs away, Steve turned and said, "Honestly, what happened next shocked me. When I pointed toward the first two rows, the ladies got up and the young men just sat there. No moans and groans. Not even a hiss." We both laughed and then he added, "But, boys will be boys!" As one young lady stood up, a young man playfully said, "What are you getting up for?" Then he saw me and smiled. All I said was, "Don't even go there." The young lady flipped her hair, straightened her dress, and stuck her tongue out at him.

Finally, something that may surprise a few parents, they cleaned up after themselves...every single plate and cup! And they said thank you. I asked Steve about the sponsor's reactions. "It was rewarding to hear the positive comments, as the students left. Comments like: Well behaved. Quiet. They asked intelligent questions. They really seemed interested." One sponsor said, "Where do they get all that energy? I was totally exhausted. And it's only 2:00 pm.".

Steve kept talking about what a wonderful day it was and what a great group of young people. And I thought, "What an excellent opportunity this service organization provided. Bravo to them! As I was driving home, Steve's story made me think about my own 31 years in education...and I smiled. I could add this story to my list of:

"Just another example of young people rising to our level of our expectations."

Take the time to organize a Shadow Day within your own community. Contact me and I will even help...just for the "youth" of it!

'These Times, they are a Changin'

"The true measure of a man is not how he behaves in moments
of comfort and convenience but in how he stands in times of
challenges and controversy."

— Dr. Martin Luther King

A few years ago, my mother told me that as a child, when I left for school every morning she would quietly say to herself, "God, he is in your hands now". Her biggest fear, concerning school security, was that I look both ways when walking to Morgan Elementary School and cross only at the lights.

As an elementary student, my idea of school security was one of those over-sized rubber bands around my Roy Rogers lunch box that my father got from the Pittsburgh Plate Glass Company where he worked. As a student at Central Junior High School, mom's security concerns consisted of,"Listen to the crossing guard". When I got to Washington Irving High School (WI)l, I was a man and she didn't worry – yea right!

While attending Central, my biggest fear was forgetting my locker combination. At WI, it was not being able to keep my priorities straight - keep my grades up so I could play sports. My apologies to my teachers but that was that was the truth. However, as Bob Dylan said in 1963, "These times, they are a changin". The entire school climate has changed and will continue to change. It is up to us, all of us, to help it change positively.

The fears we had in school in the 50's and 60's are almost laughable compared to the current fears and doubts about school safety and security. Unless you have gone ostrich (head in the sand) the last few years, every parent's fear has flashed across our television screens or has been read in the headlines of our newspapers.

The school, once seen as a haven for children is no longer a haven. Recently, we have read about teachers and administrators killed, students taken hostage, children killed and sexually assaulted. Schools have also been placed on "lock down" because of nearby violence.

It is easy to point fingers at causes and responsibilities, but be cautious when you point a finger at someone because at least three are pointing right back at you! I was an administrator in a large high school that had security cameras inside and outside of the building, a school resource officer (police), and security personnel on duty throughout the building. We practiced all the drills: fire, tornado, intruder drills, lock downs because of community violence. We had the SWAT team practice rescues. We even had the drug and bomb dogs routinely enter the schools for sniff tests.

I feel certain certain schools in my county are taking these exact same measures (if not more) to keep our students and faculty safe. However, we must not overlook the biggest and most important security resource in the schools - the students. Parents and teachers, talk with your children and make time for them to talk with you...and **Listen!** Never dismiss their concerns or take their suggestions or opinions lightly. The students know what is going on in their school far better than teaches and administrators. They know who belongs and who doesn't (as a legitimately enrolled student) and which students are possibly 'on the edge.'

As an administrator and former teacher, I always tried to know which students to talk with if things just didn't feel right around the campus. The administrators and teachers I have met since returning to the county in which I was born are no different. However, we must increase our awareness, not only for personal safety, but for the safety of everyone. Think about it: Do you walk through a shopping center parking lot at night with the same level of awareness as 30 years ago, or is it higher?

In my opinion, we must all share the responsibility for school safety. This means the adult walking or driving down the street, the shop keeper who glances out the window, the cafeteria worker in the serving line, the bus driver, the custodian in the hall, the grandmother who volunteers in the school, and the person mowing his grass. We must be aware of not only what happens in and around our schools, but throughout the entire community.

Our schools are safe, but let us do our best to prevent the tragedy and sadness that has befallen others. Nonetheless, when all is said and done and all the security measures are in place, terrible things can still happen and will happen. With that in mind, when your child leaves for school tomorrow, it might not hurt to say,

"God, they are in your hands now"!

Learning should be a joy – not a survival camp.

This is Your Life, Jim Teacher

"Even if our efforts of attention seem for years to be producing no result, one day a light that is in exact proportion to them will flood the soul." - Simone Weil

In 1952 Ralph Edwards created a television series recognizing entertainment personalities and ordinary people who contributed in some way to their communities.

Edwards said, "The lives under examination must represent something constructive, they must have given above and beyond the call of duty and passed on the help to another."

The series was called, *This is Your Life.*

My version of *This is Your Life* is dedicated to the teaching profession. For every day, teachers give above and beyond and unquestionably contribute and pass on something very special within their community… the gift of knowledge.

Jim Teacher is just one example of an ordinary person who has dedicated his life to changing the world, one child at a time. This is his life: He knew from the minute he started college he wanted to be a teacher. However, he wasn't the smartest or very athletic in high school, so paying for college wasn't easy. Like many, he had multiple loans and worked two jobs until the day he graduated. And graduate he did…with honors!

His first teaching contract was for $7,200. He once told me, "At that rate ($7,200) it will take me10 years to pay off the loans." He paid them off in seven. It always made him angry when non-teachers would say, "Boy, it must be nice to have the summers off." Teachers never have the summer off! Jim, like many/most worked a second job in the summer to help pay the bills.

Although, some summers were used for going back to school to furthering his education, eventually earning a Master's degree and an Ed.S. The only time Jim complained about summer classes was when he had to update his teaching certificate.

The school system required it, but he had to pay for it. Still, a small price to pay for doing what he loved.

He never grumbled about the long days and short nights. He was at school by 6:30 a.m.,, although classes didn't start until 7:30 a.m. and were over at 2:00 p.m. Again, his civilian friends (non-teachers) would say, "Gee, it must be nice to leave work at 2:00 p.m.." Leave at 2:00 p.m. never! He stayed at least until 4:30 p.m. grading papers, attending meetings, and preparing materials for the next day. After dinner, Jim would spend another couple of hours doing lesson plans, grading, and planning.

All-in-all he averaged working a 12-hour day, not counting weekends. This did not include the hours spent attending school plays, concerts, and athletic events. Jim always supported his students in and out of the classroom. Imagine what his salary would have been by standard union wage scales. However, he never complained even when he chose to spend his own money for classroom supplies for his children.

Over the years, Jim lost track of the days he went to school so sick he wanted to die. He didn't want his students falling behind. When a snow day canceled school, he often went anyway to catch up or worked at home. Certainly, not a day off.

He learned early in his career a teacher never gets totally caught up. Close perhaps, but never caught up. Even scheduled vacations were not total vacations. He always had papers to grade, lesson plans to write and projects to develop. Even the occasional verbal abuse by an out-of-control student didn't shake his commitment, nor did routine berating by argumentative parents who suddenly take an interest in their child's continual lack of progress - one month before school ends.

Yes, Jim Teacher is a master of self-control. The profession requires it. However, he's devoted his life to changing the world, one child at a time.

I'm sure you know Jim. He's in your school right now. Jim's your child's third grade teacher. He's teaches algebra to your middle school daughter. He's the English teacher who opened your daughter's world to Shakespeare. Jim also coaches your son's baseball team in his 'spare' time.

Thank you, Jim Teacher!

In Europe and Asia, teachers are held high by
society. What do they see we do not?

CHAPTER 14

The Shape of Mean

A Butterfly That Never Lands

"It is better to deserve honors and not have them than to have them and not deserve them." – Mark Twain

After planting my final tomato plant, I sat down to admire my spring garden. As usual, my able-bodied assistant (Merry, our black Labrador retriever) was asleep under the umbrella, or so I thought! When I went to call her to ask her opinion, I noticed she was at attention, every muscle tensed. She was about to attack and rid our yard of the first vicious trespasser of the season – a butterfly. She failed and the butterfly made an erratic, yet graceful escape to safety. What is there about dogs and butterflies?

There is something special about the arrival of the first butterflies of the season. Although they drive Merry insane, to me they are so beautiful and beneficial. Yes, I'm that old...butterflies excite me also. But, I do not chase them.

I haven't seen any monarchs yet, but it is a long trip from Mexico. Although, I did see a tiger swallowtail the other day and that means the viceroys aren't far behind. Their arrival means good news for our flowers and vegetables because butterflies are wonderful pollinators and a pretty good indicator of the overall health of our yards and community.

It's fascinating to watch them float from flower to flower. They have great vision and know exactly where they are going. Their antennae's and feet are always moving. This is how they smell and taste r before sipping nectar. It's a wonderful relationship: The flower, bloom and the butterfly, each contributing to the success and survival of the other.

Oh yes, if one lands on you, try not to startle the innocent little creature. It just smells salt. Some need it to survive. Think of yourself as a food source, if only for a few seconds. Take those few moments to really see something of grace and beauty.

However, lately I have noticed an entirely different specie of butterfly. Perhaps it may not be new or different. Maybe I just (now) have the time to really see and observe things that really matter. Unlike the monarch, with its distinctive reddish bright orange color and black veins, this peculiar butterfly comes in a variety of sizes and colors. It seems able to change its colors at will, trying to imitate its useful and beneficial cousins. It appears to care about pollinating the flower, but something is wrong.

You see, this butterfly never (or seldom) lands. It just flits and flirts from flower to flower. It nervously hovers over flowers that need its attention, but never really lands. On occasion, it may touch down for an instant, but never long enough to benefit the flower. It appears to have good intentions but it seems preoccupied with moving to the next bloom.

This butterfly seems to be saying, "The more flowers I hover over the better the garden. I can't decide! Oops, time to move on." Maybe something happened to this particular specie of butterfly as it was going through its stages of development: Egg, larva, pupa, and then adult butterfly. My observations indicate the first three were probably normal, but something changed during early adulthood. Maybe it was environmental or maybe it wanted to be an eagle instead of a butterfly. I don't know but one thing I do know is: By never (or seldom) landing, it can do little good. By never pollinating, it cheats the flower and starves itself from enjoying a fulfilling life.

It's sad that this specie is not able, or possibly willing, to learn from the monarch or the swallowtail. Those butterflies know a flowers color, form, aroma, and nectar help guide the butterfly. By doing so, the butterfly, the flower, the garden, and the community of gardens all flourish

We deserve butterflies that land and take the time to see, feel, smell, and taste. How beautiful. How essential. May the 'hovers' eventually taste the nectar.

Disclaimer: Any similarity or comparison in this story to anything other than a butterfly is purely... on purpose.

The strange butterfly is real. She flies around doing little good.
She wants to be a Queen Alexandra butterfly, the largest in
the world (12 ½ inch wingspan) but, she is more like the
African Western Pygmy. It has 1 half inch wingspan.

Know It All – Done It All

*"Sometimes the most challenging requirement of empathy is
holding your tongue when tempered to reply, to give counsel,
or to share your own stories."* – Steven Covey

We are all different. Some laugh out loud during a movie, others simply smile.

Some travel to places like Cancun and Paris for vacations while others, even if they have the means, choose to sit in the serenity of their back-yard marveling at the beauty of a butterfly. Some buy a new car every two years and others are content to 'drive'er' till the wheels fall off. I understand all that. Everyone has different needs and different ways to satisfy those needs. However, I'll never understand why some people feel the need to "Know it all – Done it All."

Oh, you know who I'm talking about: They are your neighbor. The person three pews in front of you in church. Your childhood friend. 'They' might even be you. For multiple reasons, the 'Know it alls' join every club, committee, commission and board conceivable in search of knowing it all!

At an early age, they became a true disciple of Sir Francis Bacon after reading *Knowledge is power.* Unfortunately, they never looked beyond the surface of the quote. They make it a point to know everyone's business and the entire pedigree of the family down the street before their moving van is unloaded. They can also be the master story teller, because they have 'Done it all.' No matter the topic or setting, they can top any conversation. They're charter members of the 'Bigger, Better, More Often' club.

Do any of these sound familiar: You're talking about your recent ski trip to Canaan Valley, West Virginia. 'Done it all' chimes in, "That's nice, but let me tell you about our trip to Aspen." If you had a 1964 Mustang, they had a 1964 Corvette with a 327-cubic inch engine. Much faster than your Pony's 260 cubic inch V8. Instead of saying, "Oh, we can't come. We're going on vacation." They say, "Oops, can't make it. We're going to the Italian Rivera and then to Monte Carlo." The "Done it All's" can top any and all: This winter, your cold lasted three weeks; theirs lasted four, became pneumonia and resulted in an emergency room visit.

Yes, we have all known a few "Know it alls – Done it alls." And they are not very pleasant to be around. In fact, some are very scary. I've always wondered what makes people this way: Is it misguided ambition? Are they just that insecure? Or, are they just plane mean-spirited?

Why do some people feel the need to always tell a bigger and better story? What satisfaction does someone get from knowing everyone's business? The answer probably depends on the individual. After all, everybody's different, even "Know it alls - Done it alls."

If you have someone like this in your life, my advice, "Collect your $200, pass Go and keep going." Sorry about the Monopoly reference, but it's true. Personally, I do my best to avoid these people. Of course, if this isn't possible and many times it isn't, give them the stage they desperately seek and then quickly exit stage right.

Now, the frightening part: What happens if you suddenly realize you're one of 'them?' Know it all's are incurable. You are who you are. And that is never going to change. However, if you are a Done it All, there is hope. When someone tells a story, or is excited to share some information – Listen! Become a good listener. Don't think about what you want to say. Many times, the best conversationalist is the one who says little. Let them have center stage. Ask a question or two. Show sincere interest. I know what I'm talking about. There was a time when I was a journeyman "Done it All." Fortunately, I learned early on the value of listening. As Shakespeare said, "Give everyman thy ear but few thy voice."

"Know it alls – Done it Alls," they're not very pleasant people – I know.

This story was the result of countless people in our
clubs and organizations telling my wfe Sandra and I
about all the exotic places they are vacationing.
Oh yea, they did it on purpose!

SENSELESS

"There is a thousand hacking at the branches of evil to one who is striking at the root." – Henry David Thoreau

There are many reasons why and how neighborhoods deteriorate: Vandalism that is ignored. A broken pane left unrepaired, leading to two and then three. Litter, unkempt lawns and more. However, to me, it all comes down to pride and community respect. Today, this story addresses a lack of pride and community respect. Especially, "Senseless" vandalism.

As told to me: In late spring, a man awoke to the horror of flames dancing toward the sky from his driveway. When the fire was finally extinguished, he discovered someone(s) had slit all four tires on his and his wife's cars and set his van on fire. Earlier, car windshields were broken; a car keyed (scratched), tools stolen from a front porch, a fire set in an abandoned stairwell and tires slashed on a disabled man's wheelchair.

A few weeks later, vandals broke into a country club pro shop, ransacked its contents, stole beer and flooded the floor. A week later, a gate was broken and 4-wheelers were ridden around and around on a beautiful golf course green, leaving deep ruts?

When told about these acts I just shook my head in disbelief and wondered, "Why would anyone want to commit these senseless acts? What kind of a person would deprive a disabled man of his mobility, burn and deface cars, destroy beauty? All in the name of fun!"

By the way, this vandalism happened in my own North Central West Virginia. community in back yard, not in some big gang-infested inner city or an exclusive South-Miami Beach country club. The night of terror happened in Shinnston, West Virginia and the vandalism/burglary and green destruction happened at the Clarksburg Country Club, in Clarksburg, West Virginia.

These were not mindless teenage pranks. They were serious and violent. Why? Only the one(s) responsible can that question. Hopefully, those responsible will (soon) make a mistake with the slip of the tongue, the need to brag, or fall victim to one too many beers at a local bar. Secrets are hard to keep, especially in a small town.

With substantial rewards offered in both cases, historically speaking, greed eventually turns brother against brother, friend against friend. As the 1942 slogan said, "Loose lips might sink ships." In these two cases, I hope their ships sink fast and deep.

What many fail to realize is vandalism is a serious crime, not a mindless teenage prank. I will never understand the willful destruction of private or public property. What motivates these people? Is it their desire to feel powerful or dominant? Some say its jealousy or possibly revenge: Jealousy of those who have what they don't have or revenge for a perceived past wrong.

Others lean toward the crime of opportunity explanation, "It was just there." Peer pressure, "Go ahead do it, don't be chicken." Or simply the thrill factor. Personally, I like what one person told me, "Mike, some people are just ignorant, stupid and mean-spirited. They reek with meanness! They don't even respect themselves. So how can we expect them to respect other people's property?"

Who knows what motivates senseless vandalism. One thing for sure, we'll never stop it, history teaches that. However, we can make it very painful for those responsible. My personal choice goes back to the 17th century. Unfortunately, it was outlawed as too inhumane - damn the liberals!

I guess I'm forced to support our current justice system. When caught, and they will be caught (remember loose lips), paying full restitution is a given. Follow this with good ole fashioned hard labor to repair the damage or other acts of senseless vandalism. Finally, a novel approach would be to then hire the person or persons responsible, if practical. Often, the road to respect is paved with stones of understanding. Of course, for the violent situations, lock 'm up and bend the key!

Having pride and community respect means standing up against "Senseless" acts.

If I ever catch someone vandalizing my property,
I would immediately ask myself,
"What would Charles Bronson do?"

War and Peace in the Hood

"If there is any one secret of success, it lies in the ability to get the other person's point of view and see things from his angle as well as your own." – Henry Ford

Throughout history, countries and states have gone to war over border disputes, religious differences, natural resources, human rights and several other matters too numerous to list. Even cities have gone to war (so to speak) over economic differences and boundary disputes such as road and property annexations. Families have feuded over a relative's murder, a hog, and marrying into the other family. This last example was the epicenter of the Hatfield and McCoy feud in West Virginia. Even neighbors have gone to war over a variety of issues.

However, regardless of the parties involved, most disputes seem to be centered around greed, jealousy, intolerance and/or misguided ambition. For example, let's take a fictional look at a one-such neighborhood dispute, one I call "War and Peace in the (neighbor) Hood." On one side of the street we have Bell. On the other side is Violet. Bell was new to the neighborhood but not new to town. She grew up in Ladysburg but married a career military man and was gone for many years.

Bell always wondered why it took Violet two months to introduce herself when other new neighbors were approached within a day or two. Bell always felt Violet treated her as an outsider, although this was Bell's hometown. Funny thing is, Violet looked at herself as a member of the old guard, although she was born in the Midwest and came to town after marrying a successful local banker.

Sparing all the details: Through Bell's eyes, she felt Violet was always trying to one-up her in the community or undermine her civic work. Her slurs, cutting remarks and innuendos, although subtle, seemed to always catch Bell off-guard. Bell was warned by others about the dark side of Violet but chose, in the beginning, to ignore this dark side. She was just trying to keep peace in the (neighbor) hood.

Bell admits she should have addressed the issues as they surfaced, but chose silence because, one of Bell's main character flaws is, "Take, take, and take and then explode," which she did while talking with Violet one afternoon. All the hurt and anger just spewed out. Although Bell spoke the truth, she admits it could have been said in a more acceptable way.

Now, let's look at Violet's side: She says, "I don't understand why Bell's mad. I've never said or done anything to offend her. I just want us to be such good friends and neighbors. After all, we have so much in common. I just don't understand." Being objective, Bell has written Violet but she never responds to the specific issues.

Bell has even attempted to set up a meeting but Violet (again) dodges the issue by saying,

"If you don't want to be friends, I guess the best we can do is be neighbors."

Although this story is pure fiction, unfortunately, variations of it are all too real. As I said in the beginning, most disputes come about as the result of greed, jealousy, intolerance or misguided ambition, at least that is my opinion. When I look back at the story of Bell and Violet, I remember what Paul Newman said in the 1967 movie *Cool Hand Luke,* "What we have here is a failure to communicate." In this story, Bell is trying to communicate and Violet continues to ignore her requests. One must ask, "Why?"

Talking through differences is not always easy but personally, I would rather try and fail then to never try. If you see some of yourself in this story, think about these words from Eleanor Roosevelt, "Approach each new person by trying to discover what he is thinking and feeling; understand the background from which he comes, the soil in which his roots have grown, the ideas which have shaped his thinking."

If you care enough to make the effort, you can establish an understanding relationship with people who are entirely outside your own orbit.

It's a daily fight not to become one of them.

Printed in the United States
By Bookmasters